# Burglary

Crime and Society Series

Series editor: Hazel Croall

*Published titles*
*Sex Crime*, by Terry Thomas
*Burglary*, by R. I. Mawby

# Burglary

**R. I. Mawby**

Routledge
Taylor & Francis Group

LONDON AND NEW YORK

First published by Willan Publishing 2001
This edition published by Routledge 2012
2 Park Square, Milton Park, Abingdon, Oxon OX14 4RN
711 Third Avenue, New York, NY 10017

*Routledge is an imprint of the Taylor & Francis Group, an informa business*

ISBN: 978-1-90324-032-8 paperback
ISBN: 978-1-90324-033-5 cased


British Library Cataloguing-in-Publication Data
A catalogue record for this book is available from the British Library.




Typeset by PDQ Typesetting, Newcastle-under-Lyme, Staffordshire

# Contents

# Tables and Figures

## Tables

## Figures

# Part 1: Introduction

# Chapter 1

# Setting the scene

## Burglary in debate

Public feelings about burglary are graphically illustrated by the case of Tony Martin. In April 2000, Martin was found guilty at Norwich Crown Court of the murder of 16-year-old Fred Barrass and wounding with intent Brendon Fearon.[1]

Martin was an eccentric who lived alone in a remote farm, appropriately called 'Bleak House'. He was worried about burglary, and kept a shotgun as protection, as well as other weapons, including a sawn-off shotgun. However, Martin had a history of firearms misuse, and did not have a licence for any of his guns. When Barrass and Feardon broke into his house in August 1999, he opened fire, shooting Barrass in the back from 12 feet. After a high-profile trial he was found guilty by a 10/2 majority verdict and sentenced to life imprisonment.

The Martin case provoked considerable media – and public – debate encompassing a broad range of issues, including:

- the distinction between self-defence and homicide
- the extreme ways in which those who are worried about crime may react
- the adequacy of police protection
- the extent of rural crime.
- victims' rights.

At the time, the Conservative leader pledged to reform the law to give greater protection to those who protect their home against intruders, although by the end of 2000 the Conservatives appeared to have abandoned this policy. A website was established to campaign on Martin's behalf, and – when he was refused legal aid to appeal – to raise funds to support an appeal; by March 2001 this had achieved over 2,300 'hits'.

The Martin case is, of course, an extreme example. Thankfully, very few burglary victims react in the way that Martin did. But it does, to a certain extent, caricature many of the issues that are at the heart of subsequent discussions in this text. However, before setting out the framework of the following chapters, two formalities need to be addressed. First, what do we mean by burglary; and, second, what sources will be used in discussing it?

## Defining burglary

While the term 'burglary' means different things to different people, here it is confined to illegal entry to homes and other premises such as garages, offices, shops, warehouses, etc. Even here, though, the term incorporates an enormous range of quite different acts. For example, 'distraction burglary', where a team of offenders trick their way into the home of a (usually elderly) person, is very different from a break-in where violence is deployed. And the use of a vehicle to smash through the window/bars of a shop (so-called 'ram raiding') appears, on the surface, to share little in common with a night-time burglary to a house, where the crime is effected without waking the residents. While such distinctions are clearly relevant, whether we are considering how and why people engage in burglary, how the victim is affected, or how the likelihood of future crimes may be reduced, it is equally important to set parameters.

Burglary is defined in the International Crime Victim Survey (ICVS) as an incident where someone enters property without permission in order to steal something (del Frate *et al* 1993). While this seems like an uncontroversial definition, it is not a universally accepted one, and indeed until comparatively recently the English law defined burglary very differently.

Originally, burglary was defined as *breaking and entering*. That is, in order to commit a burglary one had to physically break in. This all changed in England and Wales following the 1968 Theft Act. In section 9(i) burglary is defined as illegal entry to premises followed by theft or with the intent to commit an offence. Aggravated burglary (as defined in section 10) is where the offender commits the burglary while in

4

possession of a firearm, explosive or other weapon. Thus burglary no longer depends on the use of physical force to enter the property; merely that the offender had no legitimate or general right to be there at the time the offence occurred. The following incidents would therefore be classified as burglaries in England and Wales:

(i) Break-in to home through door or window.
(ii) Use other method (e.g. credit card) to enter through locked door or window without causing damage.
(iii) Enter through an open window.
(iv) Enter through an open door.
(v) Enter with permission, where the offender used trickery to gain access.

Interestingly, in English law there is no requirement that anything is actually *stolen* for an offence to be defined as burglary. Rather it is the illegal *entry* with intent that is decisive; so some burglaries involve no losses at all. The 2000 British Crime Survey (BCS) suggested that as many as one quarter of burglaries involve no loss (Kershaw *et al* 2000). Attempted burglary, which is covered by the 1981 Criminal Attempts Act, is where the offender is considered to have acted in a manner that is more than merely preparatory to the commission of the offence, but has not actually gained entry. Again, the 2000 BCS suggested that there were about two attempted burglaries for every three completed ones, and – for various reasons to be discussed later – the proportion of attempts relative to completed burglaries had been increasing. Attempts are – not surprisingly – more common at night or at the weekend when there is someone at home (Budd 1999). The following two examples that occurred in Plymouth have been taken from the police computer files to illustrate the difference:

Offender used unknown instrument to force open rear ground floor window. Once inside alarm activated and exit through back door. (Burglary, nothing stolen)

Front sash window forced using some form of instrument. The noise alerted the occupant. Window raised but no entry gained. (Attempted burglary)

A further distinction can be made according to the *nature of the premises* that are burgled. A common sense distinction might be between homes and other buildings associated with private homes, such as garages or sheds, and business premises. However, in English criminal statistics the only distinction made is between residential burglaries and 'other' burglaries, which will include a variety of different incidents, including for example garage or outhouse break-ins.

What is defined as a burglary, and distinctions between different types of burglary, are not therefore always as clear as they might be. The matter becomes more confused if we consider the ways in which burglary is defined abroad. In many continental countries the definition broadly equates with 'breaking and entering'. For example, in Germany both entry through an open door and entry without permission (examples [iv] and [v] above) are classified as simple thefts, whilst entry through an open window is given its own separate category. In Hungary, entry through an open window is only defined as burglary where the window is a minimum height above the ground!

One problem here concerns measurement. If we compare one year with another, or one country with another, are we comparing 'like with like'? A second problem, though, surrounds people's experiences and expectations of burglary. That is, what is the most common context within which burglary occurs? This is important because the meaning of the incident to the victim, and hence the impact of the crime, may vary markedly. For example, while newspaper headlines make much of aggravated burglaries, that is where force or the threat of force is used, these are very rare. In England and Wales in 1998–1999 for example, less than 0.7% (2,955 out of 472,960) of household burglaries (including attempts) were classified as aggravated (Home Office 2000, 50). Similarly, malicious damage *may* have a greater impact although, despite Walsh's (1980) claims, it appears rare (Budd 1999). On a less extreme level we may ask whether the burglary takes place in daytime or at night, or whether there is anyone at home at the time. The 2000 BCS, for example, found that 21% occurred at night, 26% in the evening and 6% evening or night. About half took place when the home was empty, but where there was someone at home, half were effected without anyone being aware of the burglary until later (Kershaw *et al* 2000). Commercial burglaries are even more likely to occur at night or at weekends, for obvious reasons (Mirrlees-Black and Ross 1995). However, Wojcik *et al* (1997) found that England stood out from Poland and Hungary, where burglaries were even more likely to take place in the daytime or early evening and when the home was empty. The varying social contexts are illustrated in the examples taken below from a sample of household burglaries in Plymouth in 1993:

'I was upstairs in bed at about 11.30 and I heard some glass breaking. I leapt out of bed and put all the lights on and ran down the stairs and whoever it was ran off.'

Neighbour went to bathroom in night and seeing burglars breaking in called police. Respondent was woken up by voice saying, 'Sarge, there's someone in here', and saw police officer standing in doorway. He explained that they had caught the offender coming out of the house.

'I was in the kitchen cooking on the 2nd of July, and I had the French doors open. I turned around and saw someone in the living room. I said "Oy" and they ran out.... I immediately phoned the police.'

'I came down in the morning. In the living room I had cupboards open and when I went into the bathroom the window was open. I came back in here and saw the video was gone.'

'I was out and the young lady next door saw the back door open and called the police. When I got back the police were here.'

'I came home before my husband but didn't notice anything. When my husband came home he asked where the video was and then we noticed we had been burgled.'

'I was working and a neighbour phoned me up to say we had been broken into. When I got home the police were all here. They had climbed over the back wall into the garden and my back door was all smashed in.'

'My youngest son and I were watching TV in the living room and the back door was open. My bracelet, watch, camera and Dictaphone were on the side and someone just came in and took them.'

What burgary 'means' to each of these victims may, not surprisingly, be very different. This may then have implications, *inter alia*, for the effect that the offence has on them, and their families, the relevance of different strategies aimed at reducing the likelihood of a repeat offence, and their views of the offender.

## Sources used in the book

In drawing together material for this text, a combination of sources has been used. These include local data from the author's home area of Devon and Cornwall, national data and international material. One key source of national data is the British Crime Survey (BCS), which has been carried out regularly in England and Wales[2] since 1982 (Hough and Mayhew 1983; Kershaw *et al* 2000).[3] Other national material is drawn from a raft of research studies and an ever-increasing number of policy documents and evaluations.[4] On an international level, research evidence is patchy and commonly restricted to a select group of Western industrial societies. However, the International Crime Victim Survey (ICVS) is an invaluable source that helps broaden our perspective on the nature of burglary.

The International Crime Victims Surveys have been conducted on four separate occasions. The first, in 1989 (van Dijk *et al* 1990), concentrated almost exclusively on Western industrial societies. The second, in 1992, extended coverage to the developing world and some post-communist societies (del Frate *et al* 1993), and the third, in 1996–1997 covered industrialised societies (Mayhew and van Dijk 1997), the developing world (del Frate 1998) and post-communist societies, so-called 'Countries in Transition' (Zvekic 1998). The fourth, in 2000, continued this trend towards more comprehensive coverage, although at the time of going to press its findings are unavailable. The International Crime Victims Surveys provide considerable information, for example on victims' perceptions of their experiences, reporting behaviour, fear of crime, attitudes towards the police and public views on alternative sentences.

In addition to secondary source material, considerable emphasis is placed on primary data from the author's research, both locally in the south-west of England and cross-nationally. Locally, this has involved research on and in cooperation with local agencies such as Devon and Cornwall Police (Bunt and Mawby 1994; Dale and Mawby 1994; Redshaw and Mawby 1996) and Plymouth Victim Support (Simmonds and Mawby 2000), and particularly evaluations of community safety initiatives promulgated under the Safer Cities initiatives (Mawby 1997; *ibid* 1999). In this context, the author has also benefited from his experience as a member of local committees, including the Plymouth Burglary Multi-Agency Strategy Group, Plymouth Safer Cities, Plymouth Homesafe, and Plymouth Community Partnership. However, in taking examples of local research and policy initiatives, an attempt has been made to avoid parochialism and discuss local issues as examples of wider debates.

Additionally, considerable attention is placed on cross-national research directed by the author. In contrast to the ICVS, this involved comparison of crime victims by concentrating on the experiences of burglary victims in a limited number of cities in five countries. These were Plymouth and Salford (England) and Munchengladbach (Germany) from Western Europe and Warsaw and Lublin (Poland), Miskolc (Hungary) and Prague (Czech Republic) from Eastern/Central Europe (Mawby 1992).[5]

Whereas the ICVS allows for a cross-national comparison of both reported and unreported crime and provides a broad analysis of crime patterns, our own research in contrast allows a more detailed comparison of one type of crime, household burglary, and, being a cooperative venture between academics based in the cities included, also enabled us to relate local findings to the specific circumstances pertaining to the cities concerned (see also Mawby 1998; Mawby, Koubova and Brabcova 2000).

In using both primary and secondary data, and moving between the local, national and international, the aim of this book is to provide as comprehensive an overview of burglary and policies directed at it as is possible. At the same time, the focus on our own research allows us to illustrate many of the issues. In some cases, this is integrated into the wider discussion; in others it has been presented through more detailed consideration of a number of case studies.

## The structure of the book

The following chapters cover both burglary as a problem and alternative policy responses that have been adopted in various countries. Part 2 includes four chapters. In chapter 2, burglary is considered as a contemporary social problem in terms of both the extent of the problem and public perceptions of burglary as a particular concern. At the same time, variations in both fear and risk are described and alternative explanations considered. One aspect of burglary as a problem concerns the impact of burglary on victims. In chapter 3, the effects of burglary, and the needs of victims, are discussed. Again, comparisons are drawn both with other types of crime and between the experiences of different victims. Another issue that features in contemporary debates, but is not exclusive to burglary, is that of repeat victimisation, and this is the focus of chapter 4. The emphasis of chapter 5 is somewhat different. Here attention shifts to the offender: what is known about burglars and their strategies.

In discussing research devoted to those who commit burglary, it is noticeable that much of the emphasis in the literature has been on why certain properties are targeted, with a view to recommending preventive policies. Part 3 considers various aspects of policy in more detail. Chapters 6–7 focus on crime prevention and burglary reduction. In chapter 6 the emphasis is on conventional approaches to crime prevention and individual attempts at prevention, while chapter 7 considers a range of recent policy developments in England and Wales. Chapters 8–9 then concentrate on harm reduction. The agency that most victims come into contact with is the police, and in chapter 8 the role of the police in providing – or failing to provide – support is assessed. Chapter 9 covers victim assistance programmes, especially those in England and Wales, where Victim Support initially identified burglary victims as victims *par excellence*. In contrast, commercial burglary, and victims of commercial burglary, have received less attention, and the issue of commercial burglary is the subject of chapter 10. Finally, chapter 11 is concerned with the detection and sentencing of those committing burglary.

As is evident throughout, while each burglary is unique, burglary as a crime is not. For example, many offenders oscillate between burglary and other offences, and policies may target burglary alongside other types of crime. The aims of this book thus combine an attempt to better understand burglary and policies aimed at burglary with an appreciation that by focusing on one offence type the reader might achieve a better understanding of many of the issues surrounding crime and criminal justice policies.

## Notes

1 The details contained here have been abstracted from a number of websites, including:
   http://news.bbc.co.uk/hi/english/uk/newsid_718000/718129.stm
   http://news.bbc.co.uk/hi/english/uk/newsid_717000/717511.stm
   http://guardianunlimited.co.uk/Tories/story/0,7369,409658,00.html
   http://www.tonymartinsupportgroup.org/pages/support.htm
2 Scotland is, despite it being called a 'British' Crime Survey, not included in the BCS, although separate but similar national surveys have been conducted there – and indeed in Northern Ireland – on a number of occasions.
3 A useful review of burglary from the 1998 survey is contained in Budd (1999).
4 Tarling and Davison (2000) provide a concise summary of British findings.
5 The initial research team consisted of Rob Mawby (director), University of Plymouth, and Sandra Walklate, University of Salford, England; Dobrochna

Wojcik and Zofia Ostrihanska, Poiska Akademia Navk, Warsaw, Poland; Ilona Gorgenyi, University of Miskolc, Hungary; and Gerd Kirchhoff, Abteilung Münchengladbach, Germany. The project was funded by the Central European University, contract 7/91–92, total award $55,200. Additional travel funds were supplied by NATO, contract CRG 920530, total award 277,000 BF. The Czech research involved Irena Brabcová from the Police Academy of the Czech Republic and Eva Koubová, at the time of the research a lecturer in the Faculty of Laws, Charles University, Prague. This research was funded for £5,000 by the Nuffield Foundation: ref. SOC.100(765).

# Part 2: The problem

# Chapter 2

# Burglary: the folk crime of the new millennium?

## Introduction

Burglary has not always been singled out as a major problem. Indeed, only a couple of decades ago chief constables could go on record to question the assumption that they should devote extra resources to what was, after all, 'only' a property crime. However, by the late 1980s, the status of burglary, or at least *household* burglary, had been transformed to the extent that it was seen in the UK almost as 'public enemy number one'.

There are a number of reasons behind this change of emphasis. As Tarling and Davison (2000: 6) noted:

> Burglary occupies an important position in the spectrum of crime. As the statistics reveal, it is sufficiently common to touch many individuals and households yet it is also sufficiently serious to affect victims both financially and emotionally.

During the 1980s and early 1990s, burglary rates in England and Wales were rising inexorably. At the same time public perception of burglary as a major threat was established through public opinion polls as well as the British Crime Survey (BCS). This chapter consequently focuses on the extent of burglary and public anxiety. In addition, an awareness that repeat burglaries were common fuelled concern and a variety of studies underlined the impact of burglary on its victims. These issues form the substance of chapters 3 and 4. As a result of these different pressures, as we shall see in later chapters, burglary moved towards the top of the policy agenda.

## Anxiety about burglary

The Tony Martin case illustrates one extreme in terms of an individual's fear of burglary and the extent to which many empathised with this offender-victim. On a more academic level, public concern over burglary in England and Wales was reflected in research by geographers seeking to quantify 'quality of life' (Findlay *et al* 1989; Rogerson *et al* 1988) and through public opinion polls (MORI 1994). It was most forcefully expressed in crime surveys like the BCS, and subsequently in international surveys that put the national pattern in a wider perspective.

Worry about burglary peaked in 1993 in England and Wales. In that year 26% of those interviewed described themselves as very worried and about two thirds said they were either worried or very worried (Hough 1995; Mirrlees-Black and Allen 1998). This was a higher proportion than for mugging, car theft, theft from cars and (for women) rape (Hough 1995: 55). And the proportion who were very worried about burglary was markedly higher than for non-crime problems such as home accidents, debt, illness, job-loss or road accidents (*ibid* 15).

Since then, reflecting falls in anxiety scores overall, the proportion who have expressed themselves worried about burglary has fallen, with 19% saying they were very worried in 1999. This compares with 18% who were very worried about being mugged, 21% for theft of cars and 16% for theft from cars (Kershaw *et al* 2000).

Levels of anxiety do, however, also vary according to the precise question asked. Thus in 1994 'only' 11% felt unsafe at home alone at night, whilst 36% felt unsafe when out alone after dark (Hough 1995). At the other extreme, a question about whether respondents felt they were likely to experience a burglary within the following 12 months, asked in the 1984, 1988 and 1992 surveys, elicited much higher levels of concern. In 1993 about 38% estimated that they were at least 'fairly' likely to experience burglary within the next year (Hough 1995: 13).

The International Crime Victim Survey (ICVS) uses responses to this question as its proxy measure of fear of burglary. It is therefore possible to compare anxieties in England and Wales with those in other countries and consider whether or not burglary is of international concern.

In 1996 41% of those interviewed in England and Wales felt they were at least fairly likely to experience burglary in the coming year, suggesting that on this measure at least anxiety has not declined. Moreover, apart from France, where 53% expressed concern, anxiety in England and Wales was higher than in all other industrialised countries in the survey, including Canada (30%), Northern Ireland (29%) and the USA (23%) (Mayhew and van Dijk 1997: 50). Elsewhere in the world, fear of burglary appeared extensive in most African and Latin American countries, in Indonesia (Asia) (del Frate 1998: 121), Bulgaria, Russia and Slovenia (Zvekic 1998: 84). Zvekic (1998: 84) also provided regional averages to illustrate that burglary was of most concern in Latin America, Africa and 'countries in transition',[1] followed by Western Europe, the New World and Asia. In most, but by no means all, cases these patterns parallel those for fear of street crime. None the less, they illustrate the widespread concern felt about burglary throughout the world. Whether or not such concern is justified is a question to which we now turn.

**The extent of burglary**

Entitled *Safe as houses?*, the report by then Shadow Home Affairs Minister Alun Michael (1993) illustrates the dramatisation of burglary by politicians and policy makers in the early 1990s. Arguing that household burglary was one of the most traumatic crimes experienced by individuals, Michael pointed to a rise in reported burglaries in England and Wales from 252,772 in 1979 to 664,188 in 1992, a rise of 163% in 13 years and with a particularly steep rise during the recession years in the early 1990s. Michael then went on to note regional differences, with the highest increase in East Anglia (288%) and the lowest (89%) in London. Comparing police force areas, Leicestershire (452%) and Gloucestershire (444%) experienced the greatest increases, Merseyside (31%) and City of London (12%) the least. As a result, while accepting that residential burglaries were most common in the conurbations, Michael (1993: 6) concluded that increases were most notable in *rural* areas:

> These figures show that the Shire counties have seen a surge in home burglary since the Tories have been in power, and that their rate of increase has been high whether measured from 1979 or from 1989.

This emphasis on the problems facing rural communities is ironic, given recent attacks on New Labour for allegedly ignoring the plight of the countryside, a point also underlined by many of Tony Martin's supporters. It is also misplaced. Detailed analysis of BCS data has demonstrated both lower rates of burglary in rural areas and that in such areas burglaries comprise a lower proportion of all crimes committed (Mirrlees-Black 1998). Be that as it may, since Michael's analysis the number of domestic burglaries recorded by the police in England and

Wales has declined steadily: from 661,194 in 1994 to 472,960 in 1998, a fall of 28% (Barclay and Tavares 2000: 15).

Despite these trends, it is important to remain sceptical about the validity of official statistics. Not all crimes are known about; where they are recognised, victims may choose not to involve the police; and when the police are involved they may choose not to record the crime, or may record it as something else. With regard to burglary, it is commonplace to assume that official statistics are a reasonably true reflection of all such crimes, partly because of the seriousness of the offence, partly because victims tend to be insured and the need to report the crime in order to make an insurance claim is one of the main incentives to reporting. However, a word of caution is in order, and that word needs to be amplified where we make cross-national comparisons.

The 2000 BCS indicated that some 81% of burglaries with loss were reported to the police and this was higher than for any other offence except vehicle thefts (Kershaw *et al* 2000: 7). However, only about half of burglaries where nothing was stolen were reported. While the proportion reported peaked at 73% for all burglaries in 1991, since then it has declined (Mirrlees-Black *et al* 1998: 51). Moreover, in 1999 only 77% of reported burglaries with loss were recorded as such by the police, with an even lower proportion of burglaries without loss (33%) being recorded. This reflects a steady decrease in the proportion of reported burglaries subsequently recorded by the police between 1981 and 1997, followed by a rise between 1997 and 1999. Although not conclusive, this suggests that at a time when burglary statistics came under closer scrutiny as performance indicators, the police became less inclined to accept victims' interpretations of what had happened. For example, attempted burglaries might be recorded as 'malicious damage'. Whether or not this is the case, the proportion of all burglaries (according to victims' definitions) that were recorded as burglaries by the police declined from 46% in 1981 to 32% in 1997 (based on Mirrlees-Black *et al* 1998: Tables A4.1 and A4.4, 51–53).

Data from other Western industrialised societies parallels that from England and Wales in suggesting that burglaries are highly likely to be reported – relative to other crimes – but that reporting rates for attempted burglary are lower than for completed burglary. Taking all 11 such countries surveyed in 1996, for example, 83% and 48% of burglaries and attempts, respectively, were reported, compared with 56% of robberies and 17% of sexual incidents (Mayhew and van Dijk 1997: appendix 4, Table 9). Insurance requirements were cited by 37% as a reason for reporting the incident (*ibid* 42).

However, although burglary tends to be one of the crimes most likely to be reported across the world, rates of reporting are much lower in less developed societies. Thus del Frate (1998: 88) noted that whilst most burglaries were reported to the police in the New World and Western Europe, less than half were reported in Latin America and barely a third in Asia (see Table 2.1).

Table 2.1: Percentage of burglaries reported to the police, 1992/1996, in six world regions (del Frate 1998: 88).

| | |
|---|---|
| New World | 89.2 |
| Western Europe | 79.8 |
| Countries in transition | 64.9 |
| Africa | 59.3 |
| Latin America | 49.7 |
| Asia | 35.7 |
| Average | 62.7 |

Langan and Farrington (1998: 9) showed that while in England and Wales in 1995 some 66% of burglaries were reported to the police, in the USA only half were. However, the same authors (*ibid* 11) noted that more reported burglaries were recorded as such by the police in the US (72%) than in England and Wales (55%), and whereas the proportion has been declining in England and Wales it has been rising in the USA. Combining these two considerations, it seems that in each country about 36% of all burglaries were recorded. None the less, Langan and Farrington (1998: 13) showed that over the 1981–1995 period trends in burglary rates derived from victim surveys were closely correlated to trends in recorded burglaries. In England and Wales, for example, successive British Crime Surveys revealed an increase in burglaries from 1981 to 1993, followed by a stabilisation and slight fall, from an estimated 829 burglaries per 10,000 households in 1995 to 756 in 1997. This fall was entirely due to a decrease in burglaries where the offender successfully gained entry; the number of attempted burglaries remained unchanged and thereby rose to 46% of the total (Mirrlees-Black *et al* 1998: 10–12). However, data from the 2000 BCS suggested a significant shift with a fall of 13% in burglaries and 31% in attempts (Kershaw *et al* 2000: 18).

Perhaps surprisingly, burglary rates appear to be significantly higher in England and Wales than in the USA. Langan and Farrington (1998: iv) showed that while the police recorded burglary rates in the USA and England and Wales were broadly similar in 1981, a subsequent fall in the

USA was matched by a rise in England and Wales, so that in 1996 the rate in England and Wales was double that in the USA. Titus (1997), similarly noting the declining rate in the USA, pointed out that this fall had received far less attention – from academics or policy makers – than had the declining homicide rate. Similarly, victim survey data reveal that whereas in 1981 burglary was over twice as common in the USA as in England and Wales, a steady fall in the USA combined with a rise in England and Wales meant that in 1995 the burglary rate was about 60% higher in the latter (Langan and Farrington 1998: 2).

*Figure 2.1: Trends in burglaries, including attempts, in England and Wales (Kershaw et al 2000: 18).*

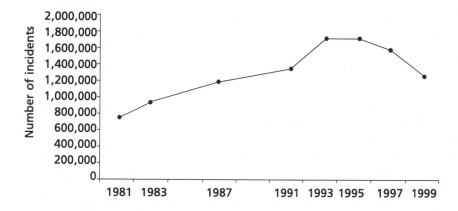

What then does the ICVS tell us about the extent of burglary in different countries? First, it is unequivocal that among Western industrial societies the risk of burglary is comparatively great in England and Wales. In 1996 no less than 6.1% of respondents described themselves as victims of a burglary or attempt within the preceding year, more than in any other country, including Canada (5.3%), the USA (4.9%) and Northern Ireland (2.5%) (Mayhew and van Dijk 1997: 21).

However, on the world stage the situation in England and Wales is less pronounced. Zvekic (1998) has illustrated that rates were markedly higher in Africa and Latin America, and lowest in Western Europe and Asia (see Table 2.2). Moreover, while these patterns broadly mirror those for crime in general, there are dramatic variations for different countries. In Africa, for example, rates for completed burglaries varied from 19.0% in Tanzania to 2.6% in Egypt; in Latin America from 8.2% in Paraguay to

1.9% in Brazil (where the latter has much higher rates for most other crimes) (del Frate 1998: 30–42); in countries in transition rates varied from 9.0% in Mongolia to 0.9% in Croatia (Zvekic 1998: 33). Zvekic (1998) concluded that while burglary rates for regions of the world varied broadly in line with overall crime patterns, national variations were marked. For example, Russia, with high rates for vehicle-related thefts and contact crimes, had a relatively low burglary rate.

*Table 2.2: Percentage of respondents who were burgled in six world regions (Zvekic 1998: 33)*

|  | Burglary | Attempts |
| --- | --- | --- |
| Africa | 8.3 | 7.3 |
| Latin America | 5.3 | 6.3 |
| New World | 4.0 | 4.4 |
| Countries in transition | 3.6 | 3.5 |
| Western Europe | 2.3 | 2.8 |
| Asia | 2.3 | 1.5 |

Following on from this, ICVS analysts considered burglary (completed and attempts) as a proportion of all crime, to ascertain which countries appear to have more or less burglary relative to their overall crime rates. In Western industrialised societies burglaries comprised some 11% of all crimes, varying from 16% in the USA and Canada and 13% in England and Wales to 6% in Sweden and 5% in Finland and Austria (Mayhew and van Dijk 1997: 31). In countries in transition the variation was even greater, from 23% in Mongolia and 20% in Georgia and Latvia to 9% in Romania and 8% in Croatia (Zvekic 1998: 41). Elsewhere burglaries comprised a staggering 38% of crimes in Botswana, 33% in Uganda, 30% in Zimbabwe, 28% in Paraguay, 25% in Costa Rica, 24% in Bolivia, and 23% in Tunisia and Indonesia, but only 9% in China and 7% in Brazil (del Frate 1998: 43). Burglary appeared most attractive in Africa, where it accounted for 26% of all crimes mentioned in the ICVS!

What, then, of changes over time? We have seen that in England and Wales police data suggest a steady increase in burglary rates, although figures levelled out and even declined slightly towards the end of the millennium. As already noted, the US national victim surveys revealed a fall during this period. While ICVS data do not cover the later 1990s, there is some indication that the earlier rise in England and Wales was greater than elsewhere in Western industrial societies (Mayhew and van Dijk 1997: 34–37). Elsewhere the picture is variable. In countries in transition,

Zvekic (1998: 43) noted that between 1992 and 1996 burglaries decreased in three countries included in the second and third sweeps of the ICVS (Estonia, the Czech Republic and Poland) but increased in three others (Russia, Georgia and Slovenia). Del Frate (1998: 56) similarly reported mixed trends from the developing world, with a marked fall in Uganda and a rise in Latin America, particularly Argentina. There are thus no grounds for assuming that a rise in burglaries is inevitable. At the same time, variations in risk and anxiety raise questions about the precise nature of such differences and the reasons for them.

### The myth of the 'average person': variations in risk

Writing about the first British Crime Survey, Hough and Mayhew (1983: 15) cited the average household that could expect to be burgled 'once every 40 years'. Of course, since then levels of risk have increased, and, on average, 4.3% of households experienced at least one attempted or successful burglary in 1999.[2] However, there were considerable variations in risk (Mirrlees-Black *et al* 1998: 29–33; Budd 1999; for more limited data from 1999, see Kershaw *et al* 2000: 19–20). On a regional level, for example, in 1997 households in the North suffered the highest risk (7.7%) and those in the East the lowest (3.1%), with London – perhaps surprisingly – nearer the national average (5.7%). This apart, four aspects might be considered in more detail to illustrate the extent of variation:

- area
- household characteristics
- design and planning features
- and other aspects of lifestyle.

Taking first area, variations in crime between different areas have been acknowledged in the literature since nineteenth century reformers condemned conditions in the 'Rookeries' of the largest British cities. The first academic analysis of the ecology of crime emerged with the Chicago School in the USA, where the inner 'zone of transition' was identified as the source of much crime, including burglary. Reppetto's (1974) study of residential burglars in Boston found that income levels were negatively associated with risk and burglaries were particularly common in areas with low levels of social cohesion (see also Lynch and Cantor 1992). Herbert (1982) also noted that burglaries in Oklahoma City were relatively rare in the more affluent suburbs. Indeed, the concentration of burglaries in socially disadvantaged areas has been a common theme of research in North America (Cohen and Cantor 1981; Waller and Okihiro 1978). Area burglary levels have also been associated with other measures of area disorganisation, such as complaints of incivilities (Rountree and Land 1996).

In Britain, researchers have also highlighted both run-down inner city areas and areas of 'social housing' (council estates) as having particular crime problems. Evans (1989), summarising earlier research, pointed to a concentration on council estates and in inner city areas, and Evans and Oulds (1984) in Newcastle under Lyme noted that all eight enumeration districts with high rates were areas of low socio-economic status. In Swansea and the Gower peninsular, Herbert and Darwood (1992) compared burglary rates in eight areas. They found variations between 7 and 138%. In areas with higher rates of burglary, residents were more likely to perceive burglary to be a problem, and perceptions of risk were closely related to levels of dissatisfaction with one's area. Summarising a variety of studies using police statistics or victim surveys, Evans (1992: 44) concluded that, 'Generally poorer households are more at risk from residential burglary, although within poor areas, higher value properties may be more at risk.'

While many of these studies relied on official statistics, the first victim surveys confirmed this overall picture, while at the same time distinguishing between – for example – high crime rate and low rate council estates (Bottoms, Mawby and Walker 1987). The BCS adds to this analysis. While it does not distinguish between actual areas, it does allow one to compare the experiences of people living in different *types* of area. Thus, for example, in 1999 6.3% of those living in areas categorised as inner city experienced a burglary, compared with 4.2% of those living in urban areas and 2.6% of rural dwellers (Kershaw *et al* 2000; see also Mirrlees-Black 1998). Even more starkly, those living in areas defined by interviewers as showing signs of high physical disorder had a rate of burglary of 11.1% compared with 3.5% for those in areas of low physical disorder.

The most common area dimension from the BCS is, however, the ACORN neighbourhood classification. Again, respondents are grouped into area types, with notable results. For example, in 1999 the lowest burglary rates were to be found in 'affluent grey' rural communities (2.8), 'prosperous pensioners' retirement areas (3.1), 'wealthy achievers' suburban areas (3.2) and 'well-off workers' family areas (3.2). At the other extreme, the highest rates were found among those living in council estates with the greatest hardship (12.6) and multi-ethnic, low income areas (8.6). However, rates were also high in some relatively prosperous areas, which possibly attracted burglars from outside: for example, among 'affluent suburbanites' (8.2) and 'better off executives' inner city areas (8.6) (Kershaw *et al* 2000).

Burglary rates are also high in some other types of area not usually associated with deprivation or disorder. For example, a rather different areal dimension was found in our Eastern European research (Mawby 2001; Mawby and Gorgenyi 1997). Second homes, or *dacha,* are a common feature of Eastern/Central European and Scandinavian societies. In some cases, these *dachas* are located in country areas a considerable distance from one's home. In other cases they may be clustered in the countryside on city perimeters. This was the case in the Hungarian city of Miskolc, where a large number of *dachas* fell under the jurisdiction of the city police. These second homes would commonly lie vacant during the week and be visited by families over the weekend. Staggeringly, almost two thirds of reported burglaries from our Miskolc sample occurred at *dachas.* Holiday areas in general also experience higher levels of burglary (Mawby, Brunt and Hambly 1999), and this is not just associated with empty properties. For example, in Cornwall, Folland and Mawby (forthcoming) found rates of burglary for static caravans in the summer to be significantly higher than for conventional housing.

The ACORN classification used in the BCS, while area-based, describes areas partly in terms of the key characteristics of residents living there. In other respects, though, household characteristics are closely linked to risk of burglary. Five distinctions can be drawn here (see Kershaw *et al* 2000; Mirrlees–Black *et al* 1998):

1   **Age.** While differences for older residents are not as marked as for other offence categories, the BCS clearly identifies households where the head of household is younger as particularly at risk. Thus the rate in 1999 was 12.0% where the head of household was aged 16–24, declining to 2.3 for 65–74 year olds, with a slight rise to 3.2 for those aged 75 and over. In Australia, Phillips and Walker (1997) found a similar pattern using data from the 1993 National Crime and Safety Survey (NCSS).

2   **Household composition.** Risk varies according to the composition of the household, with one-parent families particularly at risk (11.7%). Significantly, this is one of the few social groupings where no fall was recorded between the 1998 and 2000 surveys. Again, the findings from the Australian NCSS parallel this (Phillips and Walker 1997).

3   **Employment status.** While retired people, corresponding to their age, tend to be at low risk, generally those in employment experience less burglary (4.2%) than the economically inactive, such as students and especially the unemployed, who have a rate of 7.2%.

4   **Income.** Households with low total income (under £5,000) experience the highest risk of burglary (6.5%). Thereafter, the risk declines to 3.8 for households with incomes of £20,000–30,000, but then rises slightly to 3.9 for those with incomes above £30,000.

5   **Tenure type.** Just as areas of owner-occupation tend to have lower rates of burglary than areas of privately rented or public sector accommodation, so owner occupiers have markedly lower rates (3.1%) than either council house occupiers (6.7) or private renters (7.5).

Overall, despite the controversy over risk in rural and middle-class areas, these findings, taken together, underline the fact that it is the poor, the disadvantaged and inner city dwellers who are most likely to experience burglary (Tarling and Davison 2000).

Rates also vary according to design features – of the home or surrounding area (Newman 1973). The 2000 BCS showed that detached houses were at least risk (2.8%), with terraced houses (5.6) and flats/maisonettes (5.4) at the other extreme (Kershaw *et al* 2000). While clearly here the influence of design is clouded by the fact that social class and affluence also influence accommodation choice,[3] other differences are evident according to housing location. Thus in 1997 those living in cul-de-sacs were at lower risk (4.3%) than those living in side roads (6.2%), with main roads apparently most vulnerable (6.6%) (Mirrlees-Black *et al* 1998; see also Rengert and Wasilchick 2000). Reppetto's (1974) study of residential burglars in Boston found that design and location of dwelling influenced risk of burglary. Those more at risk included large multi-unit dwellings with at least three entry options, those dwellings located on corners, and those with insecure doors. Similarly, Evans and Fletcher (1998), focusing on residential burglaries in an affluent area of Stoke, found that houses that were readily accessible to major routeways were at particular risk.

In this respect, Jackson and Winchester's (1982) early research in Kent is particularly noteworthy. Comparing victims of (reported) burglary with other residents, they highlighted the significance of 'environmental risk':

Victim houses were for example more likely to be distant from other houses so that gardens were not overlooked and obscured from public view by trees, shrubs, fences and by virtue of being set a long way back from the road in which they stand. (*ibid* 14)

To clarify the relationship between environmental risk and victimisation, the authors constructed an index based on 14 measures of access and surveillance, including: set back from the road; accessible at both sides from front and back; and set at a distance from the nearest house. The resulting analysis was unequivocal. While the average burglary risk was 1 in 99, those scoring 0 on the index had a risk of 1 in 1,845 and – at the other extreme – those scoring 9 or more a risk of 1 in 13!

Of course, accessibility and 'surveillability' will vary in importance depending on the nature of the goods stolen. A grand piano, for example, can be more readily removed from a house with van access than from a penthouse flat! Thus Poyner and Webb (1991) found quite different patterns for burglaries involving electronic equipment and cash/jewellery.

Other aspects of lifestyle are also important discriminators. The length of time the home is unoccupied, and therefore relatively vulnerable, for example, makes a difference (Phillips and Walker 1997; Rengert and Wasilchick 2000; Reppetto 1974). Lynch and Cantor (1992), for example, found that the extent to which properties were occupied during the evenings affected burglary risk, and Mawby *et al* (1999) demonstrated that homes that were empty for longer in the daytime were more likely to experience a daylight (rather than a night-time) break-in. According to the 2000 BCS, homes empty for five or more hours on an average weekday were at most risk (4.6%) (Kershaw *et al* 2000). Jackson and Winchester (1982) also illustrated the close association between risk of burglary and occupancy. First, they noted that when their interviewers called they were less likely to find anyone at home for their victims sample compared with their nonvictims sample. Second, as Table 2.3 illustrates, burglary victims were particularly likely to state that their home was empty at different times. Finally, 'It was those victims who were most likely to leave the house unoccupied during the day who were burgled at that time and those who were most likely to leave the house unoccupied in the evenings who were burgled then' (*ibid* 17–18).

Interestingly, it also appears that those in the process of moving are also a high risk group. In an analysis of BCS data, Ellingworth and Pease (1998) confirmed Trickett, Osborn and Ellingworth's (1995) observation that those moving home had higher rates of property crime victimisation than non-movers, and that this was particularly so in the pre-move period.

*Table 2.3: Percentage of victim and general household samples who described their homes as unoccupied (from Jackson and Winchester 1982: 17).*

|  | Victim sample | Household sample |
|---|---|---|
| In last week, home mostly unoccupied during the day | 33 | 19 |
| In last week, home mostly unoccupied during the evening | 25 | 14 |
| In last year, home empty for more than two weeks | 71 | 39 |

While area, housing design, household characteristics and lifestyle factors all contribute to different levels of risk, the relationship between them is sometimes complex. Considering the relative importance of area and household features, Trickett, Osborn and Ellingworth (1995: 283) argued that target selection is determined first by area characteristics and only second by the nature of the individual household within that area:

> Thus it appears that for property crime in aggregate, the place of residence is more important in determining the risk of victimisation than the characteristics of the individual household.

Although they noted higher risks of property crime for those in rented accommodation, professionals and those of Indian origin, area differences were greater, with higher risks in areas with high levels of vulnerability (measured by proportion of single-parent households and households living in non-self-contained accommodation, poverty (measured by low car ownership) and people aged 16–24.

Combining the two, they pointed out that area and individual characteristics do not necessarily operate in the same direction:

> For instance, the proportion of no car households in an area is associated with higher risks of property crime, particularly for burglary and criminal damage. However, target choice within an area falls heavily on professional people living in detached and semi-detached dwellings. To caricature, richer people in poorer

areas suffer property crime particularly heavily. Conversely, relatively low risk is faced by poor people living in rich areas. (*ibid* 291)

On the other hand, combining household and area variables can produce stark differences. For example, Mirrlees-Black *et al* (1998: 33) drew comparisons between pairs of opposites, where differences in burglary rates are extreme. Thus only 2.3% of older households living in rural areas experienced a burglary in 1997, compared with a dramatic 19.3% of younger households residing in the inner city. At the same time, the rate was 4.2% for high income households in rural areas and 10.0% for low income households in inner cities. And whereas only 3.3% of owner-occupiers residing in rural areas were burgled, 13.6% of private renters in inner cities were.

Given that such differences emerge, it is appropriate to consider why burglary rates vary so much between and within countries. One approach to explaining variations in risk is routine activity theory (Felson and Cohen 1980). Routine activity theory attempts to explain the incidence and distribution of crime in terms of three sets of actors: potential offenders, potential victims, and law-enforcement agencies and other 'capable guardians'. It may be used to explain differences in victimisation rates between countries and in different areas of a country, but has been most commonly applied to differences over time and between victims with different social characteristics.

In terms of potential offenders, criminologists have considered conditions that appear to be associated with crime, such as unemployment, poverty, poor housing, etc. that may equally be applied to burglars. Similarly, theories such as anomie or subculture theory that associate crime with certain types of area can be applied to specific countries where population flux and underdevelopment may combine to create a breeding ground for crime. On the other hand, differences between burglary and other offences – in terms, for example, of relative rewards or different sentencing policies – may encourage or discourage offenders from committing burglary as opposed to other types of crime. Titus (1999), for example, suggested that the declining burglary rate in the USA might be partly due to a falling unemployment rate, and partly due to a switch by drug misusers from burglary to robbery. We shall revisit some of these issues in chapter 5.

Second, the role of 'capable guardians' may be significant. While there is little evidence that an increase in a police presence acts as a deterrent and results in a decrease in criminal activity (although changes in policework may affect the ways in which crime is processed), in other respects burglary may be particularly difficult to police, both in terms of prevention and detection. We shall reconsider these questions in chapters 6 (on crime prevention) and 11 (on detection). Similarly, while neighbourhood watch has been heralded as a core component in the 'fight against crime', and particularly burglary, its impact is questionable (see chapter 6).

Turning to consider victim behaviour, victimologists such as Gott-fredson (1984) and Maxfield (1987) have demonstrated that lifestyle is closely associated with victimisation. Four aspects of this have been identified regarding burglary (Cohen, Kluegel and Land 1981; Lynch and Cantor 1992), namely:

- target exposure – the visibility and accessibility of the home

- guardianship – the extent to which the home is protected

- target attractiveness – value of property that might be stolen

- proximity – distance of target from potential offenders.

Target attractiveness is often cited as an explanation for rising rates of burglary in affluent societies, where an increase in expensive (and relatively small) consumer goods such as microwaves, VDRs, and hi-fi equipment boosts the rewards to be gained. Target exposure has been deployed to explain international variations. Thus Block (1987), compar-ing the Netherlands with the USA, found that the former only had a lower risk of burglary during the daytime, a feature he attributed to its low rate of female participation in the workforce: that is, homes were less likely to be empty in the day in the Netherlands and were therefore better protected.

With regard to variations in risk between different groupings within a country, the relationships detailed above are clearly compatible with opportunity theory. For example:

- Target exposure – detached or isolated homes may be more vulnerable; houses with easy access (paths to the side and rear) are more likely to be broken into.

- Guardianship – homes that are left empty for longer periods, including holiday homes, are most at risk.

- Target attractiveness – some areas are prestigious enough to attract burglars in from outside; in general, though, within an area more 'attractive' homes may be targeted.

- Proximity – burglary is more common in poor inner city areas and areas of public housing, areas where potential offenders are likely to live.

While much of the evidence here comes from comparisons of contrasting groups of the population at one point in time, Witterbrood and Nieuwbeerta (2000) have demonstrated the importance of routine activities by comparing respondents' experiences of crime as their lifestyles changed. As people grew older, got married, had families, moved out of the inner city, etc., so their risk of burglary and other crimes changed.

However, people vary in their abilities to exercise choice. For many, life in the high crime inner city may be the only realistic choice available. The fact that area, and related measures such as tenancy status and prosperity, are so closely and consistently associated with risk suggest that proximity is the most significant factor. Other factors, like target exposure, guardianship and attractiveness, may then explain why homes in more affluent areas are sometimes burgled or help distinguish targeted homes in high crime areas. The poverty dimension is also important in the context of differential abilities to protect one's home through 'target hardening', an issue covered in more detail in chapters 6–7.

Clearly, risk is not equally distributed across the population. This raises questions about variations in levels of concern or anxiety, and the relationship between risk and fear.

## Variations in levels of anxiety

The concept of fear of, or anxiety about, crime has featured prominently in criminology. During the 1970s and 1980s, and prompted by the first British Crime Survey (BCS) (Hough and Mayhew 1983), fear was frequently seen as distinct from risk and as a problem in its own right. After all, when research suggested that older people and women, groups least at risk, were most likely to express concern, it was tempting to question the relationship between fear and risk, and indeed to question what exactly questions aimed at operationalising fear were actually measuring. This resulted in debates over the extent to which people's fears were irrational (Garofalo 1979) and policies aimed specifically at tackling fear of crime as distinct from risk (Home Office Standing

Conference on Crime Prevention 1989).

In recent years, this emphasis has changed. A notable contributor to recent debates is Hough (1995), who, in an analysis of the 1994 BCS, demonstrated the association between anxiety over crime and both demographic variables and other measurements of perceptions and experiences of crime, and then proceeded to argue that such patterns revealed a degree of rationality from respondents.

Fear and anxiety about burglary were more common, in descending order, for: Asians, inner city residents; blacks; women; those from manual households; urban dwellers, and those aged under 60. Similarly, those expressing most fear or anxiety also: worry more about noncriminal misfortunes; register higher perceptions of risk of burglary; have more direct experience of burglary; have a neighbour who has been burgled in the past year; and live in areas where they feel a lack of neighbourhood support.

Although the questions asked in the 1998 BCS were not exactly the same, Mirrlees-Black and Allen (1998) report a similar pattern, with those most at risk, those with personal experience, and those most physically vulnerable expressing most concern. For example, whilst 19% overall were very worried about burglary:

- 36% of those burgled in the last year

- 30% of inner city dwellers

- 64% of those living in areas where they perceived incivilities and petty crime to be common

- 30% of those who described their health as bad

- 26% of those suffering a disability

were categorised as very worried.

Notably, while burglary victims were more worried about burglary than were nonvictims, they were no more worried about mugging, and *vice versa*. Hough (1995: 22) consequently argued that: direct and indirect experience of crime combined with other cues about crime and disorder to shape perceptions of risk; these in turn interacted with people's social and physical vulnerability and their tendency to worry about problems in general to produce varying levels of fear and anxiety. Consequently, he concluded that people's fear of crime was rational and related to risk:

Worry about crime is shaped by respondents' relevant experience and by their knowledge of others' relevant experience.

And:

Those who are most susceptible to the consequences of crime worry more than others about becoming victims. (Hough 1995: 43)

Similar findings have been reported in the USA. For example, Rountree and Land (1996) found that fear was most evident amongst those who had experienced a burglary and among those living in areas where burglary was common. In the former case, they noted that burglary led to a 12 percentage point increase in feelings of lack of safety. In the latter, 'With each unit increase in signs of disorder in the tract, the odds of feeling unsafe increase by some 15%' (*ibid* 169).

Nevertheless, it is equally plausible to argue that at least some fear of crime is irrational. Thus, as Hough himself acknowledged, levels of fear, including fear of burglary, appear to have oscillated in the last 15 years, while the burglary rate in England and Wales has risen markedly. Yet people still tend to overestimate their risk. For example, in 1993 some 6% of households were burgled, but nearly 40% of those interviewed thought they were 'certain' or 'likely' to suffer burglary in the next 12 months (Hough 1995: 13). Although people at low risk appear less worried than those at high risk, the evidence suggests that they still considerably overestimate the likelihood of burglary. Moreover, worries over burglary, as we have seen, are relatively high compared with worries over other problems we might encounter. Finally, as Mawby *et al* (2000) have illustrated with regard to tourists, in some contexts the opposite scenario appears to apply: that is, people who are at a relatively high risk express low levels of concern.

What, then, does a cross-national perspective add to this debate? On the one hand, del Frate (1998: 120–121) noted a correlation between fear and risk:

The higher the rates of victimisation for burglary and attempted burglary, the higher the fear of this type of crime. There is a strong correlation at the regional level between perceived likelihood of burglary and victimisation rates for burglary ... The positive correlation between perceived likelihood of burglary and burglary observed at the regional level holds true also at the country level in developing societies.

On the other hand, compared with respondents from other Western industrialised countries, those interviewed in England as part of the international crime survey evidenced comparatively high rates of fear or worry (Mayhew and Van Dijk 1997). It is thus arguable that people in England and Wales worry more about crime and see crime and disorder and other problems as ever-present to a much greater extent than is justified by the actual crime rate. The same is true to an even greater extent in France, where as we have seen, anxiety levels are high but burglary rates are actually little more than average at 3.9% (*ibid* 21).

## Summary

Clearly burglary is of considerable concern to people, not just in Britain, but elsewhere in the world. Equally, some people are more anxious about burglary than are others. This raises the question of how far the extent and distribution of burglary justify such concerns. Here there is persuasive evidence that those who are most at risk, those who have recent (direct or indirect) experience of burglary, and those it is most likely to affect register most concern. However, in some cases low risk subgroups of the population express high levels of anxiety; in other cases high risk groups evidence less concern than we might expect.

Risk of burglary varies markedly according to the characteristics of the population, and following routine activity theory, we can identify the reasons for this in terms of offender and victim features and capable guardianship. In particular, it seems that victim characteristics, most notably associated with poverty and other aspects of lifestyle, are closely associated with risk. In chapter 4, we consider how far similar explanations apply to repeat burglary. In chapter 3, the impact of burglary, evidently a component of fear, is considered in more detail.

In considering the relationship between fear and risk, it is important, however, to underline one other point. While researchers have tended to debate the extent to which fear or anxiety is justified, and therefore rational, clearly burglary is far more prevalent among the disadvantaged, the poor, and inner city dwellers. Among such people, fear of crimes like burglary is a very true reflection of the reality of urban life.

An additional issue, to which we return later, is the impact that fear and experience of burglary have on behaviour. People may respond to burglary, for example, by taking sensible precautions: protecting themselves by fitting locks and alarms, or participating in neighbourhood watch. But there is a fine line between such sensible precautions and reactions that unnecessarily restrict one's lifestyle and affect quality of life. Moreover, where large numbers of people change their behaviour through fear of crime, the result may be widespread and herald a spiral of decline in the neighbourhood – for example as empty streets and disused shops themselves lead to increases in disorder and incivilities and increase the likelihood of crime (Skogan 1990).

## Notes

1 While logically the term 'countries in transition' may apply to any country in a situation of significant political change (e.g. post-colonial societies), it is restricted in the ICVS (and herein) to post-communist societies.
2 This was, in fact, lower than the 1997 figure of 5.6%.
3 In relatively affluent Kent, Jackson and Winchester (1982) found detached houses to be relatively likely to be broken into.

# Chapter 3

# The impact of burglary

## Introduction

While by no means all victims are affected by their experiences, many are. The ways in which victims are affected also varies according to the nature of the crime and the characteristics of victims. Physical injuries and financial losses are among the most obvious effects, but they are not the only ones. Emotional reactions are also relatively common. This chapter begins with a brief consideration of the impact of crime in general, and then compares the experiences of burglary and other victims. It then focuses on research on burglary victims, particularly, but not exclusively, our research in England, Germany, Poland, Hungary and the Czech Republic. The financial effects of burglary, and the extent to which insurance militates against these, are described. However, research has identified the impact of burglary to be much wider than this, and the emotional concerns of victims are addressed. Finally, the extent to which different victims are affected differently is considered.

The 1998 British Crime Survey found that 20% of victims in England and Wales described themselves as 'very much affected' by their experience and as many as 84% said that they, or someone else in their household, had experienced emotional reactions (Maguire and Kynch 2000). Responding to a checklist, 65% described themselves as experiencing anger, with 25% recording shock, 17% fear, 13% difficulty in sleeping and 11% crying. Not surprisingly, those most affected were most likely to have reported the incident to the police. Additionally, women, black or Asian victims, poorer people, those living in more depressed areas, those with restricted mobility, and single parents were more likely to describe themselves as affected.

Maguire and Kynch (2000) also noted that crime impacted rather more on burglary victims than on those experiencing other types of crime, both property and violent. As Table 3.1 illustrates, this applied whether or not the crime was reported to the police.

*Table 3.1: Percentage of victims interviewed in the 1998 BCS who described themselves as 'very much affected' by the incident, by offence and whether or not crime reported (Maguire and Kynch 2000: 5)*

|  | Reported | Not reported |
|---|---|---|
| Burglary | 39 | 31 |
| Thefts | 21 | 15 |
| Vandalism | 34 | 20 |
| Violence | 35 | 24 |
| Threats | 36 | 22 |

Similarly, while victims of violent offences described themselves as shocked and having cried more frequently than victims of burglary, as Table 3.2 illustrates, the latter were *more* likely to report difficulty in sleeping and just as likely to register fear. For each crime type, though, anger was the most common reaction. In Scotland, Ditton *et al* (1999), offering victims a similar list but 'allowing' them only one answer, also found that the most common response, by 69%, was anger, although in this case burglary victims were more likely than others to cite other reactions such as shock or fear.

*Table 3.2: Percentage of victims interviewed in BCS who described themselves as affected in the following ways (Maguire and Kynch 2000: 4)*

|  | Anger | Shock | Fear | Insomnia | Tears |
|---|---|---|---|---|---|
| Burglary | 65 | 37 | 30 | 29 | 16 |
| Thefts | 68 | 17 | 5 | 6 | 5 |
| Vandalism | 73 | 13 | 9 | 10 | 6 |
| Violence | 64 | 44 | 29 | 20 | 25 |
| Threats | 64 | 30 | 35 | 18 | 14 |
| Total | 67 | 25 | 17 | 13 | 11 |

Such findings may well be distorted by the fact that some of the most serious crimes are relatively rare, and therefore subsumed in more general categories. Certainly a number of US studies report higher levels of impact for interpersonal crimes (Kilpatrick *et al* 1987; Lurigio 1987; Norris *et al* 1997; Resick 1987). It is also worth noting that earlier BCSs have found that, in general, victims of personal crimes were affected more than victims of property crimes (Maguire and Corbett 1987; Mawby and Walklate 1994; Mayhew, Elliott and Dodds 1989). Nevertheless, burglary victims have consistently described themselves as affected more than victims of other property crimes.

It is important to stress the wide varieties of response that burglary evokes, because it is tempting to assume that the major cost to victims is a financial one, and that where victims are insured the impact is minimal. Indeed, burglars often make this point. On the contrary, burglary clearly impacts on its victims more than do many other crimes and affects people more, and in more varied ways, than other non-contact property crimes.

**Research on burglary victims**

In a small study of burglary victims in Wales, Beaton *et al* (2000) suggested that the psychological impact of burglary was considerable, and extended over a number of weeks. Taking all burglaries described in the 2000 BCS, Kershaw *et al* (2000, 78) reported that 87% of victims considered themselves emotionally affected, 29% very much so. While anger was the most common response – from 68% of victims – shock (38%), fear (33%) and insomnia (31%) were also regularly mentioned. Whether Tony Martin was reacting to the intruders he disturbed with anger or fear is, of course, a matter for speculation.

Studies that have focused on burglary victims, especially victims who have reported the incident to the police, confirm the variety of reactions. Maguire's (1980; *ibid* 1982) research in the Thames Valley area provided an early illustration of this (see also Waller and Okihiro 1978). Respondents were asked to describe, in their own words, their initial reaction. Anger or annoyance was mentioned by 30%, shock by 19%, upset/tears/confusion by 17% and fear by 9%. Moreover, at least a quarter said they were still affected at the time they were interviewed. When Maguire gave the interview data to a panel of volunteers to assess the extent to which the crime seemed to have affected victims, 13% emerged as seriously and 22% fairly seriously affected.

Asked to say what had been the worst thing about the incident, and allowing two choices from a checklist, 63% opted for intrusion on privacy, 44% emotional upset and 45% loss of property. However, Maguire noted that the effects were much broader than this. For example, given that most burglaries remained unsolved, many victims agonised over whom the offender could be and became convinced that it was someone known to them. This in turn led them to treat routine callers – neighbours, tradesmen, etc. – with suspicion:

> Victims tended to re-interpret small events in the past – arguments with neighbours, visits to the house, 'prying' questions, etc., – as related to the burglary. For example, one woman stated that she now 'suspected everybody' of being the culprit... She said she was 'racking her brains' as to who could have done it: 'You have this awful suspicion about everybody who comes near your house: the milkman, the kids, even people you have known for years'. (Maguire 1980: 264)

In our research on burglary victims who had reported their crime to the police, we also found victims to have been severely affected. Combining the two English cities in the research (Plymouth and Salford), 38% of respondents said they had been affected very much and 31% 'quite a lot' (Mawby and Walklate 1997). The impact was even greater among victims from Poland and Hungary (Mawby *et al* 1999), as Table 3.3 illustrates. Most victims also said that they (92%) or someone in their household (95%) had been emotionally affected at that time.

*Table 3.3: Percentage of burglary victims in each city affected at the time*

|  | Plymouth | Salford | Warsaw | Lublin | Miskolc | Total |
|---|---|---|---|---|---|---|
| Very much affected | 29 | 43 | 65 | 72 | 61 | 54 |
| Affected quite a lot | 37 | 25 | 24 | 18 | 30 | 27 |
| Affected a little | 25 | 30 | 9 | 10 | 9 | 17 |
| Not at all affected | 8 | 2 | 1 | 1 | 0 | 2 |
| Other | 1 | 1 | 1 | 0 | 0 | 0 |

Victims were then offered a checklist of five emotions commonly identified in the literature. As is clear from Table 3.4, 74% of all burglary victims said that they had been angry, 44% said that they had been shocked, 35% said that they had been afraid, 27% admitted to having had difficulty sleeping, and 17% reported that they had cried. Although victims who lived in households with other adults were somewhat less likely to record them as having been affected, the order of emotions described was identical. In contrast, children were most often described as afraid or tearful (Table 3.4).

The question of children's reactions to burglary is an interesting one, given an appreciation by Victim Support that by concentrating their attention on adult householders they may have been missing one group in particular need of help. Our findings here suggested that while children were not, at least according to adults from their households, as likely to be affected as were adults, they did suffer a number of effects. For example, as one respondent said:

> I feel guilty because of my children. They are devastated and there is nothing I can do. I can't afford to replace their things . . . They are still upset and staying with my mum.

In other cases, respondents cited concern for their children's safety as influencing their own responses, although overall those with children were only marginally more affected themselves. Nevertheless, concern for one's children did shape many victims' perceptions. For example:

> Mainly I was afraid to sleep there – in a sense more afraid for the children.

> I froze. They'd been in my house. They could have touched my little girl. It's horrible.

The fact that some victims were more concerned on their children's behalf than the children were themselves reflects in part the lack of awareness among very young children (Mawby and Walklate 1997). Take, for example, the following excerpt from the interviewer's notes:

> The interview took place with the parents, in the presence of their three-year-old son, some of whose toys had been stolen. Throughout the interview, the mother constantly made reference to the fact that 'everything was now alright since the nasty man had been locked up.' When I posed the question on whether the perpetrator had in fact been arrested, the victim gesticulated that the burglary remained undetected.

*Table 3.4: Percentage of respondents and, where appropriate, other adults and children, who were emotionally affected in the following ways*

|  | *Respondents* (n = 1,000) | *Other adults* (n = 760) | *Children* (n = 325) |
|---|---|---|---|
| Anger | 74 | 58 | 12 |
| Shock | 44 | 37 | 18 |
| Fear | 35 | 29 | 38 |
| Insomnia | 27 | 19 | 14 |
| Tears | 17 | 11 | 25 |

While the next section focuses on financial and material losses, the effects are clearly much broader than these.

## Financial problems

The financial costs of burglary are considerable. The 1998 BCS estimated that for England and Wales in 1997, household burglary cost in total £950 million, with damage during the burglary an additional £420 million (Budd 1999). Moreover, although the approximate cost averaged out at £1,400 per burglary, Tarling and Davison (2000) noted that the average insurance claim was far lower, implying that even when insured victims shouldered much of the cost themselves. They also found that many victims took time off work, which may also have financial implications.

The BCS provides considerable information on the financial impact of burglary. Analysis of the 1994–2000 surveys revealed that where items were stolen, the most likely to be taken – each in about a quarter to a third of all cases – were jewellery, video equipment and cash, with stereos and televisions also commonly stolen (Kershaw *et al* 2000). However, patterns seem to have changed over time. For example, television, videos and stereos/hi-fi equipment were increasingly likely to be taken in the 1980s (perhaps reflecting their worth on the resale market), but declined in popularity in the 1990s (possibly as they became less easy to fence) (Kershaw *et al* 2000; Mirrlees-Black, Mayhew and Percy 1996). About a quarter of 'successful' burglaries involved losses of less than £100, but a third involved more than £1,000. Nearly three quarters also involved damage (Kershaw *et al* 2000).

Mawby and Walklate (1996) reported that 90% of their sample of (reported) burglary victims in Plymouth and Salford said that items had been stolen and 70% that damage had been incurred; 96% said that they had suffered a financial loss due to theft and/or damage. Generally Salford victims were more likely to have suffered loss, particularly damage. However, the cost of items stolen was slightly higher in Plymouth. Overall the estimated median value of the items stolen was £717, but variations were marked, with 18% losing £2,000 or more, 7% less than £50. Electronic goods (including cameras) were the most common targets, taken in 67% of burglaries, with jewellery (41%) and cash (38%) also frequently taken. Receptacles, possibly used for carrying other items, were stolen in 22% of incidents, and credit cards, saving books, etc. in a further 17%.

Cross-national comparisons of financial loss are difficult. Del Frate (1998: 63), in comparing the developing world with more affluent societies, suggested that variations occurred according to what was readily available and the motive behind the theft:

> According to the national co-ordinators from the developing countries, stolen goods often included money, food and simple household objects such as cutlery or linen which most probably were stolen for the personal use of the burglar... Vice versa, in the more affluent regions, where most people keep their money in the bank and often jewelry and other valuable objects are kept in safes and security lockers, burglars take what is available and give preference to objects that are easily re-sold. In this respect, the most frequently stolen objects are those that are easier to place on the market of stolen goods, such as electrical appliances, TV and radio sets, VCRs, hi-fi equipment, as well as furniture and objects of art.

One impression from our research in Central and Eastern Europe was that the same types of goods were taken as in the West, with the exception of credit cards, which were less readily available there and consequently rarely stolen. But in many cases the burglars systematically stripped the home, even taking used clothes. In such cases the overall value of the burglary might have been less, but the relative loss to the victim and the consequential impact of the crime might have been more pronounced.

Cross-national comparison also reminds us of issues concerning insurance. For while the majority of burglary victims in Britain will be covered by a household insurance policy, in other societies, such as countries in transition (Zvekic 1998: 87), cover is less common and less comprehensive.

Even in England and Wales the 2000 BCS revealed that only 48% of victims of burglary with entry were insured (Kershaw *et al* 2000). Overall, 69% made a claim and 87% of these had their claim met. Victims are less likely to be insured than are nonvictims, quite simply because victims are over-represented among poorer people, and these are overwhelmingly the uninsured. Indeed, the most common reason for not being insured is being unable to afford it, and those without insurance are more likely to be: divorced, separated or single; living in privately rented accommodation; unemployed or otherwise economically inactive, and non-car owners; Asians or Afro-Caribbeans; and inner city dwellers (Budd 1999; Lewis 1989; Whyley, McCormick and Kempson 1998). Precisely those most at risk of burglary!

Given that insurance may be a major motivation behind the decision to call the police, the proportion who are insured among those reporting burglary is likely to be higher. Thus Mawby and Walklate (1997) found that among their English samples 69% of respondents were insured. Overall, 60% of victims, or 87% of those who were insured, made a claim, and only 3% of those claiming had their claim rejected. However, only 29% of respondents said that their loss was fully covered by their insurance. In many of the remaining cases victims were required to pay the first, say, £50 of their loss, whilst in other cases insurance companies disputed the value of goods itemised in claims. Clearly it is important that companies ensure that they are not defrauded by victims, but equally a number of people in our samples felt aggrieved at the way they were treated. For example, one burglary victim complained: 'They make you feel you are telling lies.' Another said resignedly: 'This insurance thing is a bit of a nuisance...We've got to accept it as a fact of life actually.'

As well as cases where the insurance claim was rejected, in others victims described the difficulties they experienced before their claim was accepted. For example:

> They are disputing the claim – the chainsaw and stuff. I went to the insurance ombudsman and now the insurance company are thinking of paying out... We have been to the Citizen's Advice Bureau and all... They knocked loads of money off. The video they only allowed us £100...

In another case, an elderly widow from Plymouth explained that her claim had been rejected:

Because they didn't break in. They just walked in, so they wouldn't pay me any insurance.

When later asked what was the worst thing about the incident she noted:

I'm upset about the insurance too. I pay £90 per year for insurance and they wouldn't give me anything.

In this case, with the victim's permission, we referred the case to Plymouth Victim Support who eventually pressured a very reluctant company to honour the spirit of the claim!

What, then, of the situation in other countries? Overall 56% of victims in England, Poland and Hungary were insured and 50% made an insurance claim, although only 16% said that insurance fully covered their losses (Mawby *et al* 1999). However, there were marked differences in insurance coverage. Thus, only 37% of Polish victims were insured, only 34% of these made a claim, and a mere 2% said that the insurance fully covered their losses. Polish victims were also highly critical of their insurance companies, and even where compensation was paid they complained about the level of payments. The following comments illustrate the depth of their feelings:

The insurance compensation covered only 50% of the losses – because of the lack of receipts from shops, and money is not covered by insurance, and the jewellery only partially.

The insurance agency estimated the value of our jewellery equal to the value of scrap-gold. We got from them only 5% of the stolen 20,000,000 (zlotis) and they took away the depreciation value of the video.

Because the burglar opened the door with a false key the compensation from the agency will be lowered by 20%.

The insurance cover was 20,000,000 (zlotis) but we have got only half the sum because in their opinion our locks were not good enough.

We did not ask victims directly for their views on the way that their insurance companies dealt with them. However, the number of unsolicited comments that we received led us to include this as an additional question when the research was replicated in Prague.

Here, about two thirds of victims were insured and 53% of all victims had made a claim 16 or so weeks afterwards. Only a quarter of all victims, however, said their claim had fully covered their losses and victims estimated their net losses at equivalent to nearly £1,400, a very high figure compared with England. Not only did insurance clearly fail adequately to compensate victims, but many complained at the treatment they received from their company. When asked directly, 24% were positive about the way their claim had been handled, but slightly more (28%) made critical comments (Mawby, Koubova and Brabcova 2000).

It is clear that for many, albeit a minority, their experience of making an insurance claim may be considered a form of secondary victimisation (see also Tarling and Davison 2000). Moreover, in few cases does insurance cover the full value of items stolen or damage incurred.

An additional matter that is not covered by insurance is the sentimental value of items stolen. Exactly half the victims interviewed in Plymouth and Salford said they had lost items of sentimental value. Those were commonly items such as jewellery or watches that had been handed down in the family, or which reminded the victim of a special occasion or the memory of a dead spouse or child. However, respondents also cited other items, such as videos of children when young, which were irreplaceable. For example:

It was his (late husband's) wedding ring and my ring from 18th. Don't have much but it's just things we bought one another.

My ring 'cos it was for my sixteenth birthday, and the other was a charm ring for Valentine's Day.

The trinket box had some earrings my gran had given me.

Jewellery ... wife's engagement ring ... daughter's christening items ... video tapes of the family growing up ...

The film inside the video camera was of the children at Christmas and past birthdays.

My mother's engagement ring which she left to me when she died. I didn't know how much it was worth. The watch was an 18th birthday present.

The wider impact of such losses is illustrated in the response of one widow when subsequently asked what her first reaction to the crime had been:

> Just burst into tears...I cried for nearly two days, every time I thought about my wedding rings – you see I was widowed...Just couldn't believe it.

Answering the same question, a Plymouth man noted:

> Anger was the main thing. The watches were the only things in the house that meant anything to me. Especially my grandad's pocket watch. That watch really meant a lot to me – it represented my family history.

Victims from other countries (Mawby *et al* 1999) raised similar points.

## Other effects of burglary

Examples of losses of sentimental value illustrate the fact that financial losses are only one part of burglary victims' experiences. When we asked victims in different European countries what was the worst thing about the burglary, some focused on the loss itself, including sentimental losses. However, four other issues were commonly cited by respondents. First, there was concern that the burglar might return, combined with a feeling that the quality of their lives had been adversely affected:

> Just worry that they're going to come back. It's always in the back of your mind, when you come home, if anyone has broken in again.

> You can't settle in proper now...lights have to be left on, doors bolted...just don't feel secure in your home.

> The lost security. I am afraid that it could happen again. I feel endangered, unsafe.

> I can't sleep. I can't live normally. I am alone now – my husband died six years ago. I can't afford holidays. I have to stay at home. I'm afraid to visit my friends.

> The fear that it can occur again. Who knows what they would do if I was at home.

Second, and following Maguire (1980), was concern over why *their* home had been targeted, with speculation that the burglar was someone whom they knew, someone who knew them. For example:

> How did they know I was away? They also burgled my sister on the same day. How did they know we were both away?

> That we were away at the time and someone came in. You wonder if it's someone you know – if someone is watching what you are doing.

> I have lost confidence in my neighbours. There are reasons to suspect that they know something about the burglary... It is a horrible feeling that there is no one to rely on.

> I became suspicious, reserved towards people.

> I don't understand why just our house was burgled.

Third, and most common, was a feeling of invasion of privacy, a feeling that their home and its contents had in some way been infected. In this respect, clearly, the saying that 'an Englishman's home is his castle' has wider international relevance, even in countries where home ownership is not the norm:

> The fact that your private belongings have been overturned. It really is upsetting... photos and private papers.

> It's an invasion of privacy – the home's the castle sort of thing.

> Not the material loss but the psychological aspects of it. Shock. The experience of a stranger entering my home. Disturbance of the privacy.

> Worst thing of all is that somebody was in my home, read my papers, looked at my photos, touched my things.

> That a stranger was in my house.

Finally, many victims expressed a feeling of injustice that they had worked hard for their possessions and that a thief had then stolen them without having to work for them. For example:

The fact that I'd saved hard for the things that were stolen and they just came in and helped themselves.

Helplessness ... feeling of injustice.

You work your whole life to have something and the thief comes and takes it.

You work through your life. Others take everything and are not punished.

## Long-term impacts: fear

Here the emphasis has been on the *immediate* impact of burglary on victims. However, while – not surprisingly – sex and violent offences have a longer lasting affect (Norris and Kaniasty 1994), as was demonstrated in chapter 2, those who have been victimised appear more fearful than nonvictims, suggesting that burglary may have a longer-term impact. In one of the few longitudinal studies conducted, Norris *et al* (1997) found differences between victims and nonvictims of property and violent crime on several scales. Most notably, on scales measuring fear and avoidable behavior, victims of property crimes registered significantly higher scores than nonvictims, although their scores were lower than those of victims of violence.

The long-term impact is often much wider than this, given that fear affects behaviour. Where fear operates to constrain social behaviour by discouraging victims from leaving the home (Liska, Sanchirico and Reed 1988; Rountree and Land 1996) and, in the case of burglary victims, leaving the home unprotected, quality of life deteriorates.

Given the relationship between victimisation, fear, and perceptions of one's neighbourhood as a safe and desirable place to live, burglary may also result in people moving home. Thus Dugan (1999) found that being the victim of a property crime increased the likelihood of moving within the following year by 12%, and that revictimisation accentuated this. Interestingly, and contrary to her initial hypothesis, she also found that property crime had a greater effect on moving home than did violent crime. Given that poorer people, who are more affected by their crime, are less likely to have the resources to move, this also suggests that many victims are virtually 'imprisoned' in areas where they feel unsafe.

**Differing impact**

The findings from our European research were notable in that victims from different countries expressed broadly similar feelings. Burglary does not, however, affect everyone in the same way or to the same extent. Two distinctions might be drawn. First, we might hypothesise that victims with different characteristics might be differently affected. Second, we can assess how far the different circumstances associated with the burglary make a difference.

Focusing first on the characteristics of victims, Maguire (1980) noted that women appeared to be more affected than men, and that among women, separated, divorced or widowed women were most affected. There was also a tendency for working-class women and those living alone to be worse affected. Citing data from the 1988 British Crime Survey, Mawby and Walklate (1994) also note that women, older people, those living in households with no other adults, and divorced victims were most affected. Those on lower incomes, renters and non-whites were also worse affected.

Our European research revealed four sets of differences (Mawby *et al* 1999; Mawby, Koubova and Brabcova 2000):

- **Age.** While there was no clear pattern with regard to older victims, those aged under 30 were significantly less likely to be affected.

- **Gender.** Although men were more likely to register anger, in all other respects women described themselves as more affected. For example, they were more likely to say that they had been very much affected at the time and twice as likely as men to say that the burglary had left them feeling afraid.

- **Family structure.** The number of single-parent households was small, but respondents from such families consistently described themselves as most affected. At the other extreme, single-adult households appeared least affected. There was also some indication that those with children were more affected than those in households without children.

- **Prosperity.** Those who were poorer, as measured for example by lack of car and not having holidayed abroad in recent years, consistently described themselves as most affected.

While differences according to victim characteristics are commonly identified, variations according to the nature of the crime are less evident. Thus, according to Maguire (1980), night-time burglaries appeared to have no more impact than daytime burglaries, and offences that occurred when the home was occupied no more affect victims than those where the home was empty. Nor did 'successful' burglaries evoke more concern than did those where nothing was stolen. In fact, the only situational difference Maguire found was that incidents involving damage had a greater than average affect.

In our European study we were also able to consider the extent to which variations in the nature of the offence impacted upon victims (Mawby *et al* 1999): that is, whether victims were differently affected according to when the burglary occurred, whether the home was empty at the time, whether their property was damaged, and whether they were insured. The findings suggested that victims who were not insured – and consequently lost more – were more affected by the crime. However, although victims of night-time burglaries were more likely to admit to shock and sleeping difficulties, and those who were alone in the home at the time of the offence registered higher levels of shock and fear, in other respects daytime burglaries and offences committed when the home was empty were, if anything, more likely to affect respondents. Apart from the extent of financial loss, there was thus, contrary to expectations, no convincing evidence that among burglary victims the nature of the offence had any impact on the extent to which they were affected.

A similar point can be made with regard to burglaries of second homes. Although victims of weekend home burglaries were more likely to be repeat victims and more likely to experience wanton damage, we had anticipated that the impact of the offence would be less, simply because attachment to the home would be one step removed. This was, however, not the case. There was some indication that victims of 'normal residence' burglary experienced the most fear, possibly because they felt more vulnerable to burglary when they were present. On the other hand, the fact that weekend homes were empty and unpoliced for much of the time meant that they were a constant source of worry for their owners, who felt powerless to protect them further. And when they were subject to break-ins, victims experienced broadly similar emotions to victims of domestic burglaries. If burglary of one's home threatens the security of one's 'castle', weekend home burglaries appeared to undermine the principle that one is able to escape from the city to the peace and tranquillity of the *dacha*.

## Summary

Far from being 'only' a property crime, burglary appears to have a marked effect on many victims. Financial losses are often considerable, and rarely fully covered by insurance, even where an insurance policy has been taken out. Moreover, stolen items may have a sentimental value that makes them irreplaceable. Additionally, most victims describe themselves as emotionally affected in some way, and although anger is the most common emotion mentioned, shock, fear, sleeplessness and tears are also frequently reported. In many cases, the effects last for some considerable time. As Coupe and Griffiths (1996: 4) expressed it in describing their interviews with 200 burglary victims in the West Midlands:

> The survey of victims revealed that the burglary caused some disturbance, either emotional or physical, to the victim's life in 92% of incidents. It also had longer-term effects on a majority of victims, particularly women, with levels of worry remaining high for at least 18 months after the burglary. These effects concerned the fear of another burglary that often resulted in greater security consciousness and nervousness. Nearly 30% of victims were so concerned by what had happened, and frightened by the risk of it happening again, that they wanted to move house to a less vulnerable area and dwelling.

Nevertheless, not all burglary victims are affected to the same extent and, interestingly, it seems that the nature of the burglary is less important in distinguishing between reactions than are the social characteristics of the victims themselves. In general, victims who are more vulnerable in the first place are affected the most. Allied to the findings of chapter 2, that the deprived and more vulnerable were more at risk of burglary, this raises questions of social justice, that are also considered in regard to repeat victimisation. It also has implications for the delivery of services – that is, whether or not victim assistance programmes successfully target those in most need – that are addressed in chapter 9.

# Chapter 4

# Repeat burglary

## Introduction

Repeat victimisation, also sometimes known as *revictimisation* or *multiple victimisation*, refers to the notion that – within a given time period – an individual or household falls victim to more than one crime. Indeed, it is predicated on the assumption that once one has been victimised once, the risk of a second or third crime experience actually increases. To state the hypothesis colloquially, lightening does strike twice!

However, in testing the theory, there has been some confusion over how precisely to measure the concept. If we consider burglary, for example, should repeat victimisation be confined to cases where a household experiences more than one offence, or more than one burglary? In the latter case, should it cover the property rather than the victim? That is, if a property is broken into on more than one occasion, even though the occupants have changed, should this qualify as revictimisation?

Other difficulties emerge regarding the practicalities of carrying out research. For example, attempts to determine repeat victimisation from police statistics have been limited by the fact that a specific address may be recorded differently on different occasions (Anderson, Chenery and Pease 1995). On the other hand, if victim survey data are used, these refer to (usually) a 12-month time period, whereas ideally one would like to take the offence in question as the start or end date and consider other experiences of victimisation in the following or preceding period. The difficulties of approximating repeat victimisation in this sense are well illustrated if we consider a hypothetical example from the 2000 BCS. Someone who was burgled in November 1998, March 1999 and January 2000, but experienced no other crimes in 1999 would be counted as a 'single incident' victim, since only the burglary in 1999 would count.

Accepting such approximations, the remainder of this chapter addresses repeat victimisation in the context of burglary. After a brief history of research into repeat victimisation, it focuses on the extent and time course of repeats, the extent to which certain victims are more at risk of a repeat burglary than others, and explanations offered for repeat burglaries. While much of the research to date has covered these questions in some detail, rather less attention has been directed at the *impact* of repeat victimisation, and our European research is taken as a case study to illustrate some of the issues arising here. Finally, the implications of research for policy are noted.

## The history of the concept

The term 'recidivist victim' was coined in the USA by Johnson *et al* (1973) to describe victims of serious violent crime who made regular hospital visits with newly inflicted injuries. It was subsequently used by Ziegenhagen (1976) in a study deploying police records for victims of violence (Farrell 1992). At much the same time, Sparks, Genn and Dodd (1977), in carrying out the first victim survey in England, noted that the number of crimes cited by victims did not follow a normal distribution. Applying statistical analysis (the Poisson model) to their data, they concluded that the finding that certain households experienced a substantial proportion of all crimes showed more than merely 'bad luck'; once victimised, one's chance of a further victimisation increased (see also Sparks 1981; Genn 1988).

While in the USA, multiple victimisation continued to be referred to in the context of violence (Hindelang, Gottfredson and Garofalo 1984), in Britain later victim surveys began to accept that it applied across a range of offences. For example, the first Islington Crime Survey referred to it in the context of violence, vandalism and burglary (Jones, Maclean and Young 1986). Similarly, analysis of successive British Crime Surveys has drawn attention to the phenomenon, following Gottfredson's (1984) discussion of multiple victimisation in the context of differential risk.

A further strand to the debate was introduced by the Kirkholt Burglary Prevention Project (Forrester, Chatterton and Pease 1988; Forrester *et al* 1990). This crime reduction initiative, based in a high crime area of Rochdale (see chapter 7), identified multiple victimisation as a key problem facing the estate. The significance of the Kirkholt project, perhaps, is that it effectively translated repeat victimisation from an academic conundrum to a key policy issue.

## The extent of repeat victimisation

Repeat victimisation is clearly most common where the offences in question are somehow linked to one another in a series, for example where violence centres on the same perpetrator repeatedly injuring the same victim. Thus, not surprisingly, violence is often considered a prime offence for 'repeats', and indeed feminist writers have assumed repeat victimisation to be the norm in the domestic arena without considering it part of a wider phenomenon of multi-victimisation.

Findings from the BCS illustrate this (Budd 1999). For example, in a review of data from the first four surveys, Ellingworth, Farrell and Pease (1995) found that between 48% and 59% of personal offences were suffered by victims who experienced five or more such offences. The equivalent figures for property crimes were lower, but at 24–39% still significant. Moreover, for both crime groupings not only did victimisation increase the risk of a second victimisation, but each victimisation increased the risk of a subsequent victimisation. For example, the 1992 BCS demonstrated that those who were the victim of a first property crime had an 18% chance of a second property victimisation in 1991; those who were the victims of two property crimes had a 34% chance of a third!

While this analysis threw up evidence of considerable fluctuations between difference years, later surveys have indicated that repeat victimisation continues to be a common feature. Analysis of the 1998 BCS, for example, by Mirrlees-Black *et al* (1998: 41), revealed that among burglary victims 19.5% were victimised more than once; the equivalent figures for vehicle-related thefts and violence were 23.5% and 31.1% respectively.

A similar pattern has emerged from local surveys. For example, the Kirkholt project identified multi-victimisation as a particular feature of the high burglary levels on the estate. Once a house had been burgled, the likelihood of a subsequent burglary increased fourfold (Forrester, Chatterton and Pease 1988a; *ibid* 1998b). More recently, in a comparison of burglary and car crime in Huddersfield, Anderson, Chenery and Pease (1995: 10–11), using police records, were cautious about the exact degree of revictimisation, for the reasons outlined above. However, they concluded that over an 11-month period 16% of domestic burglaries were definitely repeats and a further 23.5% were possibly repeats.

These studies have concentrated on victims or offence situations to identify the extent of repeat victimisation. A less common alternative is to focus on the offenders themselves. For example, Ashton *et al* (1998) considered a sample of 186 burglars under the supervision of West

Yorkshire Probation Service, and found that no less than 31% admitted to breaking into the same place on more than one occasion. Interestingly, 'repeat burglars' tended to be those who committed most offences and were more established career criminals.

The commonality of repeat burglary has also been noted in North American research. For example, Polvi *et al* (1990) considered dwelling burglaries in Saskatoon, Canada and found that the chance of a revictimisation within one year was about four times what one would expect. A later Florida study concluded that between 1992 and 1994, 1.2% of residents of Tallahassee experienced 29% of all reported burglaries (Robinson 1998). In the Netherlands, Wittebrood and Nieuwbeerta (2000, 104) also highlighted the phenomenon, concluding that: 'For burglary, the odds of being a victim versus not being a victim of this crime in any given year is about 1.7 times higher for individuals who have previously been victimized than for individuals who have not.' In a further Dutch study, Kleemans (2001) has also underlined the extent of repeat burglary. Analysing ICVS data, Farrell and Bouloukos (2001) also concluded that repeat victimisation was common in many industrialised societies for a range of offence categories, including burglary. For example, the proportion of burglaries that were repeats in 1996 was 12% in England and Wales but higher in: Northern Ireland (17%); the Netherlands (21%); Switzerland (19%); France (17%); Finland (25%); Sweden (13%); the USA (33%); and Canada (15%).

Not all the evidence is quite as dramatic, however. Some countries included in the ICVS – such as Scotland (6%) – had much lower levels of repeats, while in Australia Morgan (2001) concluded that repeat burglary was less evident in Perth than earlier Anglo-American studies might have suggested. Our European study although not focusing on revictimisation as such, did ask burglary victims whether or not they had been the victim of a burglary within the preceding five years. While 34% of Salford and 26% of Plymouth respondents answered in the affirmative, with the exception of weekend home victims (see below), the proportions on continental Europe were much lower: 18% in Lublin (Poland) and Miskolc (Hungary), 14% in Münchengladbach (Germany) and 12% in Warsaw (Poland) (Mawby 2001).

## The time course of repeats

While that study covered a five-year period prior to the current burglary, and many analyses have concentrated on a 12-month time period, much of the research has concluded that repeat victimisation is most likely within a few weeks of the first incident. In the Netherlands, Kleemans (2001) recently concluded that the rate of repeat buglary within a month of the first offence was ten times what one might have expected. In perhaps the most detailed study, Polvi *et al* (1990) tracked burglary victims for 12 months after the initial offence, and subsequently extended the time period to four years (*ibid* 1991). They found that the elevated risk of revictimisation lasted for only about six months, and after that risk fell to normal levels. Moreover, within the first six months, a repeat burglary was most common within the first month; it then fell dramatically, punctuated only by a rise at around four to five months.

This pattern was reproduced in Huddersfield as is illustrated in Figure 4.1.

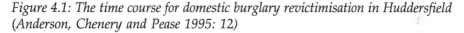

*Figure 4.1: The time course for domestic burglary revictimisation in Huddersfield (Anderson, Chenery and Pease 1995: 12)*

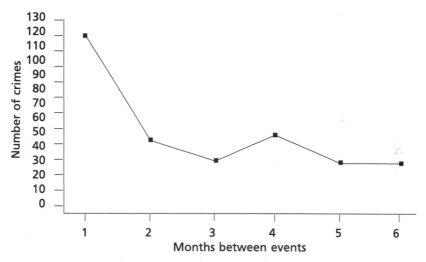

Even more dramatically, Robinson (1998) found that in Tallahassee, Florida, 25% of the revictimisations that occurred over a 52-week period took place within the first week! Again, Robinson noted a slight rise at around weeks 16–17.

## Differential risks

Although repeat victimisation appears to be common, it is clearly more common for some victims than others. Perhaps the most notable and consistent finding here is that those living in the most disadvantaged and high crime areas appear most at risk of both initial and *particularly* repeat victimisation. The fact that revictimisation was so high in Kirkholt was thus no coincidence. More detailed analysis of the BCS has confirmed this. For example, secondary analysis of the 1982 BCS revealed that as the crime rate in an area increased, so did the incidence of multiple victimisation (Trickett *et al* 1992). Subsequent analysis of the 1988 BCS revealed that property crime had become more concentrated and that this was largely due to 'victim prevalence', that is, a growth in revictimisation in high crime regions. In addition, the 1998 BCS (Mirrlees-Black *et al* 1998: 41) showed that those living in the inner city, council estates and areas of high physical disorder were at least 25% more likely than average to experience a second burglary within the year. Conversely, revictimisation is far rarer in rural areas. Analysis of the 1996 BCS revealed that in rural areas 83% of burglary victims were victimised only once and 3% on three or more occasions, compared with 76% and 10% respectively in the inner cities (Mirrlees-Black 1998).

More focused analysis of recorded burglary in South Nottinghamshire (Ratcliffe and McCullagh 1999) provided further detail about areas where repeat burglaries were particularly common. Over a two-year period, the authors concluded that homes in deprived areas were far more susceptible to repeats than were those in affluent areas:

> It would appear that the occurrence of repeat victimisation is found much more extensively in enumeration districts with a high deprivation index.
>
> (*ibid* 42)

Equally, in the Dutch city of Enschede, Kleemans (2001: 62) found that 'in neighborhoods where many dwellings are burglarised, there are also relatively many repeat burglaries.'

A rather different areal dimension was found in our Eastern European research (Mawby 2001; Mawby and Gorgenyi 1997). As already noted, almost two thirds of reported burglaries from our Miskolc sample occurred at *dachas*, a finding we attributed to the lack of capable guardianship. Furthermore, 67% of victims of *dacha* burglary said they had been burgled previously within a five-year period compared with 18% of victims of 'conventional home' burglaries.

Other aspects of lifestyle are related to the risk of a repeat burglary. For example, the 1998 BCS (Mirrlees-Black *et al* 1998: 41) showed that while overall 19.5% of burglary victims were revictimised during 1997, this rose to 22.9% among low income households and a startling 36.6% among single-parent families. Rather differently, Bottoms and Costello (2001) in Sheffield noted that not only were offenders themselves at relatively high risk of burglary, even controlling for the fact that they lived in high crime areas, but that they were particularly susceptible to revictimisation! Finally, our European research suggested that, even excluding *dacha* burglaries, repeat victimisation was most common where the home was left empty for longer periods of time (see Table 4.1).

*Table 4.1: Percentage of repeat and first burglary victims who said their home was empty for at least six hours on weekdays in the daytime*

|  | Repeat victims | First victims | Total |
|---|---|---|---|
| England | 45 | 32 | 36 |
| Poland/Hungary | 61 | 51 | 52 |
| Total | 53 | 45 | 47 |

### Explaining repeat victimisation

In seeking to explain repeat burglary victimisation, at least three questions arise (Farrell 1992). First, why does victimisation increase the risk of revictimisation? Second, why are some victims more susceptible than others? Third, how does the time frame of repeats enter the equation? Essentially, two perspectives have been offered. The first focuses on the reasons why a person or household was targeted in the first place (risk heterogeneity); the second on the effects of the first incident on independently encouraging repeats (event dependency) (Bennett and Durie 1999; Farrell, Phillips and Pease 1995; Morgan 2001; Polvi *et al* 1991).

On the one hand, it seems reasonable to assume that a property that has proved attractive to a burglar would – other things being equal – continue to appear attractive to future burglars. This would seem to underpin our finding that weekend homes were particularly vulnerable to both first and repeat burglaries, and the close association between repeats and lifestyle (Mawby 2001). In this respect, Wittebrood and Nieuwbeerta (2000) and Morgan (2001) also concluded that revictimisation among their sample was largely due to lifestyle variables.

On the other hand, such explanations fail to account for the short time frame of revictimisation and many specialists in the area have argued that the experience of committing a particular burglary may itself increase the likelihood of a repeat. For example, returning to a familiar building may be considerably easier for a burglar than stumbling into the unknown; and knowing that a property is inadequately protected may encourage a return visit. Moreover, waiting until insured goods have been replaced might ensure that there is a good range of new items to steal, which might itself explain the rise in the risk of repeats 4 5 months after the initial offence. In such cases, the original burglar may make a return visit, or information may be gleaned from the criminal grapevine by other burglars.

Interviews with repeat burglars by Ashton *et al* (1998) highlighted five reasons for returning to reburgle a property:

- Because the first time was easy.

- To steal goods the offender was unable to carry on the first occasion, or for which a buyer had subsequently been identified.

- Because breaking into a familiar property was easier: 'Once you have been into a place it is easier to burgle because you are then familiar with the layout, and you can get out much quicker'.

- To steal goods bought to replace those originally taken (see also Clarke, Perkins and Smith 2001).

- Because of a grudge against the victim.


**Case study: the impact of repeat victimisation**

Interestingly, while considerable attention has been directed at identifying and explaining differential risk of revictimisation, somewhat less emphasis has been placed on assessing its impact. Indeed, where it has been debated, discussion has more often than not been restricted to a few case descriptions that demonstrate the severe impact of revictimisation (see for example Anderson, Chenery and Pease 1995: 16–17). This can be termed 'the straw that broke the camel's back' hypothesis, or for convenience the 'last straw' hypothesis. That is, if victimisation is a traumatic experience, the experience of a second offence will increase the trauma. This would also tie in with the findings reported in the previous chapter that associate vulnerability with impact.

In further analysis of our research in Europe, this assumption was questioned (Mawby 2001). A second hypothesis, 'the shock of the new', was put forward. That is, the impact of a second burglary may be cushioned where one has learnt (for example, how to get help or what to expect after completing an insurance claim) from the initial experience. In contrast, those experiencing a burglary for the first time may be affected more where, for example, they hold unrealistic expectations of the police, do not know where to look for support, etc.

To test these competing hypotheses, we compared the responses of first and repeat burglary victims. The findings here are quite clear. On the one hand, asked to describe their reactions at the time of the incident, first time burglary victims expressed themselves at least – if not more – affected than did repeats. For example, 53% said they had been 'very much affected' compared with 43% of repeat victims. On the other hand, repeat victims were more likely to indicate longer-term effects. Thus they were less satisfied with the area in which they lived, more likely to say they planned to move, and – as Table 4.2 demonstrates – less likely to feel secure.

*Table 4.2: Percentage of repeat and first burglary victims who said they felt safe at home alone at night*

|  | Repeat victims | First victims | Total |
|---|---|---|---|
| England | 67 | 76 | 73 |
| Poland/Hungary | 55 | 70 | 58 |
| Total | 61 | 72 | 69 |

The evidence here, then, suggests that while 'the shock of the new' may influence first time burglary victims' *initial* reactions to the crime, revictimisation heightens feelings of insecurity and may even result in drastic actions, such as moving home.

## Discussion: policy implications

The Kirkholt project introduced a policy dimension to the debate over multiple victimisation. If, it was argued, a high proportion of crime was focused on a small proportion of the population, targeting crime prevention initiatives at this group was both socially just and the most effective way of distributing scarce resources; put another way, it enables one to 'get the grease to the squeak' (Farrell and Pease 1993; Pease 1991). On a local level, one of the key thrusts of the Kirkholt initiative was directed at repeat burglary. On a national level, the National Board for Crime Prevention (1994) in Britain chose repeat victimisation as the theme for its first working paper and concluded:

Research findings and demonstration projects have put the prevention of repeat victimisation high on our crime prevention agenda. The Board feels that it is now time for policy makers, senior managers and practitioners in all relevant organisations to integrate the prevention of repeat victimisation into their crime reduction thinking and planning. (*ibid* 13)

In this context, it is notable that burglary reduction policies in England and Wales have incorporated an emphasis on repeat victimisation, and especially repeat burglary, that is quite distinctive. Following Kirkholt, targeting repeat burglary became a priority of the Safer Cities programme and has been continued in more recent central government initiatives, as well as through local Community Safety Partnerships.

## Summary

While revictimisation is commonly associated with violent crime, it is also evident with burglary, where studies in England and Wales, and some other Western societies, have identified it as common, especially in the few weeks following the first incident. Variables that have been associated with initial risk also appear to be linked to repeat victimisation, although it also seems that a successful burglary may in itself generate a repeat. In contrast, less attention has been paid to the impact of repeat victimisation, although what evidence there is suggests that those who suffer a second burglary are more affected in the long term.

Those who are most susceptible to a repeat burglary tend to be most vulnerable in other respects: coming from high crime areas and areas of deprivation and being disproportionately poor or from one-parent families. This ties in with the findings from chapters 2–3. That is, the most vulnerable in our society are most likely to experience burglary, are most likely to suffer a repeat, and are most affected by the crime(s). This alone raises powerful arguments regarding the need for government intervention, a point to which we return in chapters 6–7.

Since the Kirkholt evaluation, more emphasis has also been placed on crime prevention in the context of repeat victimisation, where, it has been argued, targeting resources at those who have already been victimised may be a cost-effective stategy. Again, these crime prevention issues are covered in more detail in chapters 6–7. Before that, however, the following chapter concludes this section by focusing on those who commit burglary.

# Chapter 5

# Burglars

## Introduction

In contrast to the considerable amount of research carried out on victims of burglary, relatively little research has focused on offenders. This is partly because, with a low detection rate (see chapter 11), known burglars are unrepresentative of burglars in general. It is also because traditionally etiological research has considered offenders in general, rather than those committing a specific offence, a strategy that seems partly justified by evidence that most burglars either commit or have in the past committed a wide range of offence types.

Most research on burglars has concentrated on 'captive populations', usually on probation or in prison, and indeed the more detailed studies have tended to exclude juveniles (Bennett 1989; Bennett and Wright 1984; Butler 1994; Maguire 1982; Rengert and Wasilchick 2000; Wiersma 1996). Some detailed studies have been even more selective. For example, Cromwell, Olson and Avary (1991) used a 'snowballing' sampling technique to recruit 30 active burglars. Subjects were only accepted if they admitted committing at least two burglaries per month and fulfilled two out of three other criteria, namely: had a criminal record for burglary; defined themselves as burglars; and were perceived by their peers as burglars.

However, the extent to which convicted burglars are typical of burglars in general is questionable; they may be more typical of 'failed' burglars! The dangers of sampling convicted burglars is well illustrated in an account by Wright *et al* (1992) of their research in Missouri, again based on 'snowball' sampling but in this case including burglars who had evaded detection. Their sample of 105 included 28% who had never been arrested for a serious offence, whereas only 25% had ever been convicted of burglary. Yet whilst one third of their sample averaged five or fewer burglaries per year, 7% committed 50 burglaries or more per year, and burglars who had never been arrested averaged twice the number of burglaries of those who had been arrested!

Bearing this qualification in mind, this chapter describes the characteristics of known burglars and the extent to which they are – or are not – distinct from other 'blue collar' offenders. One offence that has traditionally been seen as distinct from burglary concerns drug misuse. However, burglary is commonly seen as a means of funding a drug habit, and the following section consequently explores the relationship between burglary and drugs. Other explanations for burglary are then considered. The emphasis here is upon rational choice theory: that is, the processes whereby individuals become drawn into a criminal career centred on burglary. This necessarily involves a discussion of burglars' social networks. The chapter then concludes with a discussion of burglars' choices of targets, providing an ideal link into the material covered in part 3.

## The characteristics of burglars

As part of the Kirkholt project (see chapters 4 and 7), probation officers and social workers interviewed all offenders convicted of a burglary (dwelling) in the Rochdale area in early 1986 (Forrester, Chatterton and Pease 1988). Most were male (95%) and lived in council accommodation (95%) and 70% were unemployed. The modal age band for the sample was 21–25. Perhaps surprisingly, only 36% said they had committed the burglary in question on their own.

Data for Plymouth were abstracted from police records for the whole of 1993. During that year only 242 domestic burglars were identified who lived within the Plymouth police division and these were formally linked to 280 burglaries. In contrast to Kirkholt, almost exactly three quarters of detected burglaries involved one offender, with 20% committed by two and 6% by three or more. In all, 81% of offenders were arrested for only one burglary, 19% for two or more. Although two or three offenders were linked with multiple offences, there was therefore no evidence here to suggest that most offences were committed by a small number of prolific offenders.

Most known burglars (93%) were male, with none of the 17 female offenders involved in more than one offence. Three quarters were single and 34% were recorded as having children. Almost all (97%) were white.

Perhaps most notably, they were relatively young. Some 26% were under 20, 35% 20–24, 23% 25–29 and only 11% 30 or more.

Home addresses were available for 91% of known burglars, of whom the vast majority lived inside the Plymouth city boundaries and police division. Considering only those living in the 20 Plymouth city wards, there was a marked concentration of offenders' addresses in certain parts of the city; 31% for example, lived in three inner city wards and offender rates per 100,000 households ranged from nil to 291. Comparing rates for known burglars with ward data from the 1991 census on a range of socio-economic indices, the pattern produced was as unambiguous as it was predictable. Known burglars were disproportionally found in areas with high levels of council housing, low owner-occupancy, low social class, high levels of both male and female unemployment, low rates of car ownership, high levels of overcrowding, and high proportions of one-parent households. They also tended to live in areas with high turnovers of population. Notably, with one or two exceptions, areas with high rates of burglary also had high rates of burglars living there.

The picture of the typical residential burglar in Plymouth complimented that of a recent study in the Netherlands:

Most offenders are male. They often start at an early age. Levels of drug and alcohol consumption are relatively high among burglars. The level of schooling is poor and most are unemployed. (Mutsaers 1996: 13)

This association between deprivation and offending is similar to that found in the criminological literature for offenders in general, where it has traditionally been tied to determinist explanations for offending, such as subculture theory or *anomie*. It has not, however, gone unchallenged. For example, while acknowledging that most burglars in their suburban research were unemployed, Rengert and Wasilchick (2000) argued that many gave up jobs to concentrate on burglary. In some cases, this was simply because burglary was more profitable; in other cases, it proved impossible to 'reschedule' working hours around a 'burglary timetable'. Thus:

In many cases, unemployment is not what caused crime. Crime caused the unemployment. Time conflicts forced individuals to choose burglary or their jobs. The resolution of the conflict led directly to unemployment. (Rengert and Wasilchick 2000: 47)

## Specialising in burglary

The above portrait of the 'typical' burglar is little different from that painted of offenders in general. Not surprisingly, then, comparisons of burglars and those convicted of other offences suggest some contrasting patterns but also a considerable amount of overlap. This is notably the case where researchers have attempted to utilise offender profiling in burglary cases. Take, for example, Farrington and Lambert's (1994; *ibid* 2000) analysis of police files in Nottingham, comparing burglars with 'stranger violence'.

The research utilised data on 655 offenders from Nottinghamshire Constabulary's CRO in 1991. Cases were included where a burglary or serious violence offence was detected, but where nobody (victim, witness or police) knew the offender at the time of the offence. Where offences combined burglary with violence, they were classified as violent.

Analysis of the 345 burglars in the sample revealed that most (95%) were male, white (91%), born in the Nottingham area, single (80%), unemployed (61%) and living with their parents (55%). Compared with those convicted of 'stranger violence', they were more likely to be male, white, under 21, lighter and of smaller build, born locally, unemployed, and to have no children. Burglars (69%) were also more likely than those convicted of 'stranger violence' (55%) to live within a mile of the scene of the crime, although older offenders did travel further to commit their burglaries. This suggested that despite sharing many characteristics with violent offenders, the typical burglar was significantly different in a number of respects.

Burglars were also significantly more likely to have a prior conviction (89% compared with 79%) and to have at least ten previous recorded offences (36% versus 24%). Just over half the burglars but only about a quarter of violent offenders had a prior record for burglary. Conversely, nearly half the violent offenders but only about a third of burglars had a previous conviction for violence. During the nine-month research period 183 offenders committed two or more offences: 753 pairs of offences could be compared for this group, comprising 638 pairs of burglary offences, 69 pairs of violent offences and 46 pairs combining both burglary and violence. This suggests that burglars were the more prolific offenders and that where they offended on more than one occasion the second offence was more likely to be another burglary.

This raises a second issue: namely, the extent to which offenders specialise in burglary. Farrington and Lambert's work suggested a degree of specialism, and others have argued that specialisation seems to occur later in an offender's career (Blumstein *et al* 1988). However, the general consensus is that those committing burglaries tend to commit various other offences as well (Butler 1994; Maguire 1982; Walsh 1986; Wiersma 1996).

This does not, however, mean that offenders select their offences 'cafeteria style' (Klein 1984) from a menu, regularly varying their options and demonstrating a wide ranging choice. Rather, they may alternate within a suite or theme, such that, for example, burglars may commit other property crimes but rarely violence. As, Donald and Wilson (2000, 204), noted, 'although the individual crimes may be different, they may belong to the same theme of behaviour such as violence, dishonesty, or sexual crimes.' This, in turn, relates on a policy level to the notion of displacement (see chapters 6–7).

What, then, of different types of residential burglary?

Following Walsh (1980), Merry and Harsent (2000) distinguished between burglars according to the extent to which there was an explicit interpersonal dimension to the burglar's motive (i.e. the burglar aimed to harm the victim, vandalise property, etc.) and evidence of craft or skill. According to these distinctions, four ideal types were identified:

- intruders: explicitly interpersonal and low craft
- pilferers: implicitly interpersonal and low craft
- raiders: implicitly interpersonal and high craft
- invaders: explicitly interpersonal and high craft.

While the image of the malicious, destructive burglar identified by Walsh (1980) and subsequently dismissed by Maguire (1982) and Tarling and Davison (2000) forms a part of this typology, the second aspect refers to professionalism and planning that will be considered later in this chapter. There are, of course, a number of other facets to the notion of specialisation. One, the extent to which burglars specialise in domestic or commercial burglary, will be considered in chapter 10. One other aspect that is of contemporary relevance is the relationship between burglary and drug use.

## Drugs and burglary

The relationship between drug use and property offences such as burglary is the subject of considerable recent debate (Inciardi 1981). There is a widespread assumption, for example, that financing a drug habit is a primary motive behind much property crime, and, in England at least, the public generally support this idea, blaming drug misusers for the current crime problem (Charles 1998).

Perspectives on the matter have, however, changed over time. In the early 1970s, for example, Penn and Hegner (1971) in California, comparing random samples of burglars and drug offenders, found that the profiles of the two groups were quite different. They concluded that those arrested for burglary and drug offences were drawn from different segments of the criminal population and that there were no significant common points in their offending patterns to indicate any relationship between burglary and drugs. The relationship may, however, be more complex than this. A subsequent study in California compared two samples of juveniles arrested in 1966 on drug charges (Penn 1973). One sample had been arrested in the following five-year period for a burglary, the second had not. The burglar sample stood out in a number of respects: for example, they were more likely to be non-white. It thus seemed that while some groups of drug users might be drawn into committing property offences such as burglary, others were not.

In contrast, more recent research has underlined the close association between drugs and property crimes. In the USA, Johnson *et al* (1985) suggested that up to two thirds of burglars were either addicts or recent drug misusers and in England a sizeable minorities of burglars interviewed as part of the Kirkholt project said that alcohol or drugs played a part in their offending (Forrester, Chatterton and Pease 1988).

In the USA, Rengert and Wasilchick (2000) also noted a close association between drug use and burglary, while *all* Cromwell, Olson and Avary's (1991) sample of burglars were drug misusers, with heroin and cocaine the most common drugs of choice. While the researchers were initially sceptical about generalising their findings, they eventually concluded that the extensiveness of their interviewing strategy, whereby they gradually gained the trust of their subjects, allowed them to uncover levels of drug misuse missed by other researchers.

They also found that most of their subjects committed their first burglary before they began to take drugs on a regular basis. As their offending behaviour became more profitable, they began to spend some of the proceeds on alcohol and drugs. As they became reliant upon drugs, so crimes such as burglary came to be seen as a means of financing a drug habit. Legitimate work became more difficult to maintain, and they became more closely drawn into a drug-using, criminal subculture and a deviant lifestyle.

On the other hand, while some burglars in need of a fix committed desperate acts of burglary, the authors argued that in general depressants were an *aid* to committing a successful burglary. They helped to calm the nerves and, more importantly, helped them 'concurrently attend and respond to stimuli and events both inside and outside the burglary site, and to the movements and actions of accomplices, neighbors, passersby, and occupants' (Cromwell, Olson and Avary 1991: 60; see also Rengert and Wasilchick 2000). In contrast, cocaine, a stimulant, detracted from the burglar's effectiveness. A similar process applied in the selection of targets. Thus those using heroin and marijuana at the time of the interview consistently expressed caution in their choice of a target's suitability, whereas cocaine users were more likely to take risks.

A more recent comparison of prior drug use by offenders incarcerated in English and American prisons has lent further support to the drugs–crime link (Taylor and Bennett 1999). Comparing prisoners subject to urinalysis, the authors found that drug use was widespread among prisoners and that (with the exception of cocaine – a US phenomenon) this was evident in both countries. While this was, not surprisingly, the case among those arrested for alcohol/drugs and public disorder offences, it also applied for property offenders. For example, 71.1% of US and 64.4% of English prisoners arrested for property offences tested positive. However, while in England property offenders were more likely than those arrested for other crimes to test positive, only in the case of marijuana (51.3%) did more than a quarter of property offenders in England test positive for any one drug. In comparison, in the USA 43.5% of property offenders tested positive for cocaine and 39.8% for marijuana.

Taylor and Bennett (1999: 34–35) also noted that those who tested positive had higher illegal incomes than arrestees who tested negative. However, while this lends support to the 'burglary as a means to fund a drug habit' theory, it should be noted that there are other illegal sources of income that are commonly utilised by drug misusers, such as prostitution and drug trafficking.

Evidence that the association between drug misuse and burglary is changing also comes from more recent English research on urine testing and self-reported drug use among arrestees (Bennett and Sibbitt 2000). The authors concluded that drug use among arrestees had increased between 1997 and 1999. The average illegal income spent on drugs over the preceding year was £5,535, and 47% of arrested drug misusers said that they had supported their habit through property crimes, compared with 19% who had supplemented their income through dealing. A small subgroup (9%) of heroin or crack-cocaine users were identified as prolific property offenders, admitting to an average of at least 20 offences per month and responsible, in total, for 52% of the crime committed by the entire sample! Nevertheless, although drug misusers were three times more likely to commit burglary than were non-users, drug misuse was more closely associated with shoplifting and robbery than with burglary.

Research in Australia has also uncovered high levels of drug misuse among incarcerated burglars. Dobinson (1986), for example, interviewing 225 property offenders in New South Wales prisons, found that 40% were regular drug users.[1] Users tended to be more dependent upon crime as a source of income than did non-users, with 50% stating that burglary was their primary form of property crime, and were more likely to commit burglaries on a regular basis. Among drug misusers, notably, drug use tended to precede rather than post-date regular property crimes. The message here is that some, but not necessarily a majority of, burglars repeatedly offended in order to finance their drug habit, but it leaves unanswered the question of whether most *burglaries* are committed by drug misusers. Conversely, not all burglars use drugs, and certainly not on a regular basis. This raises the question of why some people commit burglaries.

## Explaining burglary

Explanations of why individuals commit burglary span a variety of perspectives from determinism to free choice. According to determinist theory, individuals may be predisposed to commit burglaries because of factors in their personality, upbringing or wider social environment. Different theorists have placed the emphasis in different directions; however, the key point is that offenders to some extent lack free will. Data such as that described above, on the concentration of offenders in impoverished inner city areas, with poor schooling and limited employment opportunities, fuel such perspectives. These perspectives, however, fail to explain why – for example – not all youths from a run-down estate turn to crime, or why they opt for burglary rather than, say, car crime. As a result, theorists have tended to shift towards a softer form of determinism that accepts that everyone has some degree of choice while acknowledging that the range of options available may be more restricted for some than for others. Financial reward may, for example, be a common goal, but for some paid employment may be a more viable means of achieving it, for others crime. Equally, in the latter case, changes in security measures or readily available items to steal may make burglary more or less attractive than car crime at different points in time.

Rational choice theorists, while generally adopting this softer form of determinism, have 'focussed on the rational processes by which an offender chooses a criminal career, selects targets, and carries out criminal acts' (Cromwell, Olson and Avary 1991: 9). That is:

> It is concerned with how offenders go about their business; the kinds of things they do or fail to do before and during the commission of a crime. It attempts to understand their perceptions of the risks and rewards involved in criminal activity, particularly in residential property crime. Of particular interest are their perceptions of the sanction threat of the criminal justice system and how their perceptions are formed and evolve, and are modified over time. It is further concerned with how residential burglars select targets, how the presence of co-offenders influences decision-making processes, and how narcotics and drug abuse influence the prevalence and incidence of residential property crime, as well as what role drugs play in target selection and the risk–gain calculus employed by burglars. (Cromwell, Olson and Avary 1991: 13)

The primary motive for committing burglaries appears, not surprisingly, to be financial (Cromwell, Olson and Avary 1991; Rengert and Wasilchick 2000; Reppetto 1974). Income 'earned' in this way is generally used for alcohol, drugs, gambling, partying, and other manifestations of a 'fast and expensive' lifestyle, although in England, Forrester, Chatterton and Pease (1988) placed rather more emphasis on need. Thus a majority of their sample saw their lack of employment as a factor and 41% admitted to being in debt.

Excitement has also frequently been cited. For example, Reppetto (1974) and Cromwell, Olson and Avary (1991) found it to be particularly mentioned by younger burglars. Rengert and Wasilchick (2000) also noted that identification of premises as potential targets by groups of offenders took on many of the characteristics of a game, and Wright and Decker (1994) identified some burglars who sought adventure by targeting occupied homes for night-time burglaries.

## Social networks: co-offenders and fences

Much of the research on household – but not necessarily commercial (see chapter 10) – burglary has concluded that most burglars operate alone. There has, however, been some discussion of joint operations. For example, Shover (1973) argued that where burglars worked together members might perform distinct tasks within the group, but found little evidence of hierarchy or leadership.

Psychological studies of group decision making have tended to suggest that groups are more likely to make 'risky' decisions than are individuals working alone. Cromwell, Olson and Avary (1991), comparing burglars working alone with those operating in pairs provided some degree of support for this perspective. Those working in pairs or groups, for example, were more inclined to indulge in a spree of burglaries. However, in deciding whether or not a burglary was worthwhile or too risky, co-offenders tended to point out hazards that a lone burglar might not have noticed, and groups consistently rated properties as more risky compared with lone burglars. It thus seemed that burglars perceived more risk cues when working in a group and were consequently more cautious in their choice of target.

Even where burglars operate alone, they may depend on others to provide information on possible targets (see below), or to dispose of stolen property. Networks may, consequently, be an important aspect of burglars' working practices. Burglars, like other property offenders, may make use of a professional fence – that is, a known figure in the criminal underworld who has direct contact with offenders and specialises in buying and selling stolen merchandise (Klockars 1974).

However, many offenders dispose of goods in a variety of other ways, including selling individual items in pubs or at car boot sales. Cromwell, Olson and Avary (1991), noting that access to professional fences may be problematic for younger, inexperienced burglars, even suggested that professional burglars may block access to fences and act as intermediaries themselves. Analysis of 50 police reports that contained information on where arrested burglars disposed of stolen property, revealed that 9 burglars sold their proceeds to pawn shops, 11 traded them for drugs, 10 sold them to friends or acquaintances, 10 sold them to strangers and 9 sold them to employees in legitimate businesses. They concluded that most burglars disposed of their hauls to either 'avocational receivers' (i.e. those who dealt in stolen goods on a part-time basis) or members of the public who bought items for personal consumption.

Similarly, in England, Forrester, Chatterton and Pease (1988) noted that 43% of their sample of burglars disposed of goods through shops or dealers, rather than fences. While burglars normally stole items and then sought a buyer, in some cases they 'stole to order'. More recently, Sutton (1998a; ibid 1998b) used BCS data to show that 11% of respondents said they had purchased stolen goods within the previous year. Males aged 16–24 and those living in poorer, high crime areas were most likely to have bought stolen items. Further interviews with burglars and those handling stolen goods led Sutton to conclude that while professional (and less professional) fences were often used, stolen items were also sold to 'friendship networks', small business owners and directly to the public. Car boot sales were, contrary to popular rumour, rarely used. Some goods, including proceeds from commercial burglaries, were 'stolen to order', but this was rare for domestic burglaries.

While US research has tended to focus on either case studies of professional fences (Klockars 1974; Steffensmeier 1986) or police operations (see chapter 11), one Dutch study has analysed data on 318 fences whose operations were closed down in the mid-1980s (Roell 1989). These largely small-time fences were predominantly male (90%), with an average age of 33. Men tended to become fences for economic reasons, but some of the women were drawn into fencing to provide outlets for goods stolen by family members. The most common route into fencing was via experience as a fraudster. Interestingly, the research suggested that burglars tended to use fences from their own ethnic group.

## Burglars' targets

### Area

Research on burglars' choice of target may take at least two forms (Rengert and Wasilchick 2000). First, we might ask why burglars target particular *areas*. Second, we may consider why they target particular *properties*.

With regard to area, a number of researchers have noted that while in general city centres are high crime areas, if we focus on residential areas then areas with high rates for burglary tend to be areas where burglars live. Of course, given the low detection rates for burglary, official statistics are especially problematic in this respect. Nevertheless, a comparison of ward burglary rates and rates for arrested burglars' home addresses in 1993–1994 for Plymouth revealed a highly significant association between the two. This may also explain BCS findings that where victims had some knowledge of their burglars' identities, in a third of these the burglar was well known to them (Budd 1999)!

The Kirkholt research also identified burglary as an essentially local enterprise, with 85% saying they committed their offences within five miles of home and 77% having walked to the target address, leaving the researchers to conclude that 'domestic burglary in Rochdale takes on an almost claustrophobically local aspect' (Forrester, Chatterton and Pease

1988: 3). More recently, Bennett and Durie's (1999) Cambridge research and Barker's (2000) research in a small English town confirmed that burglars operated relatively locally, but the latter also suggested that as they gained in experience they tended to travel slightly farther afield.

Baldwin and Bottoms (1976) noted that burglary in Sheffield was generally a local enterprise, with 42% of offenders committing their offences within a mile of their homes. Subsequently, Mawby (1979) found the same pattern for the nine residential areas of Sheffield included in his study, but noted that this did not mean that offenders necessarily committed their offences locally, or indeed that most burglaries in a high crime area were committed by locals. Rengert (1981) made a similar point. In Philadelphia between 1967 and 1972, he concluded that 'most burglars reside and most burglaries are committed in the central parts of the city' (*ibid* 196). However these were also the areas where the rates of burglary by nonresidents and the rates of nonlocal burglary by local residents were highest. Nevertheless, Rengert accepted that the most attractive areas (i.e. where the availability of valuable items to steal was greatest) were most likely to attract burglars from outside, although Rengert and Wasilchick (2000) subsequently argued that burglars were deterred from targeting high status areas where they would look conspicuous and instead chose medium status areas.

This attraction of 'rich pickings' was also stressed by Maguire (1982). High status areas in the Thames Valley were likely to attract burglars from outside, especially more professional older burglars who planned their offences well in advance. In contrast, juveniles tend to act more spontaneously and commit their offences locally. Baldwin and Bottoms (1976) also noted that in Sheffield juveniles were more likely than adults to commit their offences locally and, in general, offenders were likely to travel further to commit burglaries against more attractive targets.

But the relationship between where offenders live and where they commit their crimes is more complex than that (Rengert and Wasilchick 2000). Burglars may commit crimes in other areas as the result of planning, but they may also act spontaneously and burgle properties they pass en route to somewhere else; for example between their home and the city centre. Cromwell, Olson and Avary (1991) compared 300 previously burgled homes with 300 that had no record of having been burgled. Burgled residences were significantly more likely to be closer to schools, churches, businesses, traffic lights and main roads. They concluded:

'These results tend to suggest that as burglars go about their everyday activities, traveling to and from activity hubs such as school, work, and recreational facilities, they come into contact with residential sites near these facilities. When burglars stop at a traffic light or stop sign they have a brief opportunity to view the sights nearby and may choose a potential target during these moments. (*ibid* 46)

## Property

Another consistent theme in the literature is the distinction between 'amateurs' and professionals, or opportunist/spontaneous burglars compared with those who plan their jobs. Most researchers suggest that burglaries tend to be planned, and few are opportunist (Butler 1994; Maguire 1982; Nee and Taylor 1988; Wiersma 1996). It could be that research on juvenile burglars would reveal a different picture, although Wright and Logie's (1988) study of ten juvenile burglars suggested otherwise. Bennett and Wright (1984) distinguished between 'opportunistic' offences, 'search offences' – where the offender decided to commit a burglary and went looking for a suitable target – and 'planned', where there was a time gap between the choice of target and the burglary. They argued that very few from their sample could be defined as opportunist, with slightly over half their burglars committing planned offences. However, as Wiersma (1996) pointed out it could be that burglars exaggerate their levels of professionalism when interviewed.

Cromwell, Olson and Avary (1991) used what they called 'staged activity analysis' to collect their data. Subjects, who were paid, were asked to reconstruct and simulate their past burglaries during extensive interviews and trips to sites of their (and others') burglaries. They argued that burglars tended to exaggerate the extent of planning, a process they called 'rational reconstruction', and that it was only some way through the series of interviews that their subjects began to acknowledge that their levels of planning had been rather more haphazard. Nevertheless, their findings support a 'limited rationality' model.

Very few committed their offences at night. Rather, burglars tended to choose times when the home was empty; that is, they adjusted their work pattern to their targets' lifestyle (Cromwell, Olson and Avary 1991; see also Rengert and Wasilchick 2000). They may determine that the house is unoccupied through careful planning, which may include determining that the householders are away on holiday. A good example of this is a local burglar who paid his peers who committed office burglaries to photocopy any holiday rosters that they came across.[2] Alternatively, they may check for occupancy on the spot, for example through knocking or phoning.

Cromwell, Olson and Avary (1991) argued that burglars were not completely rational in their choice of targets. They did not, for example, seek out perfect targets, merely satisfactory ones. This they termed a 'satisficing strategy'. Out of all the burglaries reconstructed in their research, none were opportunist in the way defined by Bennett and Wright (1984) but 75% fitted the 'searcher' ideal type. The remaining 25% could be described as committed by 'planners'.

None the less, in comparisons of burglars and a control group, both Cromwell, Olson and Avary (1991) and Wright *et al* (1995) suggested that the former were better at recognising certain 'burglary relevant' environmental changes than were the latter.

The extent to which burglaries are planned or opportunistic clearly has implications for policy. It is, moreover, striking that the focus of so many studies of burglars has been on planning, choice of targets, factors which attract or deter them, and consequently the implications for crime prevention (Bennett and Wright 1984; Butler 1994; Cromwell *et al* 1991; Nee and Taylor 1988; Wiersma 1996; Wright and Logie 1988; Wright *et al* 1995).

These studies distinguish between different features of the property (burgled or hypothetical) that might encourage or discourage the potential burglar. They include the physical layout of the property – for example whether it is overlooked, ease of access, etc. – and the perceived value of its contents, as well as whether security devices such as special locks and alarms have been fitted, and the presence of the occupier, neighbours (and neighbourhood watch) and security patrols.

Cromwell, Olson and Avary (1991) identified three types of cues used by burglars in assessing risk:

- **surveillability** – the extent to which the premises are overseen by passers-by and neighbours

- **occupancy** – as suggested by the presence of a car, noise, lights, etc. (see also Forrester, Chatterton and Pease 1988)

- **accessibility** – including the presence or absence of window locks, an alarm, open windows, etc.

The findings from other studies have been somewhat mixed. For example, Maguire (1982) stressed the significance of occupancy, the potential value of goods, privacy, ease of access/escape and the presence of burglar alarms (which at that time were relatively rare). Bennett and Wright (1984: 155) considered that '"surveilability" and "occupancy" were the most important situational cues influencing burglars' choice of targets', including here alarms as 'occupancy proxies'. Wright *et al* (1995), in their comparison of burglars and a control group, also noted that burglars were less likely than controls to be deterred by factors such as the fact that the house was occupied, extra door locks and property marking. It is also notable than whilst Wright and Logie (1988), amongst others, stressed burglars' choice of more prosperous targets, the clear evidence from research on actual targets (see above and chapter 2) is that crime is more prevalent in *poorer* areas, a further example, perhaps, of rational reconstruction.

Overall, then, the research findings support a theory of limited rationality, what Shover (1971) termed 'alert opportunism'. As Scarr (1973) concluded in his research in Washington, most burglars tend to exploit the opportunities available, rather than carefully plan their crimes, but they do so with a certain degree of expertise based on prior experience.

## Summary

The amount of research on burglary has been limited, at least partly by a recognition that known burglars may be very different from successful ones, and indeed research that has used 'snowball' sampling to identify burglars who have evaded arrest, suggests that these are distinctive in some respects. Nevertheless, burglars tend to evidence many of the characteristics of offenders in general, being drawn from more deprived areas and lacking educational qualifications. At the same time, there is very little evidence that most offenders who commit burglary are actually specialists, a point to which we shall return in looking at commercial burglary in chapter 10. One notable distinction that will be drawn there is the fact that for some types of commercial burglary, such as ram-raiding, burglary is a team enterprise, whereas for domestic burglary the general consensus is that most burglars operate alone. Networks may, however, be important in the distribution of stolen goods, although the extent to which professional fences are involved has perhaps been overstated.

Much of the recent research on burglars has rejected narrowly determinist explanations and treated burglars as rational actors, whose offences involve at least a minimum amount of planning. Findings on the extent to which certain types of property, in certain areas, tend to be targeted links in with victim survey research on differential risk that was discussed in chapter 2, although the likelihood of burglars 'rationally reconstructing' their professionalism is illustrated by the fact that burglars tend to exaggerate the extent to which they choose prosperous targets. Many of the findings discussed here have direct implications for crime prevention policies, and are reassessed from this perspective in chapters 6–7.

Finally, the relationship between drug misuse and burglary has been considered. It appears that a greater proportion of burglars use drugs than was the case in the past, although the extent to which drug users commit burglary rather than other property crimes is questionable. Nevertheless, programmes that target drug misusers may be an alternative approach to preventing further burglaries, a point considered in chapter 11.

What is generally lacking from the research, though, is any detailed appreciation of burglars' careers. True, there is some indication that older burglars tend to be more specialist than younger ones, and that they tend to travel farther afield, and spend more time planning their 'hits', etc. However, this is gleaned from research on burglars of different ages. Although there have been some early studies of individual offenders, the problem of identifying samples of burglars and gaining their cooperation has generally prevented longitudinal, or even retrospective, studies that would allow us to better understand, *inter alia*, how individuals first got involved in crime, why they opted for burglary, how their offending patterns changed, and – perhaps – what made them give up offending. Yet it is the answers to questions like these that can best inform policy.

## Notes

1 Marijuana use was not counted here.
2 I am grateful to Linda Green of Dorset Probation Service for this example.

# Part 3: The policy response

# Chapter 6

# Alternative approaches to burglary reduction

## Crime prevention

The past decade has seen a dramatic shift in emphasis towards crime prevention rather than the detection of crime and the treatment of offenders, and burglary reduction programmes have lain at the heart of this development. Rising crime rates and increased public concern together with low detection rates, and a minimal relationship between alternative sentences and recidivism rates (the so-called 'nothing works' philosophy of the 1970s) have contributed to this redirection of emphasis. However 'crime prevention' means different things to different people (Bright 1991; Clarke 1980; Gilling 1994; Pease 1997). On the one hand, a distinction may be made between *primary*, *secondary* and *tertiary* crime prevention; primary, where the emphasis is placed upon eliminating criminogenic environments; secondary, where the focus is on changing potential offenders; and tertiary, where preventing reoffending is prioritised.

On the other hand, many commentators contrast *social* and *situational* crime prevention. Social crime prevention is concerned with offenders and potential offenders and initiatives to prevent them continuing with or turning to crime; situational crime prevention refers to the offence situation and with making potential targets less vulnerable, and has been particularly directed at burglary. Chapter 11 will consider some initiatives aimed at tertiary or social crime prevention. In this and the following chapter, the emphasis is on primary and situational crime prevention.

We may make one further distinction here with regard to burglary reduction, depending on the techniques used. First, initiatives that prioritise the *guarding* of property, by public police, private security, neighbourhood watch (NW) groups or individual action are discussed. Second, *target hardening*, through burglar alarms, window locks, and other security features, which have become more common in Western societies in recent years, is considered. These initiatives are not, of course, mutually exclusive, and government initiatives such as the Safer Cities Programme have incorporated a cocktail of approaches (Ekblom *et al* 1996a, 1996b; Tilley 1992; Tilley and Webb 1994).

Chapter 7 addresses coordinated government initiatives that have become a key aspect of local government in recent years. Here the emphasis is upon more traditional approaches and individual initiatives. We start by considering the role of the police.

## Crime prevention and the police

It is well recognised that the English police tradition was based on the principle of uniformed officers on patrol providing a visible presence and so deterring potential offenders. However, the idea that increased police personnel could prevent crime has suffered a number of setbacks. For example, evaluations of police patrol practices, principally in the USA, have given little credence to the notion that an increased police presence would prevent crime, whether this presence was by car or foot patrol (Sherman *et al* 1997; Walker 1992). Similarly, evaluations by the Home Office in England concluded that it would require an unrealistic increase in police resources to impact upon crime levels (Burrows *et al* 1979). The increased budgetary restraints of the 1980s, with the commensurate requirement that police justify increased resources, further undermined any efforts to enhance a police presence 'on the streets', no matter how popular such an initiative might be. Populist demands for more 'bobbies on the beat' and more sophisticated critiques arguing for a dramatic change in police philosophy (Bayley 1994) were further rebuffed in England and Wales by the Posen (1994) inquiry that questioned the widening of police roles (Home Office 1995) and by the report of the Audit Commission (1996) on preventive policing.

The preventive potential for policing is, moreover, weaker in the case of offences like residential burglary (Mawby 1979). There are at least two reasons for this. First, police resources tend to be concentrated on crime hotspots (city centres, areas of entertainment, etc.) rather than residential areas. Second, police patrols are restricted to public space. The police do not routinely check private property. The likelihood of a police presence acting as a deterrent, therefore, depends either on the shaky assumption that potential burglars will be readily identified as they travel to their target or on the equally shaky assumption that they will be visible to a passing police officer when in the act of breaking in.

## Private policing

In the midst of debates over the current role and organisation of the British police, the issue of who should be responsible for policing and for the maintenance of public order is a critical one. Rising crime and restrictions on funding for the police service have led to a plethora of alternative sources whereby policework – and especially crime prevention – can be done 'on the cheap'. At one extreme are police-encouraged initiatives such as neighbourhood watch, expansion of the Special Constabulary and any number of variations on that theme such as parish constables and wardens. At the other extreme lie vigilante movements involving local people patrolling the streets and setting out their own form of justice. Rather differently, private security provides an alternative approach whereby citizens may join together to employ private police to patrol their community. Indeed, the expansion of private security is a worldwide phenomenon that is accounted for partly by financial constraints, and partly by the spread of 'mass private property' developments like shopping malls, where access of the public police is constrained (Johnston 1992, 1999; Jones and Newburn 1995, South 1988).

Private policing initiatives against burglary have a long history. In the eighteenth century, for example, Societies for the Prosecution of Felons (Shubert 1981) provided much the same service prior to the introduction of a public police. But until recently most of the private security business in Britain has concentrated on organisations, rather than ordinary members of the public, as clients. However, in some cases recently local authorities have also contracted private security firms to patrol city centres or residential areas. Moreover, at a time when the government's review of core policing tasks is likely to encourage the subcontracting of work from the public police to private security, and when recent figures show that the number of private security staff has grown almost to parity with police service employees (Johnston 1999; Jones and Newburn 1995), there has also been a concerted effort from the private sector to sell its services to local communities. Private security firms are now involved in patrolling residential neighbourhoods in a number of police force areas, including Devon and Cornwall. In Plymouth, the first private security firm paid to patrol a residential area began operations in 1993. However, private security – or at least the presence of a resident caretaker – is less common in England than in some other industrialised societies such as France, Canada, the USA and the Netherlands (Mayhew and van Dijk 1997: 52).

In general, the police have been sceptical about private security, arguing that this level of increased patrolling will have little effect on overall crime rates, that problems surround the lack of regulation of the private security industry, and that at best the result will be increased protection for those who can afford to pay at the expense of more deprived areas. A further key issue concerns payment by local residents; what happens about those in the area who do not pay for the extra patrols? Interestingly though, very little is known about the views of the public. What do people think about private security, and would they be prepared to invest in it?

## Case study: public perceptions of private security in Plymouth

In order to assess public reaction to this growth in private patrols, we carried out a postal survey of Plymouth residents in early 1994 (Dale and Mawby 1994). Four of the 20 wards in Plymouth were included in the study. Data from the 1991 Census and police records were used to identify four contrasting areas. Using census data on unemployment, housing tenure and levels of car ownership, two relatively affluent areas were chosen to contrast with two more deprived areas of the city; and police data on recorded crime and various property offences were used to distinguish two high crime and two low crime areas. The result was the selection of four areas: one middle-class ward on the outskirts of the city with a low crime rate; one middle-class ward within walking distance of the city centre, which had a high crime rate, notably for burglaries; one working-class area with a lower than average crime rate; and finally one working-class area with a high crime rate. In each ward 100 households were selected randomly, ensuring that residents of all parts of the areas were included in each sample. In all, 190 replies were received, a response rate of 48%. Overall 53% of replies were from men, 41% from women and the rest were completed jointly. Details of income, collected from the questionnaire, confirmed census data on class differences between the areas.

Members of the public were asked for their views on the police and, more generally, the criminal justice system, and then for their attitudes towards alternative approaches to preventative policing, notably private security patrols. In presenting the findings, responses from the four wards have been amalgamated, but where differences emerged between wards, or indeed according to the age or gender of respondents, these have been noted.

Views on public policing provide the background within which attitudes towards private security can be contextualised. It is notable then, that while 92% of those answering felt that the addition of 'more bobbies on the beat' would reduce crime, 69% were dissatisfied with current levels of patrolling by the Plymouth police and 65% felt that the public had lost confidence in the police. Interestingly, residents in the high crime working-class area were least likely to feel that more police could reduce crime, most satisfied with policing levels and least likely to feel that the police had lost the public's confidence. On the other hand, those in the middle-class low crime area (presumably those with least direct experience) were most likely to feel that the public had lost confidence in the police's ability to control street crime. While these findings may provide little by way of encouragement for the police, it is notable that more people (88%) felt that the public had lost confidence in the courts.

Given this apparent indictment of public agencies of social control, one might have expected citizens to be receptive to the involvement of non-state agencies. However, while 74% felt that the public were sometimes justified in taking the law into their own hands – and this was particularly the case in both high crime areas – any endorsement of private security was somewhat muted.

First, we asked: 'If the police are unable to patrol your street due to lack of manpower and other demands on their services, which of the following would you prefer to see in their place?' From the list provided, a large majority (86%) selected the Special Constabulary, either alone (28%) or jointly with other alternatives, and 43% cited neighbourhood watch. In contrast only 18% opted for private security firms. Older residents were rather more likely to vote for traditional solutions like the Special Constabulary while young respondents were more likely to cite private security. However, even among those aged 40 or less, 81% opted for the Special Constabulary and only 31% for private security.

Only 12% said they had in fact been targeted by a private security firm offering protection, and these almost all lived in the two more prosperous wards. These are clearly areas where firms believe residents can afford their services, but are not necessarily areas that, according to crime figures, might require additional security. When asked whether they would be interested in paying for private patrols, only 15% replied in the affirmative, with 68% stating that they would not. Those in the middle-class low crime area were *least* likely to express a willingness to pay, confirming that criticism of the public police does not necessarily mean that people will be willing to 'dig into their own pockets'. On the other hand, younger respondents expressed a greater willingness to pay for security patrols, although even here the figure was only 20%.

The reason for this lack of enthusiasm for private solutions is clear when we consider answers to a deliberately loaded question, 'Would you resent paying for protection?' In all 71% said they would resent it, with residents of the two low crime areas most likely to object. Of those replying in the affirmative, 50% felt that since they already paid taxes they should not be expected to make additional payments. Members of the public however put forward a wide range of reasons why this was not a favoured option. For example:

It would lead eventually to mafia-style protection racket.

Because we have a very good police force if only the government would spend money on them.

Wouldn't trust them enough to pay, could abuse their position.

To be effective one would need 24 hours' surveillance and this would be impractical.

These quotes illustrate that public concerns over the concept of private security patrols ranged much wider than an unwillingness to 'pay up'. For example, 62% felt that it was *possible* for the police and private security to work together but 43% felt that private security would undermine the work of the police. Moreover, 59% said that they would feel aggrieved if non-members benefited from private patrols, illustrating the potential for community conflict in areas where not everyone was willing to contribute.

It would be rash to draw too many conclusions from a local survey that took place in only four areas of one city. Nevertheless, it is interesting to note that not only was there widespread agreement between those of differing ages and between males and females, but that despite our having deliberately selected four very different residential areas for our study, the similarity of responses between areas far outweighed the differences.

Indeed, the results were unequivocal. In general, members of the public considered that the police were not providing an adequate service (although many blamed the government of the time for this) and felt that the threat of crime was not being confronted. However, while private security patrols provided one possible solution to this, it was not a solution favoured by the majority of those questioned, who saw police-based responses, such as an increased use of the Special Constabulary and expansion of neighbourhood watch, as preferable. Additionally, many felt that the paid police, not just organised volunteers, should be more clearly directed towards preventing residential crime. Increased resources were one means of achieving this; another was a renewed emphasis on community policing, in terms of locating the police in residential areas.

Since this survey was conducted there has been little indication of significant additional resources for the police! On the other hand, the previous government's push towards hiving off many police responsibilities has lost momentum, and our own research in Devon and Cornwall suggests that it gained little public support and that, again, people were particularly sceptical of an increased role for the private sector (Mawby 2000). At the same time, the organisation of the police in Plymouth has shifted towards an emphasis on ward-based teams, and retrospectively it would seem that this shift has public approval. The message is clearly that the public wants and expects the public police to handle local crime. At present there is little support for private security. It is, however, important to guard against complacency. If public perceptions of the proper place for the police are not matched, it would not be surprising to see increased dissatisfaction with neighbourhood crime reflected in a further shift towards endorsement of the private sector.

Some indication of a shift in public attitudes might be gleaned from Noakes' (2000) recent survey of a small private security firm providing security patrols in a residential area of a city in 'Southern Britain'. She reported that local people were very positive about the services provided, and saw them as a necessary supplement to the work of the overstretched public police. Interestingly, the regular patrols were the most valued part of the security 'package'.

**Neighbourhood watch**

A further alternative is the use of non-specialists. In the corporate sector, Home Office research in the 1970s had suggested that the use of employees as the 'eyes and ears' of public and private sector organisations might be an effective deterrent (Mayhew *et al* 1976; Mayhew *et al* 1979). Among the general public, the US concept of 'block watch' was transported across the Atlantic and translated as neighbourhood watch (NW) (Bennett 1987; Kinsey *et al* 1986). From its small beginnings, neighbourhood watch nationwide rose to 20% in 1992 (Dowds and Mayhew 1994) and sat alongside the Special Constabulary and parish special constables (Southgate *et al* 1995) as one of a number of government initiatives aimed at increasing 'active citizenship' in law enforcement, that is, the involvement of the public in the prevention of crime.

The precise ingredients of NW have also grown. In a recent overview, Laycock and Tilley (1995: 2) cited the original definition used by the London Metropolitan Police in 1983, as:

> Primarily a network of public spirited members of the community, who observe what is going on in their own neighbourhood and report suspicious activity to the police. In simple terms, the citizen becomes 'the eyes and ears' of the police, looking out for the usual and the unusual to protect their home and that of their neighbour, thereby reducing the opportunities for criminal activities.

However, by the 1990s the concept had expanded to include, *inter alia,* more emphasis upon community-based organisation, a greater emphasis on opportunity reduction and crime prevention, police advice on property marking and target hardening, and clearer definitions of what is an appropriate neighbourhood strategy (*op cit.*; see also Turner and Alexandru 1996).

Although schemes emphasise a variety of crimes, such as vehicle-related thefts and vandalism, the prevention of burglary has been at the heart of the NW initiative.

Nevertheless, from the start NW has suffered from three major problems. First, NW has developed more readily in middle-class, low crime rate, more affluent areas. On the other hand, inner city areas, public housing estates and blocks of flats – areas where burglary is most common and need consequently greatest – have found it most difficult to start and sustain NW initiatives (Dowds and Mayhew 1994; Hope 1988; Husain 1988; Laycock and Tilley 1995). A survey in Devon and Cornwall, for example, found that in 1988–89 schemes tended to be located in areas of middle-class owner-occupation, and the relationship between the introduction of a scheme and area burglary rates was tenuous (Mawby

1990a). Similarly, analysis of the 1992 BCS revealed that schemes were most common in low risk areas (see Table 6.1) and that members in such areas played a more active part in their schemes than did members in high crime areas (Dowds and Mayhew 1994).

*Table 6.1: Neighbourhood watch membership rates in areas with contrasting crime rates (from Dowds and Mayhew 1994: 2).*

|                    | 1988 | 1992 |
|--------------------|------|------|
| Low crime areas    | 17   | 25   |
| Medium crime areas | 8    | 14   |
| High crime areas   | 10   | 14   |

Second, the implementation of NW is patchy. This means that what precisely is entailed varies from one scheme to another, confounding evaluation studies. Moreover, schemes may differ from one year to the next, for example by wilting as the initial enthusiasm dies away. Sustaining the momentum is thus difficult, both in low crime areas where schemes see little action and in high rate areas where intra-area conflicts pressurise members to opt out. There is also some evidence that co-ordinators are disillusioned with the service they receive from the police, and that many police officers have reservations about the effectiveness of NW (Turner and Alexandrou 1997).

The third problem surrounds the effectiveness of NW. That is, although members of NW schemes appear more likely than other people to report suspicious incidents to the police (Dowds and Mayhew 1994), rigorous evaluation of NW suggests that it has little impact on burglary rates (Bennett 1990; Nicholson 1995), albeit fear of crime seems to be lessened (see also Laycock and Tilley 1995). In the USA, evaluation is scarcely more optimistic (Rosenbaum 1987a; 1988).

Laycock and Tilley (1995: 7) thus concluded:

Given that implementation has characteristically been very partial and that the prevailing crime rates in areas in which Neighbourhood Watch has most readily been established are typically already low, failure consistently to find crime reductions following the introduction of Neighbourhood Watch is unsurprising... Evidence exists that Neighbourhood Watch can and sometimes has produced reductions in crime, notably burglary. There is, though, no reason to believe that it will always do so. Where Neighbourhood Watch has been found to be associated with falls in crime it is not clear how these were achieved. Indeed, the literature raises some doubts about the implementation and efficacy of some traditional Neighbourhood Watch measures.

In response, the authors argued that NW needs to be adjusted to provide different services according to the nature of the area.

While neighbourhood watch is frequently identified as an Anglo-American phenomenon, it has also spread in many other Western societies, such as Australia (Bayley 1989). It has, moreover, a long history as part of the community safety culture of Asian countries such as Japan (Mawby 1990). Indeed, ICVS data suggest that it is most common in the New World and Asia, with the UK an exception in Western Europe (del Frate 1998). In the Philippines almost half of those interviewed said they belonged to a neighbourhood watch-type organisation! However, in many societies where more formalised NW structures are missing, it is common for householders to ask their neighbours to 'police' their homes. As is clear from Table 6.2, such informal arrangements are far more common. However, while in Africa and Latin America these informal arrangements to some extent compensate for the lack of NW, elsewhere the patterns are similar. Thus both formal and informal procedures are the norm in Asia and the New World, but are relatively uncommon in Western Europe and countries in transition.

*Table 6.2: Percentage of households involved in neighbourhood watch and less formal arrangements (del Frate 1998: 126).*

|  | Neighbourhood watch | Informal neighbour help |
| --- | --- | --- |
| New World | 43 | 69 |
| Asia | 38 | 76 |
| Western Europe | 18 | 46 |
| Africa | 10 | 53 |
| Latin America | 9 | 54 |
| Countries in transition | 9 | 46 |

## Target hardening

Where public faith in the preventive abilities of neighbours or police is undermined, target hardening provides an alternative mechanism of primary or situational crime prevention. This may take the form of window locks, extra locks or bolts to doors, property marking, timer lights/sensors, burglar alarms, etc.

However, there is some evidence from the BCS that NW and target hardening, rather than being distinct entities, are closely related. Thus Dowds and Mayhew (1994) found that NW members took more precautions than non-members and were also more likely to interpret incidents as suspicious and report them to the police. We might therefore expect target hardening strategies to follow similar patterns to NW membership.

In England and Wales, ownership of home security devices has increased in recent years. According to BCS figures, in 1997 no less than 72% of households had double or deadlocks on the outside doors of their homes and 71% had window locks. Although window bars or grills were comparatively rare (8%), a sizeable minority also had internal (23%) or external (38%) timer or sensor lights, or a burglar alarm (24%) (Mirrlees-Black *et al* 1998: 49). Moreover, with the exception of window bars or grills these figures showed an increase on 1995. It was also notable that experience of a burglary led to a marked upgrading of security. As Table 6.3 shows, for example, whereas only 47% of burglary victims had window locks at the time of the offence, by the time of their interview this had risen to 70%!

*Table 6.3: Percentage of burglary victims with different home security devices, 1997 (Mirrlees-Black et al 1998: 49).*

|  | At the time of the burglary | When interviewed |
| --- | --- | --- |
| Burglar alarm | 22 | 32 |
| Double/deadlocks | 45 | 75 |
| Window locks | 47 | 70 |
| Timer/sensor lights |  |  |
|     Internal | 10 | 23 |
|     External | 19 | 40 |
| Window bars/grills | 5 | 13 |

Although the ICVS also suggested that the proportion of households that target harden their homes in industrialised countries has increased, albeit at a slower rate, clearly England and Wales has led the industrialised world in security consciousness. The 1996 survey revealed, for example, that 76% of respondents had a burglar alarm, special door locks or grilles on windows/doors, compared with 71% in the Netherlands, 66% in the USA, 41% in Northern Ireland and 31% in Finland (Mayhew and van

Dijk 1997: 52–55). Alarms were possessed by 27% of those interviewed in England, compared with 21% in the USA and under 10% in Sweden, Austria, Switzerland and Finland. Overall, the authors conclude that security measures were more common in countries with higher burglary risks.

The pattern is somewhat different in countries in transition, where:

A pattern that is consistently observed in all the countries in transition is that of a low use of crime prevention measures despite a relatively high level of perceived likelihood of burglary and fear of crime. (Zvekic 1998: 85)

Burglar alarms were found to be rare, being most common in Hungary (7.4%) and Russia (7.0%). In some countries, such as Kyrgyzstan (19.5%), Hungary (18.7%) and Romania (18.1%) special grills were relatively common. Most noticeable, perhaps, was the deployment of a guard dog. The ICVS found this to be especially common in Poland (33.7%), Romania (32.2%), Hungary (29.8%) and the Czech Republic (26.5%) (Zvekic 1998).

Watch dogs and window grills are also a common source of protection in the developing world (del Frate 1998: 123–132). Window grills were found to be particularly common in Costa Rica (66.0%), Tanzania (64.3%), and Indonesia (54.9%), with a high proportion of respondents in Bolivia (65.7%), the Philippines (44.9%) and Paraguay (40.2%) opting for a watch dog. Burglar alarms were uncommon in most developing societies, the exception being Argentina, where 21.2% of those interviewed had alarms, the proportion being especially high in Buenos Aires. However, del Frate noted that the proportion of households in the developing world with alarms actually fell between 1992 and 1996, a trend she attributed to maintenance problems and the lack of spare parts.[1]

Another aspect of crime prevention that distinguishes some developing societies is the use of firearms for protection (del Frate 1998: 130–132; Zvekic 1998: 87–88). Gun ownership is particularly common in Latin America, where in the mid-1990s as many as 19.7% said they owned a firearm, and the New World, where 14.2% answered in the affirmative. Moreover, 14.3% of respondents in Latin America said they kept a gun for crime prevention purposes, far more than in Africa (3.7%), the second ranked region. Del Frate (1998: 132) also noted that gun ownership as a crime prevention measure was more common in regions with higher rates of burglary and amongst individuals who were more worried about the likelihood of a future burglary. The extent to which this results in the fatal shooting of burglars, as in the Tony Martin case in England, is however, unknown.

But how effective are such initiatives? As already noted in chapter 5, burglars' views on the extent to which they were deterred by such measures have been mixed. Equally, one of the first research studies to evaluate their deterrent effect, by Jackson and Winchester (1982), reached somewhat pessimistic conclusions. Nevertheless, noting a dramatic increase in the ownership of security devices between 1987 and 1995, Mirrlees-Black *et al* (1996) argued that two findings from the BCS are suggestive of a positive effect. First, it seemed that homes with better security were more likely to be subjected to attempted (i.e. failed) burglaries rather than completed ones. Second, comparing non-victims' levels of security with those of victims at the time of the offences, 'The level of protection among non-victims is higher than for victims at the time of their break-ins – highly suggestive of a security effect' (*ibid* 40). Thus only 14% of burgled households had a burglar alarm, compared with 20% of non-victims, and the differences for door double/dead locks, window locks, light timers/sensors and window bars/grills were even greater. The point is reiterated in the report on the 1998 BCS (Mirrlees-Black *et al* 1998: 11), where as is indicated in Table 6.4, possession of home security was generally highest among the total population and lowest among victims of burglary with entry. The authors also suggested that the increase in home security between 1995 and 1997 contributed to the fall in burglaries with entry (see also Kershaw *et al* 2000: 18).

*Table 6.4: Percentage of households with different home security devices, 1997 (Mirrlees-Black et al 1998: 49).*

|  | All households | Victims, at the time of the burglary | |
| --- | --- | --- | --- |
|  |  | Attempted | Burglary with entry |
| Burglar alarm | 24 | 25 | 19 |
| Double/deadlocks | 72 | 50 | 41 |
| Window locks | 71 | 55 | 41 |
| Timer/sensor lights |  |  |  |
|     Internal | 23 | 11 | 8 |
|     External | 38 | 21 | 17 |
| Window bars/grills | 8 | 8 | 4 |

These arguments are reiterated for industrial societies as a whole (Mayhew and van Dijk 1997: 53–55). The authors demonstrated that:

- Those without an alarm were more likely to be burgled.

- Those with an alarm were more likely to experience an attempt than a successful burglary.

The problem here, though, is (as with NW) that there is evidence that those who are best able to afford such extra security are, arguably, least at risk of future burglary, whilst poorer inner city residents or those on the most deprived council estates are least likely to increase their security following a burglary. BCS data for England and Wales, for example, revealed that while rural dwellers were least at risk of a burglary, they invested more in target hardening. In 1995, for example, 22% had a burglar alarm, as against a national average of 20%, whilst 51% had timer or sensor controlled lights compared with 28% among those living in inner city areas (Mirrlees-Black 1998; see also Tarling and Davison 2000).

Wojcik *et al* (1997) discovered that – following a burglary – victims in England, Poland and Hungary increased their ownership of a range of security devices, although overall target hardening was less evident in post-communist societies. However they also noted variations by income. For example, at the time of interview, 22% of burglary victims had a burglar alarm, but 33% of more prosperous victims had one compared with 10% of less prosperous victims. These patterns, moreover, were reproduced for community-based crime prevention measures, such as NW involvement. In Plymouth, where data on area crime rates were also available, it emerged that 48% of victims residing in low burglary rate areas subsequently owned an alarm, compared with 36% of victims from high rate areas. Corresponding figures for NW membership were 21% and 7% respectively.

What emerges from such research is that if crime prevention is to be applied where it is needed then it is impractical to expect individual householders to take the initiative. Support, including financial help, is needed from (central or local) government, police, housing authorities, victim support, probation, etc. This theme is further developed in the following chapter, which focuses on recent coordinated burglary prevention initiatives in England and Wales.

## Summary

In this chapter, a wide variety of strategies deployed in crime prevention have been discussed in the context of burglary. Ironically, as crime prevention has gained wider acceptance, so the assumption that a greater police presence can help reduce crime has been largely rejected. Equally ironically, though, this has not prevented the expansion of private security to replace the apparently overstretched public police, even though the same constraints apply to the private sector. Other alternative approaches to patrols include neighbourhood watch, which has expanded rapidly in England and North America since the 1970s. However, although – as we saw in chapter 5 – 'surveillability' of property is accepted as a deterrent by burglars themselves, NW does not appear to have fulfilled its potential, and certainly its emergence in areas where burglary is common has been restricted.

Alongside neighbourhood watch, target hardening has expanded during the last decade. Again, this has been most notable in England and Wales, although as with NW, individuals' approaches to securing their property vary in different parts of the world. Whereas in England and Wales householders may protect their property using window and door locks and burglar alarms, in the developing world dogs and firearms may be more common responses. As with NW, however, it seems that more prosperous people living in lower crime areas are more able and willing to increase their protection, highlighting the need for government support for the most vulnerable.

However, this presupposes that such measures are effective. On the one hand, there is little indication that NW is an effective deterrent against burglary, although it may help reduce levels of anxiety. On the other hand, there is some support for the claim that homes that are 'target hardened' experience less burglary. This leaves open the possibility that crime may be displaced, an issue we return to at the end of chapter 7.

## Note

1  The problem of maintaining equipment is not confined to developing societies. For example, in London, Bright (1985) found that about half the entry phone systems in blocks of flats were out of action.

# Chapter 7

# Comprehensive strategies for burglary reduction

## Introduction

Much of the emphasis of chapter 6 was on the promotion of active citizenship and government encouragement for citizens to take personal responsibility for their own and their community's safety. However, there are limits to such initiatives. On the one hand, as was illustrated in chapter 2, crime in general and burglary in particular are targeted predominantly at the poor and those located in poorer areas. On the other hand, as the research described in chapter 6 demonstrates, it is precisely in such areas that neighbourhood watch is so weakly developed (Hope 1988; Husain 1988) and where the financial impediments to increased security hardware are most severe (Wojcik *et al* 1997). As a result, numerous crime prevention initiatives in deprived areas, especially areas of predominantly public housing, have involved government investment (Allatt 1984; Forrester *et al* 1988; Foster and Hope 1993). Such initiatives are not exclusively British. For example, Rubenstein *et al* (1980) have described the introduction of improved locks in public housing projects in Seattle and Chicago. However, initiatives in England and Wales are a good illustration of the emergence of a co-ordinated central government strategy, the Safer Cities Programme being a significant addition (Tilley 1992).

This chapter, however, begins with a review of a range of other integrated initiatives in Britian. First, the Secure by Design initiative is briefly described. Then, the Kirkholt project is discussed. The Safer Cities initiative is then reviewed. In Plymouth, this spawned a number of burglary reduction initiatives, which are considered in more detail as case studies. The chapter then continues by focusing on ongoing Home Office funded programmes and the role of Community Safety Partnerships in their implementation. Finally, the success of these initiatives is considered against the possibility of displacement.

## The Secured by Design initiative

The Secured by Design (SBD) initiative was devised in 1989 in the southeast of England (Pascoe and Topping 1997). Underpinned by research on burglars' strategies that suggested that many offenders were rational opportunists (see chapter 5), and flowing from Newman's concept of defensible space, the initiative was police-led, with police architectural liaison officers involved in vetting new housing plans.

> The vetting covered an extensive list of criteria for estate design and house security. For example, the estate criteria included estate layout, entrance to the estate, access to the public, paths, communal areas, street lighting, landscaping, boundaries of dwellings, gates and car parking. House security involved standards for all potential points of access, lighting, alarms and fire security. (Pascoe and Topping 1997: 162)

By 1997, SBD initiatives were in place in about 3,700 new estates across the country. In a review of these developments, Pascoe and Topping (1997) argued that SBD aimed to foster easy surveillance and community consciousness through a combination of strategies, principally: seeing cul-de-sacs as the ideal and otherwise curtailing through-traffic and pedestrian through routes; opting for mixed housing to maximise overall occupancy levels; using fencing and hedging to clearly demarcate private space; and ensuring physical security in the home was to a high standard.

## The Kirkholt Burglary Prevention Project

The Kirkholt project developed in the late 1980s as a partnership in crime prevention between the police and probation service in Greater Manchester, in conjunction with other agencies such as the local housing department (Forrester, Chatterton and Pease 1988). Kirkholt is a large council estate on the edge of Rochdale, Lancashire, which had a notorious reputation and a rate of recorded burglary considerably above that of the typical high risk area. As Tilley (1993: 3) noted:

> The recorded rate in the year preceding the Burglary Prevention Project stood at 25% of households. This compares with a national rate for recorded burglary of 2% in 1988, a British Crime Survey rate of 5% for 1988, and a maximum BCS rate of 13% for the sorts of area most vulnerable to burglary.

The project team, coordinated through the University of Manchester, collected and analysed a wide range of data, using police records and interviews with local offenders, victims and other local people. On the basis of the information collected, a number of crime prevention strategies were implemented. These included:

- **Removal of prepayment gas and electricity meters.** A distinctive feature of British public housing has been the inclusion of prepayment meters. These have provided a reliable source of income for burglars, and in Kirkholt about half of all burglaries involved theft of cash from meters, with over a quarter exclusively so. The replacement of these meters thus provided an obvious means for cutting burglaries by reducing the reward that the average burglar might anticipate.

- **Target hardening.** In conjunction with the housing department, funding was made available to upgrade the security of burgled homes and some other dwellings to standards specified by crime prevention officers.

- **Enhanced community support.** Eleven community 'self-help' workers were employed with a mandate to liaise with burglary victims, offer support, and refer them where appropriate to other agencies. These workers also carried out security surveys, postcoded valuables, and helped establish 'cocoon' neighbourhood watch.

- **Establishing 'cocoon' neighbourhood watch.** This was a proactive approach to setting up neighbourhood watch in an area that, as we saw in chapter 6, would not otherwise be considered fertile NW territory, with the added feature that it focused on small pockets of housing adjacent to burgled properties. Seven months into the project, the authors reported that 75 schemes had been established (Forrester, Chatterton and Pease 1988: 17).

As we discussed in chapter 4, one of the main emphases of the Kirkholt initiative was on repeat burglary, and many of these elements gave priority to those who had been recently burgled, on the grounds that by targeting them one could more easily 'take the grease to the squeak', that is, allocate resources where they would have most impact.

Early analysis suggested that there was a significant decrease in burglary in Kirkholt compared with the rest of the police subdivision and that in Kirkholt the contribution of repeat burglaries declined dramatically (Forrester, Chatterton and Pease 1988: 19–24).

Phase II of the project was described in a subsequent publication (Forrester *et al* 1990). With a change of emphasis, the role of the probation service increased (see chapter 11) and the part played by community support workers was scaled down. Other social crime prevention initiatives included the establishment of a credit union and a coherent schools strategy. Target hardening and 'cocoon' neighbourhood watch, however, remained as central features of the project.

Subsequent evaluation demonstrated the success on the project (Forrester *et al* 1990: 29–43). In the year preceding the initiative, there were on average 44 burglaries per month on the estate: in the following three years the average fell to 19, 14 and 11 respectively. Moreover, there was no evidence of displacement to other parts of the subdivision. Burglary rates declined most for longer-term residents, who had presumably adapted more readily to the new 'crime prevention culture'. With the replacement of prepayment meters, the extent to which this type of property was taken fell from 48% of all burglaries to 1%. Interestingly, by the end of the monitoring period a much greater proportion of burglaries were occurring at night to unoccupied homes, suggesting both that target hardening made it more difficult to effect a break-in quickly and quietly and that, consequently, *modus operandi* displacement may have occurred.

The Kirkholt initiative informed subsequent projects in a number of ways (Tilley 1993). One was to emphasise the importance of multi-victimisation, spawning projects focused on repeat victimisation for burglary, vehicle crime, domestic violence, etc. Another was the emphasis on diagnosing and then responding to a particular crime problem, that has since been incorporated into the Crime and Disorder Act and Community Safety Strategy Groups. Third, it heralded an emphasis on multi-agency working that has become the catechism of recent governments. Finally, it demonstrated that where a coordinated strategy could be funded from outside, crime prevention could be enhanced even in high crime areas. It is fitting, then, that the Kirkholt scheme was funded in its later stages through Safer Cities, since it provided a key justification for the Safer Cities strategy.

## The Safer Cities programme

Safer Cities was part of the government's Action for Cities programme, established to address crime problems in designated cities (Tilley 1992). The initiative aimed to reduce crime and the fear of crime through targeting extra resources towards local areas where particular crime problems had been identified. Phase 1 ran from 1988–1995. In each of the 20 areas included in Phase 1, a partnership, or multi-agency approach was adopted. A local coordinator, funded by the Home Office, was appointed to work with a steering committee comprised of local agencies including the police, probation, local government, voluntary bodies and the private sector. In each case, the strategy involved an analysis of local data to establish crime patterns and priorities, the adoption of policies designed to address specific problems, and an evaluation of the policies. During Phase 1 about 3,600 initiatives were put in place, of which over 500 focused on domestic burglary.

In an evaluation of these, Eckblom, Law and Sutton (1996a, 1996b) concentrated on 300 burglary reduction initiatives, which received on average £8,700 each from Safer Cities, with about a third of the initiatives also funded from elsewhere. Schemes tended to consist of:

- target hardening, e.g. improved door or window locks, alarms, and security lighting

and/or

- community-oriented action, e.g. encourage the development of neighbourhood watch or employ staff to raise security awareness.

Eckblom, Law and Sutton (1996a, 1996b) used 'before and after' household surveys and a six-year analysis of police statistics. They compared three types of area: those not covered by a Safer Cities programme; those covered by a programme but where no burglary reduction initiative was in operation; and those where a burglary reduction initiative was in place. In the latter case they also distinguished between initiatives with different levels of intensity. The residents' surveys revealed that the burglary prevalence rate rose in areas without a burglary reduction programme but fell in those with a programme, and especially those where a high intensity programme was in operation. In general, burglary incidence rates fell in all areas, but the fall was greatest in areas with burglary reduction programmes, especially high intensity programmes (see Table 7.1).

*Table 7.1: Survey data on burglary rates in Safer Cities areas with no burglary reduction programmes and those with low, medium and high intensity programmes, and other areas (from Eckblom, Law and Sutton 1996a: 13–14)*

|  | | Safer Cities | | | Other cities |
|  | None | Low | Medium | High |  |
|---|---|---|---|---|---|
| *Prevalence rates:* | | | | | |
| 12 months prior | 8.9 | 10.3 | 12.7 | 13.4 | 12.0 |
| 12 months after | 10.2 | 9.5 | 9.9 | 7.6 | 12.4 |
| | | | | | |
| *Incidence rates:* | | | | | |
| 12 months before | 14.0 | 14.6 | 18.7 | 24.0 | 18.5 |
| 12 months after | 13.6 | 12.8 | 13.1 | 12.9 | 17.3 |

A similar pattern emerged from police statistics, where a decline in burglaries in the year after the programmes were introduced was sustained in the following year only in the areas where high intensity initiatives were operating.

Eckblom, Law and Sutton (1996a, 1996b) also assessed the extent to which there was crime displacement, in terms of burglars either switching to other areas or committing offences other than burglary. Whilst each of these occurred to some extent where low intensity programmes were operating, for medium and high intensity programmes there was no evidence of displacement, and indeed in some cases there was some indication of a 'diffusion of benefit': that is, burglaries in surrounding areas and other crimes in the targeted areas were also reduced.

The researchers then compared the impact of programmes on burglary according to whether the programme involved target hardening, community-oriented action or both. They concluded that a comprehensive range of initiatives was most effective, although target hardening alone had some impact. However, community-oriented action was ineffective unless supported by other measures.

On the other hand, there was less evidence of any reduction in fear of crime. To a large extent, this was because the public was generally unaware of the Safer Cities programme. For example, even in high intensity areas only about a quarter of residents had heard about it (Eckblom, Law and Sutton 1996a). However, among those who had heard of the programme, it seemed that where the initiative was of low intensity, this served to *increase* anxiety, but where the initiative was of high intensity anxiety was reduced.

Even assuming that the impact of the programmes was short-lived, they were cost-effective, especially in high crime areas where the costs per burglary prevented were considerably lower. The researchers therefore concluded that the Safer Cities programme was a cost-effective approach to burglary reduction, particularly where a comprehensive range of strategies was deployed.

A more detailed evaluation of selected burglary reduction initiatives from Phase 1, by Tilley and Webb (1994), was somewhat less positive, suggesting *inter alia* that success depended on good publicity, that victim-centred target hardening reduced revictimisation but not necessarily area burglary rates, that target hardening of nonvictims considered particularly at risk was ineffective, and that multi-agency initiatives were highly vulnerable where some key agencies failed to 'deliver'. However, they also concluded that comprehensive and high intensity packages of measures were particularly effective.

Phase 2 of the Safer Cities programme was initiated in 1994, when seven cities were included, followed in 1995 by a further 20. Burglary reduction initiatives were again a central feature of the programme, and they were given extra momentum by additional funding in seven areas from Direct Line Insurance (Webb 1997). Direct Line Insurance agreed to fund a target hardening burglary prevention initiative in the seven cities managed by Crime Concern, in Plymouth, Merthyr Tydfil, Lambeth, Greenwich, Blackburn, Burnley and Manchester. The sponsorship went under the general name of Homesafe, but the way it was implemented varied in each city and was moulded on a local level both by Safer Cities and the interagency framework of which Safer Cities was a part. In each city a deprived area of rented accommodation with a burglary rate of some two to three times the national average was chosen. The broad objectives of Homesafe were to reduce both burglary and fear of burglary and to increase public awareness of risks so that local people adopted crime prevention strategies for themselves.

In an evaluation of the first 12 months of the initiative, Webb (1997: 40) concluded:

Where data were available, it was found that domestic burglary was reduced in all the Homesafe areas, and at a greater level than in the Division or Sub Division of which they were a part. Targeting burglary victims had the effect of reducing repeat victimisation, though offering the service to all residents seemed more effective than concentrating on victims or selected areas. Other benefits consisted of improved and focused single- and multi-agency working, and a greater willingness of residents to become involved in the fight against crime. Tackling burglary reduction appeared to be a springboard for other crime prevention initiatives in the area.

Both the wider evaluation of Phase 1 and the more focused evaluations of Phase 2 give good grounds for optimism; crime and fear of crime seem to have been reduced (Ekblom *et al* 1996; Tilley and Webb 1994; Webb 1997). The following sections of this chapter assess the local situation by asking how the results from Plymouth, one of the cities included in Phase 2 and part of the Homesafe initiative, compare with the national picture.[1]

## Case study: burglary reduction initiatives in Plymouth

Plymouth Homesafe was, in fact, part of a much wider series of crime prevention initiatives that were generated within the city in the 1994–95 period. Central to these was Plymouth Safer Cities. Plymouth was incorporated in Phase 2 of the Safer Cities programme, beginning in 1994. The objectives of the programme were to reduce crime and fear of crime and to improve quality of life through effective crime prevention and community safety work. To this end £100,000 per annum was made available to Plymouth Safer Cities for the period 1995–98, with project running costs being met centrally. Plymouth Safer Cities was one of 12 programmes in Phase 2 that was managed by Crime Concern, but operated locally through an inter-agency Steering Committee. This committee agreed to target domestic burglary along with violence and youth crime.

At broadly the same time the Chief Superintendent of the Plymouth Division of the Devon and Cornwall Constabulary established a number of inter-agency committees to address key local problems. One such committee, arguably the most significant, was the Domestic Burglary Strategy Group (DBSG). This group included representatives of the Probation Service, Victim Support, the Local Authority Housing Department and Plymouth Safer Cities as well as the university. Its aims were to reduce both burglary and fear of burglary, throughout the city but especially in one targeted high crime rate area, to provide a consistent and enhanced response to victims, and to target repeat victims and especially vulnerable victims. To achieve these aims it adopted a cocktail of approaches, some preventive and others reactive, some focused on victims or potential victims, others on offenders.

While Plymouth Safer Cities and the DBSG themselves provided a range of funding and other resources aimed at tackling burglary, a major impetus was provided by Crime Concern when it successfully negotiated a sponsorship deal with Direct Line Insurance, which agreed to fund a burglary prevention initiative in the seven cities managed at that time by Crime Concern. In Plymouth the Homesafe initiative became part of the Plymouth Safer Cities and the DBSG programmes and included in addition to the Direct Line funding, grants from Plymouth Safer Cities and Plymouth City Council (Housing Department).[2]

The Homesafe programme incorporated five main elements:

(i)     a security check administered by a fitter trained by the police
(ii)    the fitting of security locks to doors and windows, plus, for the most vulnerable, security chains
(iii)   the fitting of smoke alarms
(iv)    property marking
(v)     provision of crime prevention leaflets.

### The Homesafe initiative in Mount Gould

Phase 1 aimed to tackle crime and fear of crime in a high crime area of the city, by providing a free service for those unable to afford increased protection. The initiative concentrated on improving security in one area of the city where burglary was a problem. Within that area the focus was on local authority housing stock but from the start it was intended to include a smaller number of adjacent privately owned homes.

The area chosen – Mount Gould – exhibited many of the problems associated with inner city residential areas, although deprivation levels were not so great as to undermine any cost-constrained initiatives such as Homesafe. For example, it rating third (from 20 wards) on poor household amenities and male unemployment and had the second highest burglary rate in the city in 1993, although it only had an average proportion of known burglars living in the area. Neighbourhood watch was however poorly established, with fewer schemes and members than all but one other ward.

The initiative was evaluated in two main ways (Mawby 1997). First, police statistics on reported household burglaries in the core streets of the initiative were collated on a monthly basis for 1994–1996. To assess the possibility of displacement or wider changes in crime rates these were compared with figures for Plymouth as a whole. Second, a sample of residents who had had their home security improved was interviewed on two occasions.[3]

A total of 451 local households were served by the initiative, of whom about 90% were local authority tenants. Interviews were conducted with 81 of these, of whom 37 had been victims of burglary in the previous 12 months:[4] 63 respondents were subsequently re-interviewed, on average 383 days after the first interview.

In using the initial interview data we evaluated two features of the scheme:

- Were those receiving the service the ones the initiative was designed to help?

- What were their feelings about Homesafe and its effects?

Additionally, by comparing responses with those from earlier surveys and, nationally, people interviewed in the BCS we can assess:

- Whether the additional security impacted upon victims' feelings about the area in which they lived.

- Whether the enhanced service had a 'knock on' effect on their views of the police.

- Whether the Homesafe initiative affected people's concerns over crime.

In terms of the social characteristics of clients of the service, most were relatively old (mean 58.6). Reflecting this, 35% were widowed, with 31% married or cohabiting and 21% separated or divorced. Slightly over half (53%) lived in households with no other adults (i.e. aged 16 or over) and only 16% had children living with them. In these respects, respondents were atypical of the Plymouth population. They were also distinctive in being relatively poor. For example, only 37% had cars and only 20% had holidayed abroad within the previous two years.

Plymouth itself has a low proportion of purpose built flats and this is reflected in the fact that 72% occupied houses, with 14% in purpose built flats and 18% in flats within houses. Most (70%) had lived in the area for ten years or more.

On this first criterion we can therefore state that the initiative met its objectives. It successfully identified a relatively poor and vulnerable group who would have been unlikely to have acted to improve their security without outside help.

What then of our second criterion: how was the initiative perceived by its recipients?

We were concerned to ensure that residents benefited from the service, particularly since other studies have suggested that crime prevention initiatives may, by sensitising people to the problem, raise concern. We therefore gave respondents a checklist and asked whether having the work done had made them feel any differently about crime, either when they were first approached (time a) or when the work was carried out (time b). As is clear from Table 7.2, replies indicated that people's reactions were overwhelmingly positive. The majority were reassured and only 27% said that initially it made them worried about burglary. Moreover by the time the work was carried out this figure had dropped to 12%, suggesting that the fitter had successfully reassured people. On the other hand only some 40–50% said they had been made more aware of the risks, implying that in attempting to reassure residents the project staff may have underplayed other crime prevention messages.

*Table 7.2: Respondents' reactions to having home security work done when first told about it (Time a) and when work done (Time b) (percentages)*

|  | Time a | Time b |
| --- | --- | --- |
| Made me feel someone cared about victim's problems | 53 | 51 |
| Made me aware of the risk of burglary | 49 | 41 |
| Reassured me that the scheme would help prevent burglary | 87 | 89 |
| Made me worried about burglary | 27 | 12 |

The fact that the operatives dealt sensitively with recipients of the service is emphasised where we asked – again using a show card – how the work had been carried out. As Table 7.3 illustrates, responses were overwhelmingly positive.

*Table 7.3: Respondents' evaluation of the service (percentages)*

| | |
| --- | --- |
| The man who did the work was efficient | 98 |
| The man who did the work was careful | 91 |
| The man who did the work was polite | 96 |
| The man who did the work was reassuring | 93 |
| The man who did the work was in too much of a hurry | 5 |

Certainly respondents indicated that they felt less worried since their security was improved. Asked directly if they felt safer now, 73% answered in the affirmative. Moreover, in response to an open-ended question on the main advantage of having the work done, 93% cited a greater feeling of security or safety. For example:

I went on holiday soon after, I felt happier leaving the house. Knowing it was more secure.

I don't feel scared about leaving the house empty. It does make you feel a lot safer.

Feel more secure with double locks and chain.

The data here unambiguously suggest that respondents were very positive about the Homesafe initiative and felt safer as a result. However, it is difficult to be certain that fear or worry had been reduced: on the one hand we have no measure of householders' perceptions prior to the initiative; on the other hand we have no control group of citizens who did not receive the service. These problems are compounded by the fact that Homesafe was targeted at poorer, inner city people, that interviews included disproportionate numbers of the elderly and women, and that we over sampled burglary victims; in all these respects we would expect, on the basis of earlier research, that attitudes would be atypical of the whole population (Hough 1995; Mawby and Walklate 1994; Mirrlees-Black and Maung 1994). Our own findings confirmed that women and prior burglary victims expressed most concern.

We attempted to overcome this difficulty by comparing our sub-sample of burglary victims with an earlier sample of 200 burglary victims taken from Plymouth as a whole as part of our cross-national research and by comparing our total sample with British Crime Survey data for lower class, inner city residents (Hough 1995). In each case the comparisons suggested lower levels of fear or worry among our sample. Moreover, residents' feelings about crime and their area were broadly the same when interviewed a year or more later. The initiative thus appeared to have had a relatively long-term impact.

However, were locals right to feel safer? Had their risk of burglary declined?

One indication of the answer to this question comes from the follow-up interviews, which showed that only three had suffered any sort of burglary in the year or more since, and two of these were attempts only. This rate is considerably lower than expected. Additionally, we monitored police crime statistics.

We abstracted data on burglaries from computerised police records on a monthly basis for the year preceding the initiative (1994), the year in which the target hardening was carried out (1995) and the next year (1996). In Table 7.4 the figures for Plymouth as a whole have been compared with the records on the 18 roads at the core of the initiative. As is evident, for Plymouth as a whole the rate of recorded burglaries fell, by 10% in 1995 and to 71% of the base figure in 1996. This largely reflected a fall throughout the force area, but it might also indicate a slight impact of PSC and the DBSG in the division. In the target area the fall was even more marked: the 1995 figures were only 79% of those in 1994 and by 1996 the number of burglaries stood at 55% of the baseline. It thus seems that the Homesafe initiative impacted upon burglaries in addition to any effects that the wider anti-burglary strategies had.

*Table 7.4: Annual burglary figures (excluding attempts) in Plymouth and core roads targeted by Homesafe*

|      | Totals (number) | | Change from 1994 | |
|------|-----------------|----------|------------------|----------|
|      | *In core roads* | *Plymouth* | *In core roads* | *Plymouth* |
| 1994 | 121 | 4,009 | 100 | 100 |
| 1995 | 96  | 3,598 | 79  | 90  |
| 1996 | 66  | 2,860 | 55  | 71  |

The Plymouth Homesafe initiative aimed to tackle crime and fear of crime in a high crime area of the city, by providing a free service for those unable to afford increased protection. Our evaluation suggests that it broadly achieved its objectives. First, the project successfully identified a high crime area, and, within the area, those provided with the additional security were a relatively impoverished group who would have been unlikely to be able to afford additional crime prevention. Second, the initiative was well received: residents felt it would be effective, and – relative to similar people living elsewhere – fear or worry over crime appeared lower than expected. Third, both follow-up interviews with residents and an analysis of police statistics suggest that the project has had an impact on burglary, in the core roads in the area and among those 'Homesafed'. It appears that the extra security provided, combined with other initiatives aimed at improving the community's own mechanisms of social control, had a significant impact on burglaries in the area and on residents' fears of future burglary.

*Targeting Homesafe at older people*

Following this initial success, additional funds were used to extend the Homesafe initiative in a number of respects. Given apparently higher levels of fear of crime among older people, it was agreed to target older local authority tenants in areas of the city where crime was of particular local concern and provide a 'package' of crime prevention help similar to that offered under Homesafe Phase 1.

Having identified an area of the city where the problem appeared extreme, the Homesafe team worked with the ward police officer to distinguish – in order of priority – repeat victims, victims of a first burglary, and those living in high incidence streets. Work was carried out at the designated addresses during a six-month period from November 1995 to April 1996. In total 147 homes were subject to the improvements.

The initiative aimed to reduce burglary and fear of burglary among recipients of the service and thus enhance the quality of life of older people in the targeted areas. The research evaluated the initiative by comparing levels of (reported) burglary before and after the initiative and through interviews with recipients of the service. However, constraints of time and resources meant that we were unable to carry out any interviews before security was enhanced or with a control group not subject to the improvements, and because of this the interview findings must be treated with some caution (Mawby 1999a).

Interviews were carried out in July and August 1996 with 122 recipients of the initiative, 76% of the total. Almost all respondents had had the extra security fitted for between two and nine months, the average being six months. Interviews were carried out with one person per household. The questionnaire used included some 30 questions covering five areas:

(i)   personal details, including poverty, age, and housing history
(ii)  experiences of burglary
(iii) feelings about the crime prevention initiative
(iv)  worries about crime
(v)   in the light of these, perceptions of the area and likelihood of moving.

Although the initiative was aimed at older people, not everyone interviewed was of pensionable age, with 7% aged under 60. This said, however, no less than 52% of those interviewed were aged 75 or more and a further 25% aged 70–74. Reflecting this, 63% were widowed and 70% were living alone. Most (73%) were women, and 70% of these were living alone compared with only 52% of the men.

Since the initiative focused on public sector housing, not surprisingly 93% lived in rented accommodation, but other indicators confirmed the relative poverty of the group. Asked about ownership of three 'luxury' items – car, video and computer – 48% owned none of them, with 48% owning a video and 16% a car. A large minority (41%) had never had a holiday abroad and only 14% had been abroad within the previous two years. Just over half (52%) had lived in the area for at least ten years, with 16% moving in within the previous two years. The picture thus confirms the characteristics that were targeted: a relatively impoverished group of older citizens, many living alone and many restricted in their mobility and so particularly dependent on the local neighbourhood.

About a third of respondents said they had heard of Plymouth Homesafe before being contacted directly by the project, the majority of these saying they had heard from neighbours or the police. Once contacted, most said the improvements were carried out within four weeks. Asked why they consented to having the work done, 39% said to make the home safer and a further 11% specifically mentioned protection from burglary. For example:

> Because of the break-ins in the area.
> Someone in the same Crescent had been broken in to.
> Because of previous break-ins.

Additionally 42% implied that they had no choice, that 'the council' had made the decision.[5] None of these, however, had not wished for the work to be carried out.

As with Phase 1, we were concerned to ensure that residents benefited from the service. We therefore gave respondents the checklist and asked whether having the work done had made them feel any differently about crime. As in Mount Gould, replies indicated that people's reactions were overwhelmingly positive. The majority were reassured and only 13 said it made them worried about burglary. On the other hand, only about a quarter said they had been made more aware of the risks, again implying that in attempting to reassure the elderly the project staff may have underplayed other crime prevention messages. Moreover, although crime prevention leaflets were routinely left, it seems that their message had not always sunk in.

Again replicating our findings from Phase 1, respondents were overwhelmingly positive in their views of how the work had been carried out. Additionally, respondents indicated that they felt less worried since their security was improved. In response to an open-ended question on the main advantage of having the work done, 93% cited a greater feeling of security or safety. Many mentioned the fact that they felt less worried about leaving the house unoccupied, or were able to sleep more soundly. The advantage of being able to lock the windows in an open position was also commented on by a large number. For example:

> You feel safer and you can go to bed at night and not worry so much.
> Peace of mind, that's the main thing.
> Sleep better... Can go out feeling the place is safe.
> I feel I can go out a little more now. And I can leave windows open.

These comments illustrate the impact of the initiative on quality of life, although they may also be coloured by respondents' feelings of gratitude for a freely provided service. In addition, at this point in the interview 5% spontaneously said they were now less likely to move. Asked directly, 87% also said they felt safer since the work was done.

In the light of these findings we might have expected respondents to register relatively low levels of fear of or worry about crime. However, it should also be noted that the targeted population again share the characteristics of those who express most fear of crime (Hough 1995, 58–62). For example, they are predominantly women, aged over 60, poor and council house dwellers. We should not be surprised to find, then, that things were not quite this simple, with older people – and women in particular – still registering relatively high levels of concern. Two points, however, are worth making.

First, most respondents felt safe alone at home at night, with 64% of males and 43% of females saying they felt very safe, and almost half said they did not worry about the possibility of a future break-in. Compared with BCS data on older people living in inner city areas, feelings of worry or lack of safety were lower, although the difference was only marked for males. For example, whilst 97% of males and 83% of females in our sample said they felt safe at home alone at night, the corresponding figures for the BCS sub-samples were 88% and 79%. Similarly, 33% of males and 18% of females from our sample said they were not at all worried about having their home broken into and something stolen, compared with 12% of males and 12% of females from the BCS sub-samples.

Second, and to substantiate this point, when asked about other types of crime or crime in general, our sample expressed more concern than older people nationally. Thus it appears that relative to their concern over street crime, respondents in our survey were less worried about home-based crimes. Overall, then, the findings suggested that the fitting of extra security did help reduce fear of burglary, especially among older men. At the same time though, it serves to warn us that improvements to quality of life are limited if people are still fearful of public space outside the home.

Be that as it may, respondents registered high levels of satisfaction with the area. A majority described it as an area where people helped each other (57%) rather than went their own way (30%), and these replies reflected a greater feeling of local community support than among the BCS sub-samples. Moreover, most also said they were very satisfied (41%) or satisfied (43%) with the area. Asked whether they were likely to move within the next two years, 74% said they would definitely not move, with a further 16% saying they would probably not. Only a minority said they were very likely to (3%) or might (12%) move to an old people's home and 62% said that the increased security had meant they were less likely to do so. While such reactions may not equate too closely with future *behaviour*, it appears that the community safety initiative had reassured many and lessened their desire to move, whether into residential accommodation or to another area.

But were burglaries less common as a result of the initiative?

It is hazardous to draw too many conclusions from a study of this kind, for a number of reasons. First, we are dependent upon official statistics, where changing crime rates may be masked by changes in reporting behaviour.[6] Second, burglaries may be displaced to surrounding areas, or to different types of crime. Third, changes in a small area or a limited time period may be 'temporary blips' rather than indications of long-term improvements.

Bearing these qualifications in mind we identified ten roads that formed the core of the initiative. Not all homes in these roads were target hardened, and other homes were also served. But 114 (79%) of the homes that had been 'Homesafed' were located in these roads. We then compared recorded burglary figures for these roads in the six months prior to the initiative (period 1) with the six months during which the work in the area was carried out (period 2) and the following six months (period 3). The results are detailed in Table 7.5, which also includes figures for the rest of Plymouth. In each case the total numbers of burglaries are presented, plus percentages using period 1 as a baseline.

Table 7.5 indicates again that the number of burglaries in Plymouth fell. In period 2 the number in Plymouth as a whole was 87% of the period 1 total; by period 3 it was 77%. However, while in the ten roads we identified the number of burglaries rose in period 2 to 113% of the level of period 1, once the target hardening was completed the number of burglaries fell dramatically. In May–October 1996 burglaries were at only 30% of the situation in May–October 1995. Put another way, on the basis of the overall figures for Plymouth, we would have expected 17.7 burglaries in the ten roads in period 3, significantly more than was the case.[7] All the indications are that the Homesafe initiative helped reduce the risk of burglary in these small pockets of housing occupied by older people, although we were unable to measure the extent to which some burglaries may have been displaced to adjacent streets.

*Table 7.5: Six-monthly burglary figures*

|  | Totals (number) | | Change from period 1 | |
|  | Ten roads | Rest of Plymouth | Ten roads | Rest of Plymouth |
|---|---|---|---|---|
| Period 1 | 23 | 1,800 | 100 | 100 |
| Period 2 | 26 | 1,561 | 113 | 87 |
| Period 3 | 7 | 1,395 | 30 | 78 |

Unlike the Cambridge research of Bennett and Durie (1999), our local research thus supports national evaluations in concluding that government-initiated burglary reduction programmes have been successful in reducing the risk and, in some cases, the fear of burglary. Partly as a result of such findings, further Home Office funding has been directed at burglary initiatives. While evaluation of these is currently ongoing, it is appropriate to describe them briefly.

## The Burglary Reduction Initiative

The Burglary Reduction Initiative was launched in 1998 as a major element of the Home Office's Crime Reduction Programme (CRP). It comprised a series of Strategic Development Projects (SDPs) in areas with burglary rates of at least twice the national average. SDPs are monitored regionally in order to evaluate the viability of different initiatives, with a view to replicating them elsewhere. However, rather than assuming that burglary could be tackled in the same way in different locations, the initiative assumed that high rates of burglary may be the result of different pressures in different areas, and consequently that strategies needed to be adjusted to meet local circumstances. Although £250 million was made available for the CRP, 60 projects were funded through the SDP, with around £60,000 being allocated to each project. The initiative was thus relatively modest (Tilley *et al* 1999).

The philosophy underpinning the SDPs is that local Crime and Disorder Partnerships would be invited to submit proposals that:

- Identified an area (in a minority of cases a 'virtual community' rather than a spatially located area) with a persistently high burglary rate.

- Identified the key causes of the burglary in that area.

- Set out a series of policies targeted at addressing the problem and reducing burglary.

In a review of the projects selected, Tilley *et al* (1999) noted that the 'key crime generators' fell under five broad headings:

(i)    **Offender related generators.** For example, areas with high proportions of known or potential burglars living there or travelling through.

(ii)   **Victim related generators.** For example, areas containing large proportions of those at particular risk, such as students, where lack of crime prevention strategies combine with a harvest of goods worth stealing.

(iii)  **Community related generators.** For example, economic hardship combined with low levels of informal social control.

(iv)   **Specific situational generators.** For example, poorly designed estates, poorly lit streets, and houses in multiple occupation (HIMOs).

(iv)   **Wider locality related generators.** For example, where local leisure facilities attracted potential offenders to the area.

Thus Tilley *et al* (1999) cited as examples of initiatives that received funding: one where defective housing design combined with an unsound housing allocation policy to create a situation where young local burglars could commit local offences with relative ease and then sell on the stolen goods to the impoverished local community; and, in contrast, another where offenders from outside the area were attracted by the easy pickings to be gained from a student population in predominantly small rented terraced housing. In Plymouth, one of the other areas where a project received funding, the emphasis was placed on the 'virtual community' of HIMOs, with high rates of burglary due to inadequate security, where the initiative aimed to encourage private landlords to target harden their property.

### Risk, fear and the elderly initiatives

Building on these initiatives, in 1999/2000 the Home Office announced up to £11 million to improve security in the homes of those aged over 60 in high crime areas throughout England, with a further £750,000 to extend the scheme into Wales.

The scheme will run in conjunction with the DETR's New Energy Efficiency Scheme, which aims to tackle fuel poverty, especially in the rented and owner-occupied sectors. Those who are eligible for home heating and insulation improvements, who are aged over 60, and who live in Police Basic Command Unit areas with burglary rates of at least double the national average will be offered security improvements, *where these are considered necessary*, by the HEES surveyor. Improvements will include, where appropriate:

- mortise locks for all exterior doors
- deadlocking rimlocks for main/front doors
- viewers and security chains for front doors
- hinge bolts on outward opening doors
- locks for all groundfloor or accessible windows.

Other developments have concentrated on 'distraction burglaries', or 'burglary artifice', that – while not common (Budd 1999) – tend to be aimed at older people. An earlier initiative against bogus callers was established by the London Metropolitan Police in 1995 (Muir 1999). Following a victim survey of older people in one London borough, the initiative was piloted with 72 people aged over 65 on one housing estate. Those involved were issued with a bracelet or pendant containing an alarm patched through to a central control centre. Although the trial was relatively small scale, it seemed to increase feelings of security among the elderly, and an extension to other parts of London was financed through Single Regeneration Fund monies. Subsequently, funding from British Gas and Help the Aged has enabled the scheme to be introduced elsewhere in London and other parts of the country, including Plymouth.

In 2000, the Home Office announced the piloting of 22 schemes aimed at tackling bogus callers. The pilot schemes have been designed in conjunction with community-based groups, principally neighbourhood watch. The pilot was due to run for six months, after which a guide for best practice would be compiled for nationwide implementation.

## The 1998 Crime and Disorder Act

Government policies during the 1990s were geared towards encouraging local government and police to enter into crime prevention partnerships at the local level, but it was only in areas incorporated within Safer Cities that local partnership working made significant headway. However, the 1998 Crime and Disorder Act, following the Morgan (1991) Report, designated local authorities and police as 'responsible authorities for crime strategies'. Acting in partnership with other agencies, including probation, health and voluntary sector bodies, these local leadership groups are required to consult with local agencies in conducting audits of local crime and disorder issues, formulate strategies for the reduction of crime, evaluate them, and publish reports on the basis of those analyses, to be submitted to the Home Secretary. They will also be required to identify long- and short-term performance targets, and evaluate the extent to which they are achieved.

As a result, local authorities have established Community Safety Partnerships as the basis for multi-agency planning. These have sought to identify priorities, and burglary has been singled out as one of the major problems by most partnerships. Local funding, and central funds – for example through the Single Regeneration Budget (SRB) – may be used to tackle burglary at local level, but Community Safety Partnerships have also been the key players in bidding for and receiving central government funds, such as Home Office money through the Burglary Reduction Initiative. One major disadvantage here is that bids for central funds may be limited to areas with high rates of burglary, thus stifling initiatives in many areas of the country. Despite this, Community Safety Partnerships provide the main conduit for the introduction of burglary reduction initiatives at local level, and have been designed to encourage initiatives to tackle directly local manifestations of the problem.

## Evaluating intervention

While the SDP evaluation is ongoing, a considerable amount of evaluation of the different initiatives has taken place. In summarising the findings of this and the previous chapter, three questions can be addressed. First, how far do different initiatives reduce the risk of burglary? Second, how do they impact upon worry or anxiety? Third, what evidence is there of displacement?

In chapter 6, the impact of NW on burglary levels was questioned, and studies that have focused on NW have generally been pessimistic about its impact. However, target hardening does appear to affect risk. BCS data suggest that homes that have been protected by burglar alarms or door/window locks are less likely to be targeted and that where an attempt is made to break in, the result is more likely to be unsuccessful than in cases where homes are less well protected. Evaluations of the Safer Cities programme provide additional evidence of the success of target hardening, but also suggest that other initiatives such as NW may be effective when combined with target hardening. Overall they also demonstrate the importance of coherent and comprehensive approaches to crime prevention. While a feature of this in England and Wales has been a partnership, or multi-agency, approach, the findings also underline the fact that an initiative is only as strong as its weakest link, and that the success of partnership work is undermined where some partners are only partly committed, or are 'pulling in different directions'.

Although the evidence regarding NW is not conclusive, there is some indication that NW developments may succeed in reducing fear or anxiety. Evidence from the Safer Cities initiative is more ambivalent, largely because many people may be unaware of local developments. Moreover, it again appears that more comprehensive programmes are more successful than limited ones. On the other hand, the Plymouth research on those who have been 'Homesafed' provides additional evidence that such programmes may reduce fear and improve quality of life.

However, the Plymouth research and BCS findings, although they suggest that improved security may reduce risk and fear, leave open the possibility that crime might be displaced rather than reduced. Essentially, displacement may occur in at least four dimensions: time, location, offence type and *modus operandi*. In terms of time, offenders may change the times when they commit offences. Thus the Kirkholt evaluation found that the time at which burglaries occurred shifted, albeit there was a dramatic fall in the number of burglaries. In terms of location, burglars may opt for different targets – for example, by burgling homes without alarms or those in areas without a NW scheme. However, the conclusions from both Kirkholt and the Safer Cities initiative were that displacement was minimal, and indeed in some cases homes in surrounding areas experienced a fall in burglaries that suggested that the benefits of the initiative rubbed off on neighbouring areas. Similarly, in Plymouth, the Homesafe initiative appeared to impact upon area burglary rates, not just those properties that had benefited from improved security. In terms of offence type, they may shift from, say, residential to commercial burglary, or to vehicle related crimes. This would seem likely where, as discussed in chapter 5, there is little evidence of offence specialisation. Moreover, where the declining domestic burglary rate in England and Wales has been matched by a rise in some other property crimes, it is arguable that burglars have switched offences. Nevertheless, evaluation of the Safer Cities initiative also found evidence of a 'diffusion of benefit' here, with rates for crimes other than burglary declining where high intensity programmes were in place. Finally, in terms of *modus operandi*, if homes are target hardened burglars may opt for distraction burglaries instead. There is, however, little evidence about this. Indeed, a more comprehensive analysis of displacement would need to consider both *offence* patterns and the *career* patterns of former burglars, something that has not, to date, been done.

Despite this caveat, there is good reason to believe that burglary reduction programmes in England and Wales have been successful and that displacement has not occurred to any significant extent. However, many people still experience burglary, and policies also need to be directed at victims and at harm minimisation. This is the subject of the following two chapters, where the roles of the police and victim assistance programmes are assessed.

### Notes

1  An alternative local evaluation in Cambridge is provided by Bennett and Durie (1999), whose conclusions are somewhat less positive.
2  Direct Line contributed £28,000 pa in 1994–95 and 1995–96 and £5,000 in 1996–97. PSC contributed £30,000 pa for the first two years and £28,000 in 1996–97. Plymouth City Council provided £25,000 pa for all three years. In 1996–97 additional funding was secured from Plymouth 2000 (£10,000) and Devon and Cornwall Housing Associaton (£5,000). Some of these moneys were used to fund other initiatives not included in this evaluation, for example for targeting repreat victims, the elderly in another part of the city, domestic violence victims and, subsequently, residents of another high crime area.
3  I am particularly grateful to Marlene Johnson, the Homesafe manager at the time, for her help in ensuring the smooth progress of the research.
4  Victims were over-sampled.
5  This was a misunderstanding.

6 We might expect those receiving the improvements to be more likely to report subsequent burglaries, so if anything police statistics might understate any improvements in crime levels.

7 Comparing periods 1 and 3, chi-squared = 15.92, p<0.01.

# Chapter 8

# Police services for burglary victims

## Introduction

Consideration of the role of the police is important for at least three reasons. First, the police are highly dependent upon the public, and especially victims, for bringing crime to their attention and providing leads on the offender (see chapter 11). Conversely, if victims feel that the police do not provide a useful service they may fail to report crimes and may even take unsanctioned vigilante action. Second, despite the emergence of victim assistance programmes in many countries (see chapter 9) the police is still the main agency with which victims have contact. As a result, police response to victims may be the most significant post-crime experience. In this respect Joutsen (1987: 212) noted:

> They are generally the first representatives of the State to come into contact with the complainant. Furthermore their intervention will come at a time when the complainant is most likely to be suffering from the immediate shock of the offence. Their attitude will considerably influence not only what the complainant decides to do but also what impression he received of the administration of justice, and of how the community as a whole regards the offence.

Zvekic (1998: 63), writing specifically about countries in transition, has recently echoed this point:

> The police are usually the first criminal justice agency with which citizens come into contact, and they will shape opinions about the criminal justice system as a whole.

Third, the police traditionally hav[...]
victims and in many cases their [...]
effects of the crime, promoting [...]
support. Moreover, this response se[...]
systems:

> There is ample evidence from in-dep[...]
> particularly sensitive to the way they are[...]ims
> police officers. According to several re[...]
> experience an acute need to be 'reassured'[...]
> state that victims expect the police to recog[...]
> someone who has been wronged by a fellow citiz[...]
> express dissatisfaction with police officers who [...]
> callous or cynical. Such observations are often viewed a[...]
> secondary victimisation... Police officers must be taught that their
> deskside manners are as important to victims as bedside manners of
> doctors are to patients. (Van Dijk 1985: 154, 162)

While criticisms of the police have been expressed most forcefully in the case of their treatment of rape and domestic violence victims, the point is no less relevant for burglary victims. In the latter case, however, the circumstances of police intervention are quite distinct. First, in most cases the police are called in to a 'cold' crime, that is, some time after the incident occurred. Second, and as a result of this, detection rates are low. Third, in most cases the status of the complainant as an 'innocent victim' is not disputed, although in some cases the police may suspect the complainant of an insurance scam or similar (including self-committed meter thefts) and in others they may blame the victim for lack of precautions. The response of the police to burglary victims may, consequently, be distinct from their response to, say, interpersonal crimes.

A number of studies have indicated that victims have very clear ideas about police performance and in many cases see the police as failing to address their own priorities about the crime situation (Maguire 1982; Shapland *et al* 1985; Squires 1998). In England and Wales, British Crime Surveys provide recent evidence of growing public dissatisfaction with the police, albeit among a minority of victims (Mayhew *et al* 1989; Mayhew *et al* 1993; Simms and Myhill 2001; Skogan 1990, 1994, 1996). Yet, with the notable exception of the Netherlands (Hauber and Zandbergen 1991; Wemmers and Zeilstra 1991; Winkel 1989), we know very little about alternative models of service provision by the police in other

Anglo-Saxon/North American experiences. It is
to assess how far alternative police systems may be
providing services that the public appreciate. Little is
ms' perspectives in continental police systems, in either
estern Europe, much less about the situation in developing

chapter thus begins with a review of victims' evaluations of the
ces they receive from the police, using data from the International
ime Victims Survey (ICVS) and focusing on victims of burglary, before
discussing the findings of our own research in different European
countries. There is, encouragingly, some evidence that police 'deskside'
(or 'crime-side') manners have improved since van Dijk was writing, and
the chapter concludes by discussing changes in the Netherlands, the
USA, and particularly England and Wales to illustrate this point.

### Policing in a cross-national context: the ICVS

The ICVS provides some rudimentary information on public and victims'
attitudes towards the police, although as noted in chapter 1, data on
public attitudes is obviously based on larger samples than is data for
victims, while burglary victims make up a relatively small number of
respondents in each country.

Taking all those countries that participated in the third ICVS, 45.8%
said that the police did a good job in controlling crime locally, with 38.8%
disagreeing. A positive response was most likely in the New World
(76.0%), followed by Asia (58.3%) and Western Europe (54.0%). In
contrast, rather less citizens from Africa (41.1%), countries in transition
(23.2%) and Latin America (21.9%) expressed themselves satisfied (Zvekic
1998: 76). Among Western industrialised societies, respondents from
Canada (80%), the USA (77%), Scotland (69%) and England and Wales
(68%) were most likely to express a favourable opinion (Mayhew and van
Dijk 1997: 47).

Intriguingly, victims' evaluations of the ways in which the police
handled their complaint followed a somewhat different pattern, with
Asian victims relatively more critical (del Frate 1998). Moreover, as is
illustrated in Table 8.1, victims of different types of crime responded
somewhat differently. Clearly, burglary victims from the New World and
Western Europe were most positive about the service they received, with
African and Latin American victims highly critical.

*Table 8.1: Percentage of victims of burglary and contact crimes who were satisfied with police service (del Frate 1998: 101).*

|                          | Burglary | Contact crimes |
|--------------------------|----------|----------------|
| New World                | 74       | 70             |
| Western Europe           | 68       | 64             |
| Asia                     | 42       | 62             |
| Countries in transition  | 38       | 40             |
| Africa                   | 29       | 47             |
| Latin America            | 25       | 34             |

If crime is a problem, the police may be seen as part of the solution. But public expectations of the police, and perceptions of appropriate policing policies and practices, may vary considerably between societies. While interaction with burglary victims is only one aspect of police work, we might none the less expect to find variations between countries with different policing traditions and different public expectations. We might assume that countries with different policing traditions might display consistently contrasting patterns – with, for example, more negative responses from former colonial systems and countries with a continental European tradition (Mawby 1990b) – but ICVS data showed no such consistency. Equally, patterns were also diverse within regions. This suggests that the policies that individual forces adopt to respond to a specific crime, such as burglary, may be more significant than 'police tradition'.

One further question from the ICVS allows us to tap further victims' evaluations of the services they receive from the police. Where victims expressed dissatisfaction, they were offered a checklist and asked what it was of which they were critical. As is demonstrated in Table 8.2, burglary victims were most critical of the police for not doing enough, not clearing up the crime, not recovering their property and not showing any interest. A broadly similar pattern emerged among robbery victims and victims of assaults/threats although the latter (not surprisingly) rarely mentioned recovery of goods. However, there were also regional differences in the criticisms made. For example, burglary victims from countries in transition were particularly likely to complain that the police had not caught the burglar (46.9%) or had not recovered their property (46.4%).

*Table 8.2: Percentage of dissatisfied victims of burglary, robbery and assaults/ threats citing different reasons for their dissatisfaction (del Frate 1998: 103; Zvekic 1998: 74)*

|  | *Burglary* | *Robbery* | *Assaults/threats* |
|---|---|---|---|
| Didn't do enough | 53 | 45 | 36 |
| Not interested | 30 | 39 | 26 |
| Crime not detected | 38 | 43 | 25 |
| Goods not recovered | 36 | 33 | 8 |
| No feedback | 22 | 20 | 18 |
| Incorrect/impolite | 13 | 17 | 20 |
| Slow response | 15 | 16 | 12 |

There were, of course, variations between countries in transition, with Zvekic (1998, 74–79; 1996) noting that burglary victims were most complimentary in the Czech Republic and Hungary, and citizens in general most positive in Slovenia and Albania. However, the same author warned against complacency by pointing out that for those countries involved in both the second and third ICVSs there was no evidence of any consistent improvement in public/victims' perceptions of policework.

Given the importance of this question in the context of the changing political situation in countries in transition (Mawby 1999b), the following section focuses on our own research in Poland, Hungary and the Czech Republic, compared with England and (West) Germany (Mawby 1998; Mawby *et al* 2001).

## Case study: police response to burglary victims in Europe

Our research on burglary victims addressed three general questions about police services: first, how do the police handle complaints of burglary; second, how far do burglary victims from East and West Europe share similar perceptions of the police; third, to what extent are their assessments of the police influenced by policing traditions, their perceptions of the crime problem and by the services provided by the police today?

In terms of the way the police became involved in the incident, there were broad similarities between countries. Almost all crimes were reported to the police by victims or others acting on their behalf. In most cases reporting was by phone, although visiting the police station in person was more common in Eastern European cities.

In almost all cases the police visited the crime scene. However the speed of response varied. On average, police response was quickest in Miskolc (Hungary), slowest in Warsaw (Poland). There was also considerable variation in the nature of police response. In England, uniformed officers were almost always involved, whereas in Germany and Poland in particular plain-clothes officers most frequently attended burglaries and in many cases no uniformed officers were involved. Details of the investigation were only partly covered in our survey, but it also seemed that bureaucratic procedures were most extensive in Hungary and especially Poland. In both countries, victims had to attend the station to sign statements and in Poland locks were commonly removed for 'analysis', and premises sealed. Such measures may sometimes be interpreted as meticulous policework, but our impression was that in Poland victims often saw this as a nuisance (Mawby *et al* 1997). Certainly there was no evidence that detection rates improved as a consequence!

Speed of response and clear-up rates, on the face of it, underpin victims' evaluations of police performance. We asked a number of questions directly about the way police dealt with the complaint. For example, we asked whether victims had been kept well informed of police progress and if they felt they should have been kept better informed; whether the police had put sufficient effort into the case; whether the police had responded quickly enough; and how satisfied they were overall. Responses to this last question are given in Table 8.3. We then constructed a scale based on these four items, where those critical of the police on all four would score 4, those uncritical on all four 0 (Table 8.4).

*Table 8.3: Percentage of burglary victims in each city expressing themselves overall satisfied with the police*

|  | Satisfied | | Dissatisfied | |
|---|---|---|---|---|
|  | Very | Fairly | Fairly | Very |
| Plymouth | 19 | 58 | 14 | 8 |
| Salford | 7 | 54 | 22 | 9 |
| Münchengladbach | 17 | 56 | 11 | 8 |
| Warsaw | 1 | 17 | 45 | 21 |
| Lublin | 3 | 20 | 39 | 20 |
| Miskolc | 20 | 55 | 13 | 2 |
| Prague | 11 | 53 | 17 | 7 |

Tables 8.3 and 8.4 illustrate the marked variations between victims in the different cities. In general victims from Poland (both Warsaw and Lublin) expressed considerably more criticism than did those from the other four countries, including Hungary and the Czech Republic. Despite this, over nine tenths of victims said that it was likely that they would report a future burglary to the police, and international differences were minimal in this respect. However, differences were pronounced when we asked those who expressed any dissatisfaction what it was about the police that they felt negatively about, using a similar pre-coded checklist to that of the ICVS and BCS. Overall victims were most likely to cite lack of feedback, the fact that the crime was undetected, property not being recovered, and criticism that the police did not do enough or were not interested. However, while lack of feedback was one of the most common criticisms in all five countries, in other respects the emphasis was different. Most notably, whereas in England victims were also most likely to criticise the police because they 'did not do enough' or were 'not interested', in Eastern Europe in general, and Poland in particular, the most common complaints were that the crime was not detected and that property was not recovered. This parallels Zvekic's (1996) findings from the ICVS.

*Table 8.4: Mean scores on scale of police criticism (0–4), where high score denotes criticism*

| | |
|---|---|
| Plymouth | 1.18 |
| Salford | 1.53 |
| Münchengladbach | 0.96 |
| Warsaw | 2.47 |
| Lublin | 2.61 |
| Miskolc | 0.79 |
| Prague | 0.91 |

Criticisms of the way the police dealt with a specific complaint are of course intimately bound to overall feelings about the police. We asked a number of questions on this, which generally suggested that victims in the Western European cities were most positive in their evaluations than those from Central and Eastern Europe. For example, we asked respondents to select up to three occupations from a list of 12 that they most admired. In England and Germany the police ranked third on this list, being selected by 24–27% of respondents; in Poland, the Czech Republic and Hungary they ranked rather lower, being selected by 16% of victims in Prague, 15% in Miskolc, 11% in Warsaw and 7% in Lublin.

It seemed that in Poland victims were critical of the police in most contexts, whereas Hungarian and Czech victims were less positive about the police in general than they were about the way the police dealt with their complaint. This is confirmed where we asked whether contact had made respondents 'feel more or less favourable to the police in general'. In Poland almost four times as many victims responded in the negative compared with the positive; in Hungary 30% said their contact had improved their views of the police while only 9% said they now felt more critical; in the Czech Republic over twice as many victims said their views had improved (23%) as said the opposite (9%).

While in this respect there is a marked difference between Hungary and the Czech Republic and Poland, in terms of police 'victim-proneness' it was clear that public images of the police were more positive and had improved in all three countries. For example, we asked respondents how sympathetic they felt the police were when dealing with victims of (i) burglaries (ii) disasters like fires and floods (iii) rape and sexual assault. Overall, victims were less likely to voice an opinion in the latter cases: only 6% said they were unsure in the case of burglary, compared with 47% for disasters and 54% for rape/sexual assault. This suggests that they were more certain where they had personal experience and that many were unwilling to make assumptions where they had not. In Table 8.5, then, those answering 'don't know' have been excluded and the others scored according to their responses, where an answer 'very sympathetic' has been scored 2, 'fairly sympathetic' 1 and 'not sympathetic' 0. Thus a high mean score indicates that victims felt the police were sympathetic towards victims.

Victims generally felt the police would be most sympathetic towards victims in the case of a disaster (overall mean 1.37), then a rape/sexual assault (mean 1.17), with burglary rated lowest at 0.97. Although responses varied with each situation, overall respondents from Poland and Hungary were about as likely as those from England to see the police as sympathetic and it was in the Czech Republic (Mawby et al 2001) and Germany, with its militaristic policing tradition (Mawby and Kirchoff 1996), that victims were least likely to consider the police sympathetic. The figures do, however, reflect a real difference in victims' perceptions of police response to the three situations, a conclusion that is in line with the ICVS data discussed above.

*Table 8.5: Mean score for burglary victims in each city on whether the police would be sympathetic towards victims of different types of incident*

|  | Burglary | Rape/sex offence | Natural disaster |
|---|---|---|---|
|  | (maximum score 2 indicates sympathy) | | |
| Plymouth | 1.12 | 1.12 | 1.50 |
| Salford | 0.82 | 1.42 | 1.68 |
| Munchengladbach | 0.79 | 0.72 | 1.19 |
| Warsaw | 1.11 | 1.25 | 1.35 |
| Lublin | 1.02 | 1.05 | 1.20 |
| Miskolc | 1.06 | 1.60 | 1.53 |
| Prague | 0.89 | 1.00 | 1.15 |

We then asked whether, over the last few years, 'the police have got better or worse at handling the victims of crime'. As is clear from Table 8.6, victims from Poland, the Czech Republic and (especially) Hungary were likely to register an improvement rather than a deterioration in this respect. Perhaps surprisingly, victims from England were less positive, although in many cases lack of police resources was cited as the main reason for a decline in police service.

*Table 8.6: Percentage of burglary victims in each city who felt that the way the police dealt with victims of crime had changed*

|  | For the better | For the worse |
|---|---|---|
| Plymouth | 31 | 21 |
| Salford | 32 | 34 |
| Münchengladbach | 15 | 13 |
| Warsaw | 29 | 4 |
| Lublin | 22 | 9 |
| Miskolc | 37 | 3 |
| Prague | 25 | 5 |

What is clear from the above is that police practices, and recent changes in police response to burglary victims, vary in a number of ways between the five countries and that victims' perceptions of the police, both in general and with regard to this particular incident, also vary. In many respects victims from Poland were most critical and those from England and Germany relatively positive, but there were at least as many differences between Poland, the Czech Republic and Hungary as there were similarities, and some differences were also evident between England and Germany.

How, then, do we account for victims' perceptions of the police in Central and Eastern Europe, and how do we explain the marked differences between Poland on the one hand and Hungary and the Czech Republic on the other?

There would appear to be at least three ways in which the distinctive patterns might be explained. First there is the argument that public perceptions of the police in some post-communist societies might be influenced by tradition; that the 'repressive' police of communist societies have survived the transition. Second is the suggestion that different perceptions of the police reflect different standards and levels of police performance. Third is the claim that perceptions of the police are closely linked to perceptions of the crime problem.

The first argument is persuasive in explaining the lower public esteem enjoyed by the police in Eastern Europe. Despite concerted attempts in countries in transition to change police personnel, the structure of the police, political connections, roles and accountability (Fogel 1994; Jasinski and Siemaszko 1995; Mawby 1999b; Timoranszky 1992), changes are inevitably slow and difficult. On the other hand, both quantitative analysis and more qualitative examination of our interviews suggest that in all three countries in transition victims drew a clear distinction between the 'old' and 'new' police. This is illustrated both by changing perceptions of the 'victim-proneness' of the police, and in verbatim comments made in the course of the interviews. For example, a burglary victim from Miskolc said:

They were nicer and kinder than seven years ago.

A Lublin respondent concurred:

They are more kind. They don't consider themselves to be above everybody now.

If public perceptions of the police are not entirely explained in terms of memories of the repressive police of communist regimes, how far is it possible to explain differences in terms of actual variations in the quality of police services? In some respects this is plausible. For example, in

Warsaw at least, police response was slow, leading to victim criticism, and in Hungary and especially Poland (see Mawby *et al* 1997) the bureaucracy involved in filing a complaint was considerable. Moreover, where inadequacies were compounded by the attitudes expressed by the police at the time, it is easy to understand victims' complaints. Take for example two Warsaw cases where victims' criticisms centred on slow police response and an undetected crime respectively:

> Five to six hours – very late. They explained that they had something very important to do.

> Police's declaration that practically nothing can be done in this case. So they left you with such an attitude, what can you expect?

However, while poor police services combined with an inappropriate attitude in explaining inadequacies may partly account for differing levels of criticism, they are scarcely adequate as the sole explanation. What then of the third explanation: that perceptions of the police are related to concern over the crime problem?

Victims in Central and Eastern Europe, and Poland in particular, were more concerned about the crime problem, more worried about future crime, and more affected by their current burglary (Mawby 1998). It is thus not surprising to find that those on whom crime had the most impact, those most worried about crime, and those most dissatisfied with their current residences, were most critical of the police. For example, victims from Poland were most likely to say they had been seriously affected by the burglary; those most affected were most critical of the police; Polish victims were most critical of the police. Polish victims were least likely to be covered by insurance; uninsured victims were most critical of the police; not surprisingly, then, Polish victims were not only most critical of the police but focused their criticisms on the inability of the police to clear up the crime and recover their property.

This is, however, only one strand to the link between crime and evaluations of the police. Another is the extent to which the police may be blamed for the crime problem. One element here is the feeling that respondents are vulnerable because the police are ineffective – even if they are more sensitive than in the past! For example, in the words of an Hungarian respondent:

> They were polite, but they didn't find the perpetrator.

According to one Polish victim, the worst thing about the burglary was:

> Lack of feeling safe. The police's inefficiency and ineffectiveness of the work.

A key feature here is the implication that the former so-called repressive police, for all their faults, were at least efficient. While this is questionable, the inefficiency of the police in communist society was certainly not as public. A second, crucial element here is the feeling that the police in post-communist societies have lost power and are thus less well equipped to respond to the crime problem. A victim from Lublin complained:

> Feeling of harm, hopelessness, frustration. There is nobody that can help. The police are helpless; they have the excuse that the law is too lenient and they can do nothing.

This was most evident in relation to questions taken from the BCS, where we asked victims if they felt the police treated people they suspected of crimes 'more fairly than a few years ago, or less fairly'. For many Polish respondents, this question was meaningless: the key issue was that the police were now too soft on suspects/offenders, as the following quotations illustrate:

> The rights of the police are too limited.

> The policemen take care of the criminals and not the victims.

> The rights of the police are too little. Offenders feel exempt from punishment.

> Now if they don't have any definite evidence against the offender, they do nothing.

In one sense, ironically, it seems that concern over crime in post-communist Poland has led to the public reacting with a nostalgic reinterpretation of the work of the 'old' police, when crime was apparently under control. Clearly this does not fully account for the differences in public perceptions of the police, especially the distinctiveness of Poland. However, while police traditions and current practices may partly explain the current relatively low status of the police, it seems that in these countries in transition differences in evaluations of police response to their burglary are more adequately understood in terms of victims' concerns about crime in the context of the changing political situation. This, in turn, acts as a salutary reminder of the importance of improving police services.

## Worldwide examples of improvements to policing

Some countries have made concerted attempts to improve police services to victims. In the Netherlands, for example, the importance of improving police service was recognised by two committees: the Beaufort Committee of 1981 and the wider ranging Vaillant Committee of 1983 (Wemmers and Zeilstra 1991). As a result, a series of guidelines for police and prosecutors, what Penders (1989) calls 'pseudo-laws', was issued for sex offences (1986) and victims in general (1987). The guidelines required the police to treat victims sympathetically, provide all the relevant information and, where necessary, refer them to other agencies, and victims now have a right to cite the guidelines should they subsequently take legal action against the police. Nevertheless, in a meticulous evaluation of the subsequent operation of the police, Wemmers and Zeilstra (1991) argued that improvements were limited, on the one hand because victims were unaware of their rights, on the other hand because the vagueness of the guidelines allowed the police considerable discretion in their interpretation.

Somewhat more positive conclusions were drawn from an evaluation of changes in police procedure and training in Zaarstrad (Winkel 1989, 1991). Improved police training in victim awareness was followed by an experimental programme whereby some crime victims were recontacted by the police some weeks · after the crime and offered a range of additional support. The experimental group of victims were far more positive about police action than were a control group, and the Winkel suggested that victims in general, and vulnerable victims in particular, drew tangible benefits from the extra service.

Other improvements may involve better referral systems. For example, Hauber and Zandbergen (1991) described how in the Hague, where victim assistance was police-based but located centrally rather than in local stations, the result was low rates of referral and poor knowledge of victim support among police officers. Rehousing victim support to local police stations resulted in improvements in police relationships and in police 'victim-mindedness'.

The commitment of the Dutch government to improving victim services is well illustrated in the 'Terwee Law' of 1995 that requires both police and public prosecution service to liaise with relevant agencies in the adoption of policies that will improve the treatment of victims, enhance the information given to victims and encourage the development of restitution arrangements (Geveke and Verberk 1996). While little is known as yet of the effects of the new law, it does seem that there may be initial resistance, and inter-agency cooperation on a policy level is not always matched by cooperation at ground level. It thus seems that even in a system like the Dutch, where considerable emphasis has been placed on victim services, changing police practices is not always easy.

This conclusion is echoed in the USA where, despite 30 years of victim-oriented reforms and the siting of many victim assistance programmes in police stations and prosecutors' offices, there is no indication that in general the police are any more 'victim-prone'.

For example, one study of police services for crime victims, in Houston, involved police following up a random sample of victims. Victims were telephoned and asked whether they needed further assistance, and where necessary referred to support services or given additional advice. In their evaluation of the initiative, Skogan and Wycoff (1987) concluded that victims involved in the 'callback programme' were no more likely than a control group to voice satisfaction with the police or to improve their crime prevention measures. This rather pessimistic conclusion paralleled Rosenbaum's (1987) research in Detroit, where a control group of police was compared with a group subjected to a three-day victim awareness training programme. Although the latter was clearly more victim-oriented at the end of the training period, four months later there was little difference between the two groups, with the experimental group rapidly losing their recently acquired 'victim-mindedness'. Furthermore, as in Houston there was no evidence that victims dealt with by the experimental group perceived themselves as receiving a better quality service

## Evaluating policing: England and Wales

Both ICVS data and our comparison of the perceptions of burglary victims from Western and Eastern European cities suggested that the public in general and burglary victims in particular in England and Wales are relatively positive towards the police. However, there are one or two blemishes on this generally favourable image. For example, burglary victims in Plymouth and Salford were somewhat likely to feel that police services to victims had deteriorated (see Table 8.6).

What these findings indicate is a broader level of concern over the nature of policing than was voiced by the public towards the end of the 1980s. Public satisfaction with the police, although generally high, fell among most groups of the population (Skogan 1990, 1994, 1996). What generated most concern among politicians was the fact that criticism of the police was greatest among those most likely to come into contact with the police: those who had had recent dealings with the police, including crime victims, were less positive than the public at large.

Victims' satisfaction with the service they received also declined in the 1980s, and although it rallied in the early 1990s it subsequently fell again (Simms and Myhill 2001). Thus, while 81% of burglary victims interviewed as part of the 1998 BCS were satisfied with police response times and 61% were satisfied with overall police performance, a significant minority voiced some criticisms (Yeo and Budd 2000). Similarly, although the proportion of burglary victims in 1999 who said the police had kept them very or fairly well informed had risen, the figure was still rather low at 37% (Simms and Myhill 2001). Coupe and Griffiths' (1996) research on burglary in the West Midlands also revealed a degree of dissatisfaction among victims. Victims were particularly critical when the police took longer than 30 minutes to attend the crime scene, when they stayed for 20 minutes or less, when police attitudes were considered discourteous or unsympathetic and when the burglary remained undetected and goods unrecovered. This led Coupe and Griffiths to conclude that, 'Although the way the police handled burglaries was generally quite well regarded, there appears to be some scope for improvement' (*op cit.* 22).

The period when public/victims' attitudes began to change coincided with government concern to ensure that sufficient detail of policing policies and practices was available for services to be comprehensively assessed. The Conservative government's interest in evaluating policing differed from traditional orthodoxies concerning accountability in at least two respects. On the one hand lay the Major government's desire to extend its control over the police – and other public services – through inspection and review procedures which themselves necessitate the production of more information on police practices. On the other hand lay government commitment to a requirement that police forces should provide publicly accessible information on performance. The first route flowed from the greater involvement of traditional agencies such as Her Majesty's Inspectors of Constabulary (HMIC) and more recent quangos like the Audit Commission (AC). The second, derived from the *Citizens Charter*, which itself included policing issues, culminated in the presumption that individual forces would produce their own police charters and the requirement that forces publish information on how they meet the standards set. In essence, these routes converged where government concerns for greater control over local police forces, and the conception of the public as consumers (Squires 1998) resulted in individual forces being required to produce a wealth of material on their performance levels. Whether or not the end product is a set of league tables (Davidoff 1993), the result is that comparative data are available as the basis for evaluating performance, assessing value for money and measuring effectiveness and efficiency.

Unfortunately, the system is open to abuse. In a world where consumers are sometimes taken in by presentation, glossy force charters may hide a multitude of ambiguities. Further, as discussion in recent years has illustrated, some statistics can be massaged to present a more favourable image of crime rates or detection levels. Indeed, a review of performance indicators now required from each force by HMIC suggests that Government has gone for details that are easily obtainable but either fairly meaningless or of questionable validity. Comparison of the performance indicators suggested by the Audit Commission, HMIC and the Association of Chief Police Officers (ACPO) reveals that in reality the Audit Commission and HMIC have taken the views of the consumer public in vain. In contrast, ACPO advised forces to ask their public's opinions of police services. For example, under the heading 'Call Management': HMIC asked for information on the number of incidents per 100 police officers; the Audit Commission for definitions, target times and outcome re 'incidents requiring immediate response'; and ACPO for levels of public satisfaction with performance of the police in relation to both 999 calls and services at police station enquiry counters.

Surveys of consumers of police services are by no means sufficient to satisfy local accountability requirements (especially where they tend to be directed at 'victim' rather than 'suspect' consumers); nor can it be denied that the imposition of central standards is often beneficial. However, where changes are being implemented allegedly in the interests of the public, the lack of interest by the Audit Commission and HMIC in pursuing consumer surveys is regrettable. Moreover, consumer surveys have provided the opportunity for the police to monitor current policies, assess local practices and promote improvements in service provision.

In the early 1990s a number of individual constabularies took the decision to establish units to monitor public or consumer opinion of police performances (Skogan 1996). Many of the surveys they undertook targeted victims, particularly burglary victims. In Merseyside, for example, an early survey of nearly 2,000 burglary victims, undertaken in 1992, concluded that most were satisfied with the services they received from uniformed officers, detectives and scenes of crime staff (Merseyside Police 1992). In Devon and Cornwall, victims' evaluations of police performance became a main focus of a newly formed Quality of Service Unit (Bunt 1999).

## Case study: victims' perceptions of police services in Devon and Cornwall

The Quality of Service Unit of the Devon and Cornwall police was established in 1991 with one of its main objectives to assess public response to police services. While the police were responsible for carrying out consumer surveys, a key initial decision was to involve outside agencies in the evaluation process. I was recruited as consultant to the unit, providing advice on sampling methods, questionnaire design and data analysis. Non-police staff already employed by the police were recruited as interviewers, with their training being carried out by an independent social and market research company. One further decision taken initially by the unit was to adopt telephone interviewing as the main research method, with postal questionnaires sent out to those not listed as having access to a telephone and those whom interviewers had difficulty contacting. As well as asking consumers for their views on the services they received, the interviews also provided the opportunity for respondents to request a discussion with a senior officer over how the incident in question was handled.

Since 1992 surveys have been conducted on a number of different consumers of police services, including victims of burglary and violence (by a non-family member), drivers in minor accidents, nonvictim witnesses, and those given fixed-penalty tickets for speeding. As well as being asked about their specific cases, these were also used, where appropriate, to gather further information on other police services. In order to illustrate the value of such surveys, data from the 1994 surveys of victims of burglary and violence are described (see also Bunt 1999; Bunt and Mawby 1994). These were conducted between January and August and resulted in interviews with 865 burglary victims and 527 victims of violence, approximately 10% and 12% respectively of all those reporting such crimes during that period.

Traditionally, in England and Wales, burglaries have been responded to by uniformed officers, with the possibility of follow-up visits by uniformed officers or various specialists (see also Coupe and Griffiths 1996). Among those contacted in Devon and Cornwall, victims of violence were more likely than burglary victims to receive a follow-up visit from the original officer (46% compared with 36%) or another uniformed officer (32% compared with 27%). In contrast, about two thirds of burglary victims were also visited by scenes of crime officers (SOCO) and about a quarter by CID, while the corresponding figures for victims of violence were far lower (8% and 14% respectively). With the possible exception of SOCO for burglary victims, these victims' experiences of a police service were therefore largely dependent upon the initial visit by a uniformed officer; the extent to which he or she is helpful and reassuring may determine whether victims consider that involving the police is a positive or negative experience.

Perhaps not surprisingly, most victims rated this officer polite, helpful and smart in appearance. Over three quarters were also satisfied with the time it took the police to arrive. What is equally important, though, is what help officers gave victims. For example, the policy in Devon and Cornwall is for the police to provide victims with six basic pieces of information: officer's name or reference number; crime reference number; telephone contact number; details of further action to be taken; information on Victim Support; and a leaflet containing information for crime victims. One key objective of the consumer surveys was to discover how far policy was being carried out in practice. That is, accepting that victims may sometimes forget information they were given, did most respondents recall being given these six pieces of information?

The results for burglary victims were reasonably positive. Over three quarters of respondents remembered being given the officer's name or number, a file number and a telephone contact number and over two thirds were told what action the police would be taking and given information on Victim Support, although only 58% remembered being given a leaflet on victim services. Over half said they received at least five of the six pieces of information.

What was crucial from the point of view of the constabulary, however, was that information from the surveys could be fed back to each division/ area, and it was noticeable that the percentage answering in the affirmative increased as local commanders found themselves invited to comment on the figures for their areas. What was also evident from the replies was that victims of violence were in most cases provided with less information than their burglary counterparts. For example, only 37% received at least five pieces of information. This was confirmed where victims were asked how satisfied they were with this first contact. While about four fifths of violence victims replied that they were at least generally satisfied, the corresponding figure for burglary victims was 93%. Moreover, those given most information by the police were most likely to express satisfaction.

At the end of the interview, respondents were asked whether they were generally satisfied or dissatisfied with the way the police dealt with the matter. Again there was a significant difference between victims of burglary and violence. As Table 8.7 demonstrates, burglary victims were markedly more satisfied with all aspects of what was done.

*Table 8.7: Overall feelings about police handling of incidents in Devon and Cornwall in 1994*

|  | Burglary victims | Victims of violence |
| --- | --- | --- |
| Satisfied with all aspects | 71 | 50 |
| Generally satisfied | 22 | 34 |
| Generally dissatisfied | 5 | 11 |
| Dissatisfied with all aspects | 2 | 6 |

Further analysis indicated that victims' levels of satisfaction were closely related to the levels of service they received from the police. Those who were provided with the most information initially and those who received further communication from the police were significantly more positive in their evaluation of the police. The apparently contradictory findings that police responses to burglaries, with low detection rates (see chapter 11), were viewed more favourably by victims than police responses to violence, with much higher detection rates, were explained in these terms. That is, it was the service that the police provided for victims at the time the crime was reported and subsequently that determined public satisfaction; the public did not have unrealistic expectations about the possibility of detection.[1]

Of course, there is a danger in becoming over-reliant on public opinion. Here, as in other surveys of the public, it is clear that different groups of the public hold different opinions of police performance irrespective of how the police actually responded. It was no surprise to find that elderly victims were more positive than younger victims, for example. Moreover, public ratings of police performance will be limited to the extent that victims are not always aware of what steps the police took, or what alternative avenues of inquiry were open to them. A doctor with a good bedside manner may none the less not carry out all the possible tests! Interestingly, then, we found that when a sample of case reviews was conducted by supervising officers, their evaluations of police actions were lower than were those of the victims concerned. We should not, consequently, allow a positive response to general questions to lull us into complacency. Moreover, while the current vogue is to ask victims of offences like burglary to rate the services they have received from the police, there is correspondingly little evidence of police perceptions with which to compare it.

Consumer surveys do not provide us with all the information necessary to evaluate police work (Squires 1998); nor do they compensate for alternative versions of accountability. However, used sensitively they do provide information on public views of the way the police operate that allows us to address key issues and improve the quality of the service provided. In this sense, at least, they are an important component of mechanisms aimed at improving the lot of burglary victims.

## Discussion

Ideally police response to crime victims should encompass a service approach alongside a concern to do everything possible to clear up the crime. However, a traditional emphasis upon action, excitement and 'real' policework means that the police have often been criticised for their lack of concern for victims and – in the case of rape and domestic violence – an unwillingness to take the incident seriously.

While these criticisms have been directed at the police in a number of societies, there is some evidence of improvements in police response within recent years. With regard to domestic violence and rape, for example, changes in police procedure have meant that in many cases the police are now more willing both to treat complaints as 'real' crimes and to place more emphasis on the service they provide to victims. With regard to property crimes, increased concern to monitor and evaluate police performance in England and Wales has in part led to a greater willingness to prioritise police *service*. Training and legislative control also provide partial means to effect changes in police response, but evidence from the USA and the Netherlands should caution us that they are no panacea.

However, this does not necessarily mean that victims' ratings of satisfaction with police response will improve. As is indicated in research in Central and Eastern Europe, victims may appreciate the new service role adopted by the police but be highly critical of police failure to fulfil their more traditional functions. This at least serves as a warning against shifting the emphasis too far. The public does expect the police to investigate their crimes and make some effort to clear them up: indeed, not to do so is to undermine the notion that the police take victims' complaints seriously. But victims also expect the police to respond sympathetically, to treat them as people rather than crime numbers, to provide help or advice where necessary, and to keep them informed of any progress regarding 'their' crime. It is against these criteria, in addition to detection rates, that police services for burglary victims need to be measured.

## Note

1 Although Coupe and Griffiths (1996) found that victims expressed more criticisms about police failure to clear up their burglaries, this might have been influenced by the research's explicit focus on detection.

# Chapter 9

# Victim assistance programmes

## Introduction

Alongside the police and insurance companies, Victim Support is the third main agency with which victims in England and Wales are likely to have contact. The genesis of Victim Support was the Bristol Victims-Offenders Group, formed in 1970 under the auspices of NACRO (Rock 1990). The first Victim Support Scheme was subsequently launched in Bristol in 1973/74 and, despite a hesitant start, the scheme expanded and victim assistance gained national recognition. In 1979 the National Association of Victim Support Schemes was formed and by 1980 there were 256 schemes nationwide. During the 1980s and 1990s the expansion continued, Victim Support extended its influence on government, central government funding became established and services were extended to cover victim/witness services in courts (Maguire and Corbett 1987; Mawby and Gill 1987; Mawby and Walklate 1994; Raine and Smith 1991; Rock 1990; Russell 1990).

Victim Support in England and Wales is of particular relevance here because, from the first, burglary was identified as the most appropriate crime for schemes to target. Thus burglary was seen as more traumatic than other property crimes, but – unlike violence – not so serious that victims would need professional help. This has not been the case as far as the fast-emerging victims' movement abroad is concerned. Consequently, while this chapter begins with an overview of victim assistance programmes worldwide, the chief focus is on England and Wales. However, given the contrasting patterns that are identified, it concludes by focusing on the international material and considering whether there is any evidence of unmet need in other countries.

## Victim assistance programmes: an overview

There are considerable variations in emphasis between victim assistance programmes, both within and between nations. Mawby and Walklate (1994) identified four broad areas within which to describe the key features of such services. First is the organisational structure of the agency; second is its relationships with other agencies; third is the nature of the service provided; fourth is the nature of the victim population targeted, or prioritised, by the organisation. For example: on an organisational level, victim assistance programmes may be state-based or non-governmental organisations (NGOs); in terms of their relationships with other agencies, they may be closely associated with the police, probation, and/or health services, or be totally independent; and they may provide any from a range of services, including practical help, financial support, legal advice and professional counselling.

Of most relevance here, we can compare the nature of the victim population targeted or prioritised. As already noted, in some countries (such as England and Wales) the needs of property victims have been prioritised. In contrast, in the USA, where services were created at a similar time, the emphasis was more on victims of sex and violence offences (Bolin 1980; Chesney and Schneider 1981; Mawby and Gill 1987; Mawby and Walklate 1994; Roberts 1990; Young 1990). There are, however, marked differences within the USA. For example, Chesney and Schneider (1981: 401) reported that in 1977 in the two Minnesota victim crisis centres the most common offence dealt with was burglary (45%), and more recently Davis *et al* (1999) noted that the programmes in their survey included burglary victims.

Differences are also marked between Western industrialised societies. In the Netherlands, early schemes varied considerably, with some prioritising victims of sex and violence offences, and this diversity has been maintained (van Dijk 1989; Groenhuijsen 1990; Mawby and Walklate 1994). Thus in 1999 only 15% of referrals involved burglaries and 31% any property crime.[1] A fourth country in which victim services developed at an early stage was Germany, where the Weisser Ring was established in 1976 (Doering-Striening 1989). However Mawby and Kirchhoff (1996) noted that much of the agency's energies went into promotional work, notably regarding crime prevention, and the few victims who did receive support tended to be victims of interpersonal crimes. In contrast the Weisser Ring rarely supported burglary victims: from their sample of 257 burglary victims in Monchengladbach, only one had had any contact with a specialist programme! Where victim services have emerged in post-communist societies, differences in emphasis are also evident. The Weisser Ring in Hungary seems to help many burglary victims, its equivalent in the Czech Republic few (Mawby et al 1999; Mawby et al 2000).

Variations are well illustrated from responses to the international crime victims survey (ICVS). At the time of the third survey, 10% of burglary victims in Western Europe said they had received assistance from a specialist agency, considerably more than in the New World (6.3%), countries in transition (2.5%), Asia (2.3%), Africa (2.1%) and Latin America (1.2%) (del Frate 1998, 75). As many as 21% of burglary victims in England and Wales received help; none in the USA sample (Mayhew and van Dijk 1997: 44–46). In Sweden, the ICVS revealed that only 1% of burglary victims received help, compared with 6% of burglary victims from the Netherlands (Mayhew and van Dijk 1997: 44–46).

What is unequivocal from these studies is the conclusion that Victim Support in Britain is distinctive in the way it has prioritised victims of burglary. The next section thus focuses on England and Wales.

### Victim Support in England and Wales

In England and Wales, the first Victim Support Scheme was launched in Bristol as an independent agency relying on the cooperation of statutory agencies such as the police, probation service and magistracy. By 1999 there were 374 schemes, including one on Jersey, one on Guernsey, 12 in Northern Ireland, and 35 in Wales (Victim Support 1999).[2] Scotland has its own, separate organisation. During the year 1998/99 1,141,198 cases were referred to Victim Support.

The extent of involvement of Victim Support in England and Wales is well illustrated if we consider public awareness of Victim Support and the numbers of victims receiving help (Maguire and Kynch 2000). The 1998 BCS revealed that as many as 74% of those interviewed – and 79% of victims – were aware of Victim Support and this level of public awareness is considerably higher than in the USA (Davis et al 1999) and elsewhere in Europe (Mawby et al 1999). With regard to contact with victims, Victim Support figures suggest that some 45% of victims whose crimes are recorded by the police are contacted by Victim Support and analysing data from the 1998 BCS, Maguire and Kynch (2000) estimated that approximately 29% of victims of crimes included in the BCS whose incidents were recorded as crimes by the police were subsequently contacted.

Victim Support operates as a coordinating and validating body. Over the 1970s and 1980s it developed a close relationship with the Home

Office, while maintaining its independence (Rock 1990) and it is separately funded by the Home Office. It employs some 53 staff, paid for by the Home Office and based in its London office. At the other extreme lie individual schemes that are affiliated to Victim Support and linked to the centre via a county structure and a number of national committees. There is a Code of Practice, which includes requirements covering service provision, training and management structure, and individual schemes that do not conform to the code are excluded from the organisation, and, effectively, from receiving police support. The national organisation is also responsible for allocating central government funding to individual schemes, which gives it an additional level of control. At local level, each scheme has a management committee, at least one coordinator, and a number of visitors who are the most common points of contact with crime victims.

Throughout the UK, Victim Support schemes are voluntary organisations and registered charities, the latter allowing them to claim tax relief. Financial support was originally gained from a number of private sponsors and from the government (Russell 1990). Since the mid-1980s, government funding has increased significantly, such that in the year ending March 1999, Victim Support (1999) reported an income of over £13 million, of which £12,725,000 came from the Home Office, although a significant proportion of this covers the expanding court-based programmes.

These developments heralded both a shift in government commitment to Victim Support and a major change in the nature of the organisation (Rock 1990; Russell 1990). Nevertheless, the bulk of the work of individual schemes today depends on volunteers. Although a *majority* of schemes in 1999 had paid coordinators, the total of 964 paid staff is dwarfed by 14,670 volunteers, of whom 9,477 visited victims, 3,456 were volunteer office staff, 25 supportline volunteers and 3,700 members of management committees (Victim Support 1999: 13).[3]

What of the *location* of Victim Support in relation to other agencies? Two of the key features of Victim Support, evident from the first Bristol scheme, were the fusion of independence and cooperation. While some schemes, especially in the early years, were located in probation offices, schemes were independent of both police and probation. At the same time, they built up good relationships with these and other agencies within the criminal justice system, and the close cooperation between the police and Victim Support has been a notable feature, contributing much to the successful establishment of the organisation (Mawby and Gill 1987; Rock 1990).

The importance of the police to Victim Support is centred on the role of the police as referrers of clients. Unlike many other European countries, almost all victims assisted by Victim Support are referred to schemes by the police.[4] Originally the police were reluctant to relinquish control of referrals, and passed on to schemes victims whom officers felt to be in need of help, a practice that resulted in a disproportionate number of elderly, and clearly fragile, victims being seen by Victim Support (Maguire and Corbett 1987; Mawby and Gill 1987). However, it is now common practice for scheme coordinators to liaise directly with the police and record all known victims of predetermined crime-types as referrals, a system known as the 'direct referral system'. Schemes will then decide for themselves which victims will be contacted or, more commonly, what sort of contact will be made. This is clearly preferable to the original practice, but does raise some difficulties. First, given that referrals have increased at a faster rate than volunteers (Russell 1990), schemes are increasingly having to make decisions about who gets visited, or what means of contact is preferable (Maguire and Kynch 2000). Second, although the police no longer act as gatekeepers, coordinators in the schemes are themselves increasingly deciding, on the basis of very little information, which victims are 'in need' of personal contact within a day or two of the offence being reported (Wilkinson and Maguire 1993). Despite these problems, however, it is arguable that the English system has achieved a successful balance and remains a distinctly separate organisation while simultaneously receiving full cooperation, by way of referrals, from the police.

In contrast, relationships with other agencies working with victims, largely from the voluntary sector, are patchy, partly because agencies may be competing for the same clients (Russell 1990), and correspondingly for what limited funding is available, and partly because of marked variations in the philosophies of the different organisations (Gill and Mawby 1990).

In relation to the nature of the services provided, Victim Support in Britain is also distinct from its North American equivalent in emphasising the service nature of its work, rather than educational or political goals (Mawby and Gill 1987). This does not mean that Victim Support is apolitical. On the contrary, as Rock (1990) has pointed out, it has quietly and uncontroversially built itself an impressive power base within the political establishment. It is consulted by the Home Office over impending changes to the law, and has on various occasions campaigned publicly or instigated working parties to push for changes that would improve the lot of the crime victim. But any such political role is tightly circumscribed. The national Code of Practice bars members from expressing party political viewpoints when representing Victim Support and from commenting on sentencing policy, other than where it is of direct relevance to victims.

For Victim Support then, the most important focus is on the service provided by volunteers for victims. Coordinators receive details of victims from the police, or directly from police files, within a day or so of the crime being reported, and decide whether or not contact is to be made and if so whether in person or by letter or telephone. In England and Wales in the early years of Victim Support, unannounced visits to victims were preferred. However, as referrals increased, various schemes began to experiment with alternative forms of contact, such as letters or telephone calls (Wilkinson and Maguire 1993). In 1998 Victim Support introduced a national telephone helpline, Victim Supportline, to facilitate self-referrals.

Contact by letter or telephone is clearly more cost-effective than unannounced visits, where in many cases no one is at home. However it does have its disadvantages: for example, take up from letters and phonecalls is low (Davies *et al* 1999; Maguire and Kynch 2000; Wilkinson and Maguire 1993) and unsolicited telephone calls may be unwelcome. Nevertheless, analysing 1998 BCS data, Maguire and Kynch (2000) found that nationwide 69% of those victims who recalled having been contacted by Victim Support said that the initial contact was by letter, with 19% citing a 'phone call and only 13% an unannounced visit. Mawby and Simmonds (2000), focusing on the work of Plymouth Victim Support during seven days in May 1998, found that from 427 crimes listed[5] in the computer printouts sent to the scheme, Victim Support responded by carrying out visits in 36 cases, phoning two victims, and writing letters to 68.

If a victim is considered in need of a visit, the coordinator arranges for a volunteer to pay the victim a visit, which will normally take place within the following 24 hours. Only in exceptional circumstances will a victim be visited when the crime is 'live'. Where contact is made, most victims will be seen only once (Maguire and Corbett 1987). Maguire and Kynch (2000) found that of all those interviewed in the 1998 BCS who said they had had personal contact with Victim Support, only 16% were seen more than once, with a further 18% having further contact by telephone. In areas with less crime, return visits are more normal (Mawby and Gill: 1987), and more serious crimes, where victims are more severely affected, are allocated markedly more time (Victim Support: 1999). Russell (1990) also suggested that those in inner city areas, where victimisation was only one of a number of problems faced, might be visited more frequently. In most cases, however, the emphasis is on four levels of support: personal support, reassurance and the demonstration that 'someone cares'; immediate practical help where the victim needs to repair windows, fit secure locks or take other crime prevention measures; the provision of information and advice on what resources or services might be available, for example on compensation or additional security; and as a link between victim and police to feed back details of case progress to victims (Maguire and Kynch 2000; Mawby and Simmonds 2000).

The original scheme, in Bristol, prioritised burglary victims, partly because of the need to restrict services to a manageable proportion, partly to match needs to what help could realistically be offered. It was 'accepted' that victims of certain types of crime, such as vehicle-based offences, were little affected and would not require assistance, whereas at the other extreme sex and violence offences were considered too difficult for volunteers to deal with (Gay *et al* 1975; Maguire and Corbett 1987). As a result, as Victim Support developed as a national service, burglaries came to dominate its case files. In 1985, for example, some 80% of referrals were victims of burglary. At the same time, only 8% of victims were victims of violent crime, 11% of other property crime and 1% noncrime victims, the latter being more common in rural, low-crime areas (Mawby and Gill 1987).

Since then, the most dramatic change has been in the increase in help for victims of more serious crimes, including violence. Partly in recognition of the unmet needs of such victims, partly in an attempt to expand services and extend credibility, and partly in response to Home Office and police willingness to turn to Victim Support for help rather than rely on more militant feminist alternatives, Victim Support has shifted its emphasis to include domestic violence, rape, homicide and so on. Special courses have been provided to train dedicated volunteers for this more intensive and demanding work; working parties have been used to set agendas, improve credibility and effect liaison with other agencies; and special projects have focused on needs and service provision. Reflecting these shifts, in 1998/99 only 38% of Victim Support's referrals were burglary victims and Victim Support dealt with 4,184 rape cases and 671 homicides (Victim Support 1999: 10). Nevertheless, Victim Support's (1995) Codes of Practice identified burglary, along with thefts (excluding vehicle related thefts), robbery, assaults (other than domestic violence), criminal damage and arson, as crimes that should 'automatically' be referred to schemes. Victim Support's continued emphasis on burglary is reaffirmed in its Burglary in Britain campaign, of which Tarling and Davison's (2000) literature review was the first stage.

Interestingly, burglary is also acknowledged by the public as an offence with which Victim Support commonly deals (Maguire and Kynch 2000).

Data from the 1998 BCS also illustrated the extent to which burglary is prioritised by Victim Support (Maguire and Kynch 2000). Burglary victims were disproportionately likely to be contacted by Victim Support (53% compared with 29% for all relevant victims), and 46% of respondents who said they had received a visit were burglary victims. Where contacted, burglary victims were also relatively likely to be visited – in 30% of cases.[6]

In Plymouth, Mawby and Simmonds (2000) focused on the work of the local Victim Support scheme. In 1998/99 Plymouth Victim Support offered support to 4,939 victims, of whom 2,376 were victims of 'simple' burglary, 71 artifice burglary and 18 aggravated burglary. However, their response differed markedly according to crime type. Taking seven days in May 1998, Mawby and Simmonds (2000) found that almost all those visited were burglary victims (89%) and indeed 82% of victims of household burglary were visited and most of the remainder (15%) sent a letter. The authors subsequently took a sample of 90 burglary victims. In only 3% of these was no attempt at contact made, with 23% written to and the remainder visited. However, only 27% of victims were actually seen by a volunteer visitor; in the remaining cases (47%) the visitor failed to make direct contact and left a note. Thus while burglary victims may be prioritised by Victim Support, the proportion who are seen in person is perhaps less than the aggregate figures imply.

In many cases, data from local schemes contrast with the national picture. The emphasis that schemes place on burglary, for example, varies according to other demands on the organisation. As Mawby and Gill (1987) demonstrated, some schemes have numerous volunteers but few referrals, whereas others struggle to provide a service with a limited number of volunteers. The result might be that in high crime areas burglary victims fall lower down the priorities than in others. Contrast the views of – respectively – the Plymouth and Salford Victim Support scheme coordinators, for example (Mawby and Walklate 1997):

> Now we have the name of the victim, the address, the age, the type of crime and a small, sort of, amount of information as to what happened. Actually it is not enough. There are things that we don't know, if people are disabled or ... often if we did it would obviously prioritise our reason for going ... We go through and pick out all the burglaries, attempted burglaries or burglaries with intent. Usually we can go by age then. If it's an attempted burglary on a young

person we very often won't do anything about it, if it's over 60 we will try and contact them...There are three ways in which we contact victims; visits, letters and telephone calls. Ideally we like to send a visitor out, but because of lack of resources, the shortage of volunteers, we can't always find people to go out...we still try to visit all the 'burglaries'. It is just that we prioritise, we try to go to the older ones first of all and then the younger ones, whatever age. The only reason we send letters to burglary victims is when we just haven't got anyone. (Plymouth coordinator)

When Victim Support started the work was predominantly burglary. I hardly ever see a burglary victim now – it's assault, victims of armed robbery and Jean – the deputy – deals with sexual assault and domestic violence. Volunteers do court work. The original reason for Victim Support has got lost. There is such a demand for serious crime and that's long-term work and very hard. We've made a policy decision to maintain contact with burglary victims. We could leave the burglary victim outside given the volunteers we've got...schemes are developing into two tier services. (Salford coordinator)

Interviews with these two coordinators thus suggested that while not all burglary victims would be contacted by Victim Support, Plymouth victims might fare rather better than those living in Salford, a poorer, inner city location. Responses to a series of questions to victims bore this out. Given a prompt card with a list of agencies that might have offered help, 69% of Plymouth victims said they had some form of contact with Victim Support compared with only 35% of Salford victims; similarly 13% of the former but only 6% of the latter said they in fact received help or useful advice from Victim Support.

Of course, the fact that victims said they had had contact with Victim Support is no guarantee that they had. Respondents may have forgotten, or confused Victim Support with some other agency. They may have rejected the offer of help. Or Victim Support may have contacted another member of their household. Mawby and Walklate (1997) therefore also analysed Victim Support files in the two cities. In Plymouth Victim Support had no record of 26% of the sample, which may have been because of a failure of communication with the police or, less likely, an initial decision not to include cases as referrals. The remainder had however been contacted in some way: 23% by letter, 3% by phone and 58% by visit, although in nearly half of these no direct contact was achieved and a personal note was left by the volunteer visitor. Salford Victim Support was more likely to contact victims by letter only and less likely to visit: 40% were sent a letter, 2% phoned and only 29% visited. However, personal contact was made with rather more of those visited (70%).

## Needs and services

In assessing the extent to which victim assistance programmes meet the needs of crime victims, two questions arise. First, are those victims who are in most need more likely than other victims to be contacted by such programmes? Second, do those who are helped receive the sort of assistance they require? The first question relates to the match between victims and support; the second to the match between needs and services.

Referring to crime victims in general, a number of studies in the USA have concluded that overall the most vulnerable victims are most likely to be contacted by victim assistance programmes. In an early evaluation, Friedman et al (1982) concluded that poorer victims, repeat victims and those with more crime-related problems were most likely to be in contact with support services. Similarly, in New York, Davis (1987) found that victims who received help were more likely to be in poor health, unemployed and badly affected by the crime. Most recently, Davis et al (1999), in a study across four US cities, noted that the neediest victims and those who had the most problems were most likely to receive assistance.

However, there are indications that even where help is offered, victims do not always receive the types of support that would be most useful. The emphasis upon immediate support and crisis counselling, very much a feature of US initiatives, and reflecting the predominance of a mental health lobby within the victims' movement and the early focus on violent crime, often produced a mismatch between needs and services, with basic services not always available (Davis and Henley 1990). Roberts (1990: 47) reported that 54% of programmes in his sample provided crisis intervention, but that only 25% provided emergency money and 12% lock repairs. Later research by Davis et al (1999) reiterated this point. Thus in their survey victims wanted help with practical assistance and crime prevention advice, whereas victim assistance programmes were more likely to offer counselling. As a result, as Table 9.1 illustrates, even where victims were in contact with victim assistance programmes, they received few of the services they needed.

*Table 9.1: Percentage of victims expressing different needs and receiving help from a victim service (based on Davis et al 1999: 108–109)*

|  | Needed help | Received help |
|---|---|---|
| Crime prevention | 52 | 5 |
| (e.g. advice, security improvements) |  |  |
| Household logistical support | 52 | 4 |
| (e.g. borrow money, repairs) |  |  |
| Counselling, advice, advocacy | 47 | 24 |
| (e.g. legal advice, someone to talk to) |  |  |
| Property replacement | 22 | 4 |
| (e.g. help with claims, replace stolen documents) |  |  |

Analysis of the 1998 BCS by Maguire and Kynch (2000) also suggested that those victims in most need were most likely to receive support. Thus among victims who had reported their crime to the police, 15% of those who described themselves as very much affected recalled some form of contact with Victim Support, compared with only 4% of those who said they were 'not at all affected'. Moreover, while only a small number recalled a personal visit, those who were most affected were 15 times more likely to have received one than those not affected. However, unlike in the US research, the relationships between contact and other measures of vulnerability/deprivation were less clear-cut. For all those crimes reported to the police, older people and poorer victims (measured by income and car ownership) *were* more likely to be contacted, but black and Asian victims were *less* likely to be contacted. Moreover, among burglary victims, the only category who were significantly more likely to be contacted than average were those on *higher* incomes. It may well be that an area effect comes into play here and that Victim Support schemes in more affluent areas, with lower referral rates and more volunteers, are better able to contact burglary victims. Be that as it may, the findings do undermine the assumption that Victim Support is able to reach most of the more vulnerable crime victims.

BCS data also allow us to consider the types of help victims felt they needed. As Table 9.2 demonstrates, for victims in general 'getting information from the police' was most commonly cited, followed by 'someone to talk to' and 'protection'. Among burglary victims, advice on security was also frequently mentioned. As in the USA, it appeared that victims who wanted 'someone to talk to' were most likely to feel they received this from Victim Support (in 51% of cases where some form of contact was made), although 26% of those wanting advice on security also said they received this from Victim Support. Moreover, victims who had had contact with Victim Support were highly positive about that contact, especially in the case of face-to-face contact, which 50% described as very helpful and 30% helpful.

*Table 9.2: For crimes reported to the police, percentage of victims saying they had wanted different types of help (Maguire and Kynch 2000: 9)*

|  | *Burglary victims* | *All victims* |
| --- | --- | --- |
| Getting information from police | 31 | 29 |
| Advice on security | 30 | 14 |
| Practical help | 10 | 6 |
| Someone to talk to/moral support | 23 | 19 |
| Help with insurance/compensation | 10 | 8 |
| Protection | 18 | 19 |
| Help in reporting to police | 7 | 9 |
| At least one type | 68 | 63 |

Research in Plymouth by Mawby and Simmonds (2000) arrived at similarly positive conclusions. Interviews were carried out with 168 victims who had been dealt with in varying ways by Victim Support. The authors found that whereas those who had had face-to-face contact were no more likely than those who were not contacted at all to say they had been 'very much affected' by the offence, they were more likely to describe themselves as afraid, upset or shocked and to say they had experienced insomnia, again suggesting that Victim Support was successful in targeting those in most need. Focusing on those victims who were seen in person, most of whom were burglary victims, Mawby and Simmonds (2000) reported that a majority said they had got 'real help or advice from Victim Support' and only 9% felt that Victim Support could have done more to help.

While many burglary victims in England and Wales will have had some contact with Victim Support (even if this contact is not always face-to-face), the same cannot be said for victims elsewhere. Evidence from the ICVS has suggested that in industrialised countries a significant proportion of burglary victims who received no specialist help said that 'the services of a specialised agency to help victims of crime would have been useful' for them. For example, over 40% of burglary victims in the USA, Finland and Sweden felt that they would have benefited from such help (Mayhew and van Dijk 1997: 46).

## Case study: identifying unmet needs in Europe

Further evidence comes from our research in England, Poland, Hungary and the Czech Republic (Mawby *et al* 1999; Mawby *et al* 2000). Respondents were first asked whether they received any help from a specialist agency. In contrast to the situation in England, very few victims of burglary in the other countries surveyed received any specialist help. Those who answered in the affirmative were then asked whether or not they had received 'any real help or useful advice' from any of these agencies, and those who had not been offered any help were asked whether 'help or advice from any of these sorts of people would have been useful.' In England, Victim Support was cited most commonly as the agency providing the most useful help or advice. In Poland, employers appeared to be the most helpful, but in Hungary no agency was mentioned by more than a couple of victims.

Given that, with the exception of England, the numbers mentioning any one agency were relatively small, answers were combined and respondents categorised into four groupings: those who were offered or asked for help and found it useful, those who were offered or asked for help but felt that it was not useful, those who were not offered any help but would have liked it, and those who were not offered any help and said that they did not need any.

The distribution was different in each country. In England, victims were unlikely to say that they needed help but were not offered any, and they were over-represented among those saying that they were offered help but it was not useful. This suggests that, in ensuring that most burglary victims received the offer of help, agencies such as Victim Support were reaching most 'needy' victims but in the process were also contacting victims who did not require help or would have benefited from a different kind of help. In Poland, by way of contrast, comparatively more victims said that they had not been offered any help but would have found it useful, and very few said that they were offered help that they did not need. This suggests that there is a considerable unmet need in Poland. In Hungary, victims were unlikely to say that they were offered any help, and the number saying that they had been offered help that they did not need was particularly low. This again suggests a lack of support, although to a lesser extent than in Poland. Finally, in the Czech Republic, while very few victims were offered any help, a majority (57%) said they did not need any help and a further 25% said they were unsure. At first sight this suggests a lack of unmet need in the Czech Republic, but it to some extent confirms the difficulty of asking people to comment on the usefulness of a service about which they have little awareness.

The extent to which help was being offered to those most in need was then assessed by considering the relationship between the four groupings identified and victims' descriptions of the ways in which they had been affected by the crime. The pattern was very clear. Those who were most affected by the crime were most likely to say that they had been offered help and had found it useful (particularly in England) or that they needed help but were not offered any (particularly in Central and Eastern Europe). Those who were least affected were most likely to say either that they had not been offered any help and had not needed any or that they had been offered help but it had not been useful.

Though complex, the findings here are unambiguous. In England, most burglary victims in our samples received some offer of help. As a result, few who registered high levels of need were not offered help, but a large proportion of those who were offered help were not markedly affected by the crime and were thus in less need of help. This is accepted by Victim Support, who would argue, first, that it is difficult to predict from police records which victims are in need of support and, second, that even victims who have not been significantly affected may appreciate the offer of help, the message that someone cares. Elsewhere, where far more victims said that they were offered little or no help, those who said that they would have found help useful registered more severe reactions to crime.

Finally, fear or worries about future crime were compared according to whether victims said that they had been offered help and whether they had needed it. It seemed that those who said that they had not needed any help and those who had been offered help but did not find it useful were least likely to express concern, again suggesting (in the case of the latter group) that these were generally people who did not need help. Although those who were offered help and said that they benefited from it were rather more worried about the future, those who had not received any help but said that they would have appreciated help registered significantly higher levels of concern. This suggests that, where victims feel that they need help, intervention at the time of the burglary may have a long-term effect in reassuring victims. It also indicates that those identified as in need of support at the time of the offense might also have benefited in the long term had help been offered to them.

## Summary and discussion

A review of victim assistance programmes across the world suggests that only in Britain are burglary victims prioritised. Yet it is evident (see chapter 3) that burglary victims are often severely affected and in need of support, and indeed ICVS data confirm a high level of demand among burglary victims across the world.

The policy implications of this are twofold. First, high levels of unmet need demonstrate that more and better services for burglary victims are required in many countries. This applies both in countries where victim assistance programmes are in operation but where burglary victims receive low priority and in countries without any such services. Second, although it would be tempting to suggest that services in England are wasted on victims who do not need them, this is not the case. On the one hand, given that it is difficult on the basis of information in police files to assess need, providing a more comprehensive service helps agencies ensure that those who are in need receive support. On the other hand, the level of service provision from Victim Support in England does vary, with personal contact being made with only a minority of victims. It is important, therefore, to ensure that the 'filter' is used efficiently and that it is the victims most in need who receive a visit from Victim Support and who are, where appropriate, referred on to other agencies.

The emphasis changes in chapter 10, which concentrates on corporate burglary. However, although the assumption is commonly made that corporate victims do not require support services, this will be challenged. The extent to which those owning or employed in businesses that experience burglary are also excluded from Victim Support will be noted.

## Notes

1 Based on a presentation by A. van Beckhoven at the Xth International Symposium on Victimology, Montreal, August 2000 (see www.victimology.nl)
2 Data taken from the annual report (Victim Support 1999) sometimes include figures for the Victim/Witness Services as well as victim assistance.
3 The remaining 1,112 were Witness Service Volunteers.
4 Some 18,000 were self-referrals in 1998/99. A Victim Supportline was established in 1998 to allow victims to telephone Victim Support direct, and received 11,500 calls in 1998/99 (Victim Support 1999, 11).
5 These included victimless crimes and crimes against corporate victims.
6 In this respect victims of violence, when contacted, were even more likely to receive a visit (39%).

# Chapter 10

# Commercial burglary

## Introduction

While there has been considerable research into household burglaries, little has been written about commercial burglary: break-ins to shops, stores, offices, factories, warehouses, etc. To some extent, this reflects a greater emphasis on crimes where individuals or households, rather than organisations or businesses, are the victims. Certainly, despite one early study in the USA (Reiss 1967), business victim surveys have only recently 'taken off' – the 1994 Commercial Victimisation Survey (CVS), conducted by the Home Office as part of a wider international survey, being a case in point (van Dijk and Terlouw 1996).[1]

In Britain at least, research is also confounded by the unavailability of official statistics on commercial burglary: police data distinguish between burglary of household premises and other burglaries but the latter may include a variety of types of incident. For example, Redshaw and Mawby (1996) drew a sample from police computer listings of all 'other' burglaries reported to the police in Devon and Cornwall for a three-week period between December 1994 and January 1995, a total of 562 break-ins. These included burglaries of individuals' sheds (9%), garages (12%) and outbuildings (10%), in total accounting for 36% of the sample. It is equally difficult to tease out from crime statistics different types of commercial burglary, such as ram-raiding (Jacques 1994).

Some research has, however, been carried out. This covers at least five broad areas: the nature and extent of commercial burglary; the effects of such offences on the companies and individuals involved; the nature of police response; crime prevention strategies; and information on the offenders.

## The nature and extent of commercial burglary

A number of studies have focused on specific types of premises or *modus operandi* and shown the extent of commercial burglary. For example, in an early study Laycock (1984) discussed the particular problem of burglaries of chemists' shops. Beck and Willis (1991) reviewed burglary records kept by 22 out-of-town superstores, while Jacques (1994) assessed data on ram-raids provided by three retailers. The extent of British media attention devoted to ram-raids in the early 1990s suggests that offences of this type were then particularly prevalent. While Jacques concurred, arguing that such crimes peaked in 1991/92 partly as a result of the 'copycat' process, he also noted that 'smash and grab' crimes have been evident for a long time. 'Smash and grab' raids became common in the 1930s, while in the 1950s forced entry to shops was effected by attaching grappling irons to window bars and using a car to force them off (Donald and Wilson 2000).

Ram-raids are, however, only a small proportion of all commercial burglaries. The Home Office's CVS found ram-raids to be relatively uncommon, although some 3% of larger retail premises experienced them in 1993 (Mirrlees-Black and Ross 1995).

There is also some evidence that commercial burglaries in general are far from rare. In one study of crime on industrial estates, for example, Johnston *et al* (1994) identified burglary as one of the most common – and serious – crimes experienced by units on five estates. Focusing on 92 units, they reported that 39 units had been burgled and 23 had experienced an attempted burglary within the preceding two years and that 'when tenants on the estates thought of "crime" they generally meant burglary' (*ibid* 106). The predominance of burglary as the most common crime was also confirmed in a subsequent analysis of 600 estates. Tilley's (1993) review of crimes against small businesses similarly identified burglary as one of the most common crimes experienced and also one of those most often feared. The CVS in England and Wales confirmed this, finding rates of burglary against retail and manufacturing premises to be higher than for households (Mirrlees-Black and Ross 1995). Among retail premises, 24% experienced a burglary in 1993, this being the second most common crime after theft by customers, cited by 47%. In comparison, 25% of manufacturing premises suffered a vehicle theft and 24% a burglary. In each case, burglary of commercial premises was considerably more common than household burglary, experienced by 4% of households in the same year. Repeat victimisation was also common. In all, 2% of retailers and manufacturers experienced over a quarter of all burglaries. As a result, Mirrlees-Black and Ross estimated that the retail and manufacturing industries suffered some 148,000 burglaries and 155,000 attempted burglaries in 1993.

The survey also found variations in the likelihood of burglary. Commercial burglaries were most common for larger retail and manufacturing premises and for those stocking 'saleable' goods such as alcohol and tobacco. Additionally, premises in certain parts of the country were particularly at risk, although the patterns varied between retail and manufacturing premises.

Van Dijk and Terlouw's (1996) discussion of the CVS in all nine participating countries[2] reiterated many of these points. For those in the retail trade, burglary (including attempts) was the second most common offence cited, after 'theft by persons'. However, the proportion of respondents who had been burgled in the preceding year ranged from 40% in the Netherlands to 14% in Italy. As well as in the Netherlands, burglary was also common in the UK and Hungary. In the Netherlands, the catering and industrial sectors ranked high risk. Countries with high rates of household burglary, such as South Africa, the Czech Republic, the UK and Australia, also tended to have high rates for retail burglary. Again, retailers stocking readily disposable goods, such as tobacco and electronics, were most at risk. Vandalism costs were also relatively high – particularly so where considerable force was used to effect entry, as in ram-raids, where the cost of damage may even exceed losses (see also Jacques 1994). Overall, the risk of burglary in the retail sector was about ten times that for households. Repeat victimisation was also a widespread problem.

In Australia, Walker (1996) found that reported rates for burglary were 38.34 per 1,000 residential dwellings but 98.29 per 1,000 business premises. According to the Australian component of the ICVS, around 4.2% of households were burgled each year in the early 1990s, but the first Australian business victimisation survey revealed a rate of 27.4%, with burglary 'the most common form of crime occurring to businesses in 1992' (Walker 1996: 283). Repeat victimisation was also common, with almost 60% of commercial burglary victims saying they had been victimised more than once during the year. More recently, a survey of small businesses in Australia found that burglary was the second most common crime experienced (after shoplifting) and that revictimisation was common (Perrone 2000).

The extent of repeat victimisation was also noted by Johnston et al (1994) and Tilley (1993) and by Redshaw and Mawby (1996) in Devon and Cornwall. While 'only' 8% of the latter's domestic burglary sample said they had been burgled before in the last 12 months, in contrast exactly half the commercial burglary sample said they had, with 16% burgled once, 16% twice and 18% on at least three occasions. Repeat victimisation is clearly then a key problem for the business sector and might be expected to be reflected in victims' views on the crime and police response.

### Case study: the effects of commercial burglary

The CVS emphasised the financial costs of crimes against retail and manufacturing premises. Mirrlees-Black and Ross (1995) estimated that burglaries cost industries in England and Wales over £300 million in 1993. The average cost of a burglary was £2,420 among manufacturers and £1,660 among retailers, compared with £1,370 for household burglary. One additional cost not included here involves the cost of crime prevention, estimated by Mirrlees-Black and Ross (1995) to be £440 million in 1993. Small businesses, with less assets to fall back on, may be particularly vulnerable, as Perrone (2000) noted in Australia.

The broad nature of the costs incurred is illustrated by our research in Devon and Cornwall (Redshaw and Mawby 1996). When asked directly, 44% of victims claimed the incident had had an adverse financial impact on their business, whilst 24% said it had had an emotional effect on themselves or their staff. Victims who indicated that they had been subject to an adverse financial impact were asked to provide details. Their comments predominantly fell into four categories:

(i)   Having to meet the cost of damage to their premises (26%). For example, one victim complained that, 'Damage from intruders is now accounting for the largest proportion of our maintenance budget' while another explained that, 'Damage cost about £500 to repair...this was only covered in part by insurance'.

(ii)  Insurance did not cover all of the costs of stolen items (22%): for example, 'I cannot claim for the loss as my excess is now so high'.

(iii) Loss of business (21%): for example, 'Loss of business due to restocking time'.

(iv)  Increased cost of insurance premiums (20%): for example, 'Lost no claims bonus on insurance – £450.'

In addition, 7% mentioned the cost of increased security as a financial impact. However since, as we shall see later, about three quarters had increased or planned to increase their level of security, clearly perceptions of the financial impact of additional security were under-stated in answer to this question.

While the emotional effect of burglary on victims of domestic burglary is well documented, there is little information on the extent of any emotional effect on victims of commercial burglary. The expectation that victims of commercial burglary can be affected emotionally by the incident was acknowledged by the Devon and Cornwall police, in as far as 49% of victims in the sample had been given a Victim Information Leaflet. This was lower than for domestic burglary, where 83% were given a leaflet (Bunt and Mawby 1994), but still perhaps higher than might have been anticipated. However Victim Support contact was extremely low, with only 3% of victims of commercial burglary stating they had been contacted either personally or on the telephone by a Victim Support worker, compared with 62% of victims of domestic burglary. A later survey of Victim Support in Plymouth confirmed this pattern: out of 102 cases of crime against businesses, Victim Support did not attempt to contact any victims in person, and only communicated by letter on one occasion (Mawby and Simmonds 2000).

Nevertheless, we found that many of the comments made related to the effect on staff within the business. For example:

My staff were very distressed and I was scared to sleep over the premises for some time.

The cleaner who comes in during the evenings is so nervous her husband accompanies her.

It also unnerved staff and made them very edgy.

Equally the effect was also felt at a personal level with comments like '...invasion of privacy' and 'we worry about the next burglary, which will happen, without a doubt'.

Overall, the findings suggested that there was a need for support for employers or employees of burgled commercial premises that was unmet, and perhaps unrecognised.

## Victims' perceptions of police services

The CVS found that levels of reporting were high for completed burglaries, at over 90% (Mirrlees-Black and Ross 1995). Van Dijk and Terlouw (1996) described a similar picture on an international level, noting that this largely reflected the commonality of insurance coverage. All UK respondents were asked to evaluate police response to local crime problems, and while over half were positive, a quarter were critical. Those who had been victimised were particularly likely to express dissatisfaction.

Johnston *et al* (1994) noted considerably more dissatisfaction among their sample, with victims criticising the police for minimal effort, poor feedback and a low clear-up rate. Respondents in general also complained at the lack of a visible police presence, with only 16% saying they saw a police officer on the estate at least once a month. Only 8% felt their estate was well policed. Conversely, Tilley (1993) noted that a desire for a greater police presence was the most common recommendation made by small business operators.

Victims in Redshaw and Mawby's (1996) survey were also asked about the service they received from the officers attending the scene. As noted in chapter 8, force policy in Devon and Cornwall at the time required officers to provide victims with six specific 'services'.[3] Victims of commercial burglary were significantly less likely to say they had received each of the six services than were victims of domestic burglaries. However, when asked to evaluate the services by the officers attending at this stage, there was no significant difference between the two samples: 83% of victims of domestic burglary and 80% of respondents in the commercial burglary survey said they were satisfied with all aspects of the service.

In contrast, victims were more critical of follow-up services, as provided, for example, by scenes of crime officers (SOCOs). They were also less likely to have been contacted again, either by the officers who first attended or by anyone else. As a result, they expressed more criticism of the police than did victims of household burglary and cited the failure of the police to keep them informed of progress or tell them the results of their investigation. Only 45% of victims of commercial burglaries thought that the police had kept them well enough informed, compared with 63% of domestic burglary victims. Yet both groups had similar expectations of the need to be kept informed. Victims who felt that the police could have done more, or who were unsure, accounted for 29% of domestic burglary victims and 35% of commercial burglary victims. When asked to explain, the most often cited answers from both groups were that the police could do or could have done more patrolling in the area either on foot or in a car (i.e. prevent crime from happening in the first place), and further detective work towards identifying the offender. This was followed by a desire to be kept informed of the progress of the investigation and the provision of security advice.

To summarise victims' experiences of police action, Redshaw and Mawby (1996) asked victims whether or not they were satisfied with all aspects of the service they had received and what they had felt most satisfied or dissatisfied again. Again there was a significant difference between commercial and domestic burglary victims: only 62% of the former compared with 71% of the latter expressed themselves satisfied. In each case, however, it seemed that victims' satisfaction levels fell over time. For domestic burglary victims, satisfaction fell from 83% to 71%; for commercial burglary victims the fall was greater, from 80% to 62%. From comments made by both groups of victims, initial satisfaction related in the main to the attitude of the police officer dealing with the incident and the initial quick response from the police. Most frequently cited reasons for particular dissatisfaction were a belief that the police should have made more effort in detecting crime, that victims were not given any kind of progress report and the perceived negative attitude of the police/ lack of interest. It could be that the difference in satisfaction levels between the two burglary groups is connected with the degree of repeat victimisation, much more prevalent amongst victims of commercial burglary, and/or the fact that victims of commercial burglary were less likely to receive further contact from the police following the incident.

### The extent of security

The commercial sector faces a particular set of problems in attempting to prevent crime. On the one hand, premises are often relatively large, empty at night and at weekends, and located in non-residential areas where the possibility of natural surveillance is limited. On the other hand, restricted public access to retail premises and commercial premises like shopping malls inhibits routine surveillance.

Not surprisingly, then, there is an emphasis on physical aspects of security, with – as we have seen – considerable financial implications. The CVS found that in the England and Wales a majority of respondents had burglar alarms and window protection, and a large minority also had security lights (Mirrlees-Black and Ross 1995). Although at that time only a small proportion had closed circuit television (CCTV), the deployment of video cameras has clearly been extended since then. Brown's (1995) subsequent evaluation of CCTV in town centres suggested that this might have a considerable impact on shop burglary rates. It might also aid detection, by facilitating a rapid response and by providing the police with more visual evidence. Private security is another option, with many firms employing their own security staff and others subcontracting out to a specialist security firm that provides regular patrols when the premises are closed. Contract security has been growing at a faster rate than in-house security in the last decade, although Button and George (1994) concluded that the latter offered a number of advantages. Another approach that has growth potential involves cooperation with neighbouring premises, either through the pooled deployment of security guards or through schemes like business watch. Again this was found to be relatively rare at the time of the CVS, but has subsequently expanded in popularity.

Similar findings have been reported from abroad. Van Dijk and Terlouw (1996: 165) concluded that, 'The anti-burglary measures taken most in all countries are the installation of burglar alarms with or without follow-up by security companies, lighting and window security.'

Redshaw and Mawby (1996) explored the extent to which commercial premises invested in security by asking victims about their security both prior to the incident and subsequent to it. Half of all respondents revealed that prior to the burglary they had had a burglar alarm installed, with other victims identifying a wide assortment of security measures. Only 11% had none of the security measures listed. Following the burglary 74% of respondents had either increased, or planned to increase, security of their business premises. Table 10.1 identifies the method of increased security this group either used, or intended to use.

*Table 10.1: Percentage of victims of commercial burglary who had improved or intended to improve their security in the following ways*

| | |
|---|---|
| Fit or improve burglar alarm | 42 |
| Put bars or grills on windows | 15 |
| Steel line or put bars on doors | 9 |
| Fit lights with timers or sensor switch | 7 |
| Add window locks | 7 |
| Improve door bolts/locks | 6 |
| Improve security personnel situation | 6 |
| Fit security cameras | 5 |
| Other | 10 |

The major change to security was either the installation or improvement of burglar alarms, followed by fitting windows with bars or grills and reinforcing doors. Only 2% had taken the step of employing a security guard when their business was closed. Given the extent of financial losses suffered by victims it is, perhaps, not surprising to find that this expensive option was scarcely ever chosen.

While public funding of improved security for the business sector is rarely an option, in the case of small businesses it has sometimes been available, for example through the Safer Cities programme. Tilley (1993) described a number of such initiatives where at least some of the target hardening costs were subsidised, most commonly to provide alarms and shutters. Some Industrial Watch projects were also born out of the initiative. He concluded that there was some evidence of a reduction in burglaries as a result (see also Tilley and Hopkins 1998).

Most recently, Bowers (2001) has evaluated the Small Business Strategy of the Safer Merseyside Partnership (SMP). This focused on businesses with fewer than 25 employees in the most deprived areas of Merseyside. A victimisation survey of businesses was used to identify those at most risk. These were then offered specialist advice from a crime prevention officer. Some of those visited were also offered grants from the SMP towards increased target hardening.

Bowers (2001) found that take-up of the grants was disappointing. Despite being eligible for up to £1,500 for improved security, many firms were deterred by the requirement for them to contribute 50% towards the additional security. However, subsequent evaluation showed that where small businesses took up the offer of a visit by a crime prevention officer, this alone led to reduced levels of victimisation, although the reduction was even greater where a grant was given for additional target hardening. For example, there was a fall of 59% in burglaries among those who received advice from a crime prevention officer, compared with an 8% reduction for the 'non-intervention group', and differences in levels of repeat burglary were even more pronounced. Bowers concluded that, with the exception of security lighting, all additional security measures proved effective, with window locks, other window security, and roller shutters particularly effective. Finally, she demonstrated that there was little evidence of displacement.

**Offending patterns**

As with domestic burglary, research on commercial burglars is handicapped in that most has been conducted on convicted burglars, especially incarcerated ones. In Britain, Walsh (1986) interviewed 45 prison inmates whose last offence was recorded as commercial burglary and Butler (1994) interviewed small samples of commercial burglars either on probation or in prison. Wiersma's (1996) study in the Netherlands involved semi-structured interviews with 83 (mainly incarcerated) commercial burglars.[4]

Most of the latter were male, aged between 20 and 30, and had had little or no schooling. However, Wiersma (1996: 218) noted: 'The majority of the offenders had been active in crime for years, and had certainly not restricted themselves to burglary of businesses.' Over half had committed residential burglaries, a large minority vehicle-related crimes and one third robbery. Commercial burglary was, nevertheless, preferred, partly because the offenders could more easily justify crimes where no individual victim was involved, partly because the courts were more severe on residential burglars, and partly because it was more profitable. Both Butler (1994) and Walsh (1986) also noted that there was little evidence of much specialisation in commercial burglary. Most of their samples had committed household burglaries or other property offences and seemed fairly flexible in their choice of offences. A Dutch survey by Kruissnik (1995) reiterated these findings.

Interviews with commercial burglars provides additional evidence on the effectiveness (or otherwise) of increased security. The burglars interviewed by Walsh claimed they were not put off by conventional burglar alarms. Similarly Butler's sample did not overall consider alarms or door or window locks a deterrent, and were more likely to be deterred by a physical presence, whether this entailed security staff or members of the public to whom potential targets were visible. In Kruissnik's (1995) Dutch survey, commercial burglars also admitted that they were put off by security staff, by silent alarms wired directly to the police station and by guard dogs, but not by other security equipment. Respondents to Wiersma's (1996) survey were also not generally deterred by security measures such as 'extra locks and bolts, compartmentalisation, roll-down shutters, warning lights, cameras, loud alarms and the presence of security personnel' (*ibid* 222). On the other hand, just over half *were* deterred by dogs, and silent (as opposed to loud) alarms, and in-house (as opposed to visiting) security guards were considered effective deterrents. Given that there is no evidence of the effectiveness of target hardening or private security, the contrast between these findings and those from burglars targeting domestic homes is intriguing.

Wiersma (1996) was somewhat ambivalent about the extent of professionalism displayed by his sample. On the one hand, many were motivated by the thrill and excitement of the act and proceeds were spent on drugs, alcohol and high living, but most also put a considerable amount of effort into planning the crime. A large majority of his sample showed cunning, resourcefulness and professionalism in preparing for and carrying out their burglaries. For example, over 80% collected advance information on access points, alarms, where valuables were stored, etc. Targets were commonly chosen because of their perceived vulnerability; for example, location on a business park or lack of burglar alarm. He consequently concluded that most could, following Bennett and Wright (1984), be described as 'limited reasoning decision makers' rather than professionals.

Unlike conventional burglary, where offences may be haphazardly planned and generally committed alone, ram-raiding is a more professional crime that is usually well planned, requires considerable skill and tends to be committed by groups of offenders working together as a team.

Donald and Wilson (2000) researched 70 convicted offenders whose most recent offences involved ram-raiding. All were male, with a mean age of 23. The majority had a previous conviction for TWOC (74%), theft (67%), handling (67%), non-dwelling burglary (63%) and thefts from motor vehicles (53%), but interestingly rather less had previous convictions for domestic burglary (30%), robbery (19%) or other violent crimes. The researchers described the typical raid as involving three to five offenders arriving at the target in a stolen car, forcing entry with sledge hammers, crowbars or bolt croppers, loading the goods and making a getaway within five or so minutes.

The distinctiveness of Donald and Wilson's (2000) approach was to consider ram-raiding groups as 'work groups', with a designated leader, specialists (such as a driver), and younger members serving apprenticeships. They described six roles within the 'work group':

- **The leader/planner** – generally with several convictions for dishonesty and often with convictions for violence, especially robbery.

- **The heavy** – who may act as a guard or help force entry; these tended to have previous convictions for violence, but rarely for dishonesty or anti-social behaviour.

- **The driver** – these showed little evidence of previous convictions for violence or anti-social behaviour; but some had records for dishonesty and all for TWOC.

- **Extras** – these tended to drift in and out of groups, with records for anti-social behaviour and – in some cases – dishonesty.

- **Apprentices** – these may be friends or family of the leader, some with previous convictions for dishonesty, but with few convictions for violence or anti-social behaviour.

- **Fences/handlers** – some had previous convictions for handling and/or dishonesty, but not for anti-social behaviour or violence.

Fences were not in many cases actual group members, but Donald and Wilson (2000) noted that in some cases they were involved in planning the raid and that goods might be 'stolen to order'. Moreover, it seems likely that as commercial burglaries are more likely to involve the theft of large quantities of the same product than is the case in domestic burglaries, fences may be a more central feature of such operations (Sutton 1998a). At the very least, the fencing process will differ in emphasis.

### Summary

What then do such studies tell us about patterns of commercial burglary? Overall, four points have been highlighted in the literature. First, considering the timing of the offences, studies suggest that commercial burglaries most commonly occur either at night or over the weekend (Butler 1994; Kruissnik 1995; Mirrlees-Black and Ross 1995; Walsh 1986). Such findings are scarcely surprising and reflect the times when premises are closed; what is most interesting is that they contrast with data for household burglary, where empty houses during the day mean that such offences are more common then. Second, it seems that out-of-town superstores are particularly at risk, a factor closely related to their poor defensible space qualities. Thus Butler found that burglars preferred superstore targets when confronted with a hypothetical choice, and Kruissink's Dutch research came to similar conclusions. Third, a number of studies have focused on the crime prevention aspects of the subject. Tilley's (1993) research of business security in Salford suggested that hardware such as shutters may reduce burglaries and Jacques argued that target hardening of superstores contributed to the decline in ram-raiding incidents. Others, though, have produced more sceptical conclusions. Finally, it appears that the recent policy drive against domestic burglary in England and Wales has passed victims of commercial burglary by. They appear to receive little or no support from victim services and a poorer response from the police than do victims of domestic burglary.

## Notes

1 A summary, in English, of a recent survey carried out for the Dutch Ministry of Justice by its Research and Documentation Centre is available on line at www.minjust.nl/b_organ/dpjs/engels/business_burglary.htm
2 From Western Europe: the Netherlands, Germany, France, Switzerland, the UK and Italy. From Central and Eastern Europe: Hungary and the Czech Republic. Elsewhere: Australia. A parallel survey was also conducted in South Africa.
3 Identification of the attending officer (name or number); a crime reference number; a telephone contact number; details of further police action; explanation about the services of Victim Support; and a crime victims booklet.
4 For further details, see note. 3

# Chapter 11

# Detection and sentencing

## Introduction

While chapters 6–7 addressed primary and situational crime prevention, the emphasis here is upon tertiary prevention and the possible use of social crime prevention strategies. However, before offenders can be sentenced, they must be caught, and all the evidence – from Britain and abroad – suggests that detection rates for burglary are particularly low. The chapter consequently begins with a discussion of the reasons for this, followed by consideration of innovative strategies that have been introduced in recent years. Policies aimed at limiting the distribution of stolen goods are then reviewed.

The second half of the chapter focuses upon the most appropriate and effective ways of dealing with known burglars. In the context of (in England at least) hawkish public opinion, the use of prison and noncustodial alternatives are considered, and the balance between prevention and treatment and deterrence assessed.

## Detection

Detection rates for burglary have traditionally been relatively low (Bottomley and Coleman 1981; Burrows and Tarling 1982; Greenwood and Chaiken 1977). In England and Wales in 1999, for example, 15% of burglaries (dwelling) and 10% of burglaries (other) were cleared up, with the corresponding figures for Devon and Cornwall being 15% and 13%. This compared with a detection rate of 25% for all indictable crimes, 65% for violent crimes and 97% for drug offences (Home Office 2000).

Burglaries are usually committed when the home is empty and in the absence of witnesses. Unlike violent offences, there is rarely an available witness to name or describe the perpetrator, and unlike drug offences the identification of an offence does not almost inevitably bring with it the identification of a suspect.

In an early study of reported crime, Mawby (1979) noted that most burglary detections were due to indirect methods: that is, an offender arrested for another offence would admit to the burglary. Direct detections were rare. Burrows (1986), following Burrows and Tarling (1982), used the terms primary and secondary detection which broadly correspond to Mawby's direct/indirect distinction. Again, secondary detection was relatively common, with two strategies predominating. On the one hand offenders pleading guilty to one offence might be induced to admit to others (TICs); on the other hand, in some forces detectives routinely visited sentenced offenders in prison to clear up cases from the files. Burrows (1986) compared burglary figures in three pairs of matched police force areas, three with low detection rates for burglary and three with high rates. He found that in two of the high detection rate areas, Syston (with a medium burglary rate) and Chappeltown (with a high burglary rate), secondary detections accounted for 75% and 89% of detections respectively, with TICs most common in Syston and prison visits in Chappeltown. Thus, high detection rates were largely a result of strategies directed at secondary detections rather than police efficiency in clearing up burglaries that were recently reported to them. Excluding the former, variations in detection rates between the six areas fell from 54 percentage points to six percentage points (Table 11.1).

*Table 11.1: Primary and secondary detection rates for burglary in six matched areas, 1983 (from Burrows 1986: 15)*

|  | Primary | Secondary | Total |
|---|---|---|---|
| *Low detection rate areas* | | | |
| Walton (low burglary rate) | 7 | 6 | 13 |
| Bitterne (medium burglary rate) | 9 | 9 | 18 |
| Clapham (high burglary rate) | 7 | 4 | 11 |
| *High detection rate areas* | | | |
| Epping (low burglary rate) | 13 | 11 | 24 |
| Syston (medium burglary rate) | 12 | 34 | 46 |
| Chappeltown (high burglary rate) | 7 | 58 | 65 |

For primary detections, Burrows (1986) reiterated Mawby's (1979) finding that the police were highly dependent on the public for information leading to an arrest. On average the police spent 3.7 hours on each burglary, but there was little relationship between time spent on investigation and outcome (i.e. a successful arrest).

This picture is confirmed in more recent research by Couple and Griffiths (1997) in Home Office sponsored research in the West Midlands. They took residential burglaries committed over a six-month period in 1994, comprising all 256 cases that were detected by primary means and an 8% sample (448) of unsolved burglaries, combining an analysis of police files with interviews with police officers and victims. They concluded that 'most primary detections were attributable to activities carried out by the first officer at the scene (*ibid* vi). Most commonly this was the result of:

- The police detaining the offender in the act or near the scene of the crime (in 43% of cases).

- Evidence provided by witnesses, especially victims, at the scene of the crime (in 34% of cases; this involved cases where the victim/witness named a suspect, provided a detailed description, or described the offender's vehicle).

In contrast, forensic evidence was the principal method of detection in only 6% of cases, and subsequent CID investigation (including surveillance and stop-checks) in no more than 10% of cases.

Although 43% were cleared up due to the offender being arrested at or near the scene, in fact only 10% of burglaries reported as 'in progress' were cleared in this way. This may be partly due to the fact that some astute victims may describe 'cold' burglaries as 'in progress' in order to receive a prompt response. However, Coupe and Griffiths (1996) demonstrated that clear-ups from 'burglaries in progress' were more common where the police responded quickly and where more than two officers attended. But:

> Although the police response time and number of officers who attended are both important in the detection of 'in progress' burglaries, their relative importance does vary, When a burglary was reported 'in progress' and the offender was on the premises a quick response time was more important than the number of officers that attended. However, when the offender had just left the premises, the number of officers that attended became more important. (*ibid* 9)

Evidence provided by victims was also important: useful information was provided by victims in 18% of cases, and their evidence was crucial in 19% of primary detections. To a lesser extent, evidence from other witnesses, especially neighbours, was also important.

The extent to which primary detections in cases of domestic burglary were effected almost immediately was illustrated by the finding that 80% of primary detections occurred within ten days of the crime and a mean time of six days between the burglary and a suspect being charged (*ibid* 26).

Farrington and Lambert's (2000) research also included details of detection methods. Burglars were most likely to be detected because: they were caught in the act (14%); shopped by an informant (12%); apprehended at or near the scene of the crime (12%); traced through stolen property or property left at the scene (10%); seen acting suspiciously in the area (8%); through a witness description (7%); and as a secondary/indirect detection (7%). Not surprisingly, victim or witness descriptions featured less frequently than in the case of violent crimes. Moreover, 61% of 'stranger violence' cases were detected within an hour of the crime being committed, compared with 43% of burglaries.

The relative significance of 'real policework' in effecting detection is reiterated in the USA (Greenwood and Chaiken 1977), where detection rates are equally low. Indeed, Rengert and Wasilchick (2000) suggested that burglary is so difficult to detect that offenders must be either very stupid or very unlucky to be apprehended! Our research in Europe also found low clear-up rates to be the norm (Mawby 1998).

However, poor detection rates are increasingly seen as a problem, and as detection rates have declined in England and Wales, the alleged inefficiency of the police as regards detection has come under closer scrutiny. In reality, however, it seems that detection rates have fallen since PACE (the Police and Criminal Evidence Act) due to the lesser influence of indirect/secondary detection in recent years.[1] In essence, burglaries are, and always have been, difficult to detect due to their very nature.

Findings such as these have had at least four implications. First, they heralded a policy shift towards crime prevention rather than detection (see chapters 6–7). Second, as performance indicators have been created, there has been a concern to distinguish between primary and secondary detection methods, and highlight the former as indicators of police success. Third, pessimism regarding the apparent waste of resources has led to a critical re-examination of the ways in which burglaries were investigated, with resources rationed in favour of more serious offences and those where the chance of an arrest seemed most likely. Fourth, and most recently, there has been a new optimism towards detection, with a variety of focused initiatives being piloted.

## Innovations in detection

A number of these initiatives either stemmed from or were evaluated as part of the Home Office's 'Police Operations against Crime' in the early 1990s. The research by Coupe and Griffiths (1996) was one such evaluation. So, for example, having identified the ways in which the police initially responded to burglary complaints as crucial, they suggested that an improvement in police response to incidents would increase the detection rate. Equally, they advocated a more planned approach to house-to-house inquiries, and a more systematic monitoring of cases so that CID and SOCO could concentrate their efforts (and resources) on those cases where there was some prospect of detection.

In a parallel study, Taylor and Hirst (1995) assessed the different approaches for police visits to scenes of house burglaries. Based on a national survey and a more detailed analysis of six schemes, the researchers evaluated the ways in which different approaches saved resources, improved detection rates, or otherwise provided an enhanced service to victims. However, although they identified differences between schemes in terms of their cost and the quality of service provided to victims, there was no conclusive evidence that any one approach led to an increased clear-up rate.

Gill *et al* (1996) also evaluated the ways in which crimes were processed within police forces and the extent to which evidence collected at each stage of the investigation contributed to an arrest. Again, the authors found little evidence that different approaches affected detection, and concluded that while the police adopted a narrow definition of a 'result', victims' views of a successful investigation were broader than this (see chapter 8): victims 'valued demonstrations of care and interest and perceived a visit to the scene and the performance of some investigative actions as indicative of this' (Gill *et al* 1996: 43).

A somewhat different emphasis has been suggested by those who see crime analysis and offender profiling as potentially able to make a greater contribution, especially where the information collected by uniformed officers, CID and SOCO is coordinated more systematically. Canter and Allison (2000), for example, have criticised SOCO information's unsystematic and incomplete nature. Crime analysis is an example of 'intelligence-led policing' that depends on accuracy and the systematic gathering of evidence. The crime analyst compares different crimes and known offenders to identify links that are not evident from routine police inquiries. Merry (2000) has advocated a more extensive use of analysts, and indeed the number of crime analysts employed by forces has increased significantly in recent years.

Offender profiling aims to improve detection through aiding in the prediction of the characteristics of offenders, using information on the offence and the victim and using victims' and witnesses' descriptions of the offender. While much of the emphasis of offender profiling has been on sex offences and homicides, research by Farrington and Lambert (2000) using information on police records for burglars and violent offenders has explored the feasibility of a statistical approach to offender profiling for property crimes.

Perhaps the UK police initiative on the investigation of burglary that has attained the highest profile has been Operation Bumblebee. This approach by the Metropolitan Police was evaluated by Stockdale and Gresham (1995) alongside Gloucestershire's Operation Gemini and a somewhat different strategy adopted in Hampshire.

Operation Bumblebee was initiated in part of the Metropolitan Police Force area in mid-1991 and extended forcewide in mid-1993. As well as aiming to improve arrest and conviction figures, the operation was directed at both crime prevention and an enhanced quality of service for burglary victims. Based around an area burglary team and a divisional burglary squad, the initiative aimed to improve investigation and detection by improved intelligence, increased provision of fingerprint and forensic evidence, surveillance of suspected 'active' burglars, curfew monitoring, a 'stop and speak' campaign in high burglary areas, and a structured system of post-sentence visits. This latter point is important because whereas the emphasis in Operation Bumblebee publicity was on primary detection, secondary detection formed a crucial element of the initiative.

Stockdale and Gresham (1995) argued that while the incidence of both household and corporate burglary fell slightly between 1991 and 1993, Operation Bumblebee had a more significant impact on detection, with the clear-up rate rising noticeably for both household and corporate burglaries. Unfortunately, and unlike Coupe and Griffiths (1996), the researchers failed to analyse the different ways in which primary detections were effected, and so it is impossible to judge precisely how patterns of primary detections changed in terms of the different aspects of the initiative. However, comparing primary with secondary detections, it is notable that over the study period the number of primary detections *fell*, and that the increased clear-up rate was due almost entirely to secondary detections, accounting for 14% of all detections in 1991 and 33% in 1993. This was the result of an increase in both TICs and prison visits. In contrast, the number of primary detections fell from 10,220 in 1991 to 9,848 in 1993, and the percentage of clear-ups that were primary fell from 86% to 67%. While the authors rather limply justified Operation Bumblebee as a success in improving detection rates, it is thus clear that this much vaunted proactive approach to detection had little or no impact on primary detections.

This is not to imply that all anti-burglary strategies will inevitably fail. However, it is important to monitor not only changes in clear-up rates but also changes between primary and secondary detections and changes in the nature of primary detections. The following section considers an alternative approach that might be adopted by the police: a concentration upon the distribution of stolen goods rather than the burglary itself.

### Operations against the distribution of stolen goods

If burglars are to profit from their crimes, they need to sell on stolen goods to either fences or members of the public (see chapter 5). It therefore makes sense for policing operations to target the distribution outlets. They may do this by paying special attention to outlets such as pawn brokers and car boot sales,[2] or by targeting fences. It is, however, widely recognised that the successful prosecution of fences is difficult (Renooy 1991; Roell 1986; Swedish Crime Prevention Council 1978).

In England, policy makers and practitioners have paid little attention to ways of disrupting the sale of stolen goods, and academic contributions have been minimal. One review that promised to provide a fresh insight by following best practice in business analysis, for example, recommended little more than property marking (Kock, Kemp and Rix 1996). A subsequent critique, however, concluded that offenders were undeterred by property marking (Sutton 1998a, 1998b)![3]

In fact, using BCS data, Sutton identified the purchase of stolen goods as thriving, most notably among young males and small businesses and those living in deprived, high crime areas. The impression was that those who suffered crime and were uninsured could minimise their losses by purchasing goods stolen from their 'neighbours'. The evidence also suggested that burglars who failed to sell on the proceeds of their crimes tended to be deterred from further burglaries, which implied that focusing on handling transactions would be a viable crime reduction strategy. Although this is a difficult area to police, Sutton did suggest that increasing regulations and surveillance (for example CCTV) might curtail sales to small businesses. Nevertheless, to date targeting stolen property outlets has rarely featured as a key factor in clearing up burglaries, which is scarcely surprising since, 'At present there is no systematic approach to using stolen property as a means of solving burglaries' (Coupe and Griffiths 1996: 34).

In the USA, more attention appears to have been directed at professional fences. The LEAA's Anti-fencing Program in the 1970s was directed at setting up sting operations to apprehend both fences and property offenders seeking to fence stolen goods in 20 areas of the country (US Department of Justice 1979; Walsh 1976). Some internal evaluations of programmes suggested that the initiative was successful. For example, Project UFO in the Greenville Police Department (1979) resulted in over 100 arrests, a 100% conviction rate, and the recovery of $250,000 worth of stolen goods. There was also a fall in the number of property crimes. On the other hand, Raub's (1983) internal evaluation of two Illinois programmes failed to demonstrate any impact on property crime. Some external evaluations have been more critical (Langworthy 1989). Weiner, Stephens and Besachuk (1983), in research on the Detroit programme, concluded that whilst it did lead to an impressive number of arrests, convictions and recoveries of stolen goods, it failed to impact on major receivers. This is perhaps one of the reasons why sting operations have lost their popularity in the USA. However, other programmes have continued to target fences, such as the Repeat Offender Program (ROP) in Washington (Trainum, Brown and Smith 1991).

## Cautions and conviction

Because the detection rate for burglary is so low, only a small proportion of burglaries result in the prosecution and conviction of suspected burglars. Comparing England and Wales with the USA, Langan and Farrington (1998: 18–19) showed that a burglary in England and Wales was less likely to lead to a conviction than in the USA. For example, in 1995 in England and Wales there were only about 6 convictions for every 1,000 alleged burglaries, compared with about 27 in 1981; in the USA the numbers, while still low, had actually risen from 10 to 14. Of course, this takes no account of the possibility that many of those prosecuted may have committed a number of offences, and not all 'cleared' burglaries result in a prosecution.

In England and Wales cautioning is commonly deployed in the case of younger offenders, and whilst this has been restricted in recent years and is in any case less common for offences such as burglary, as Table 11.2 demonstrates it is still the most usual outcome for males aged under 15 and females aged under 18.

Males aged over 15 and females aged over 18 who are arrested are, however, highly likely to be prosecuted.

*Table 11.2: Percentage of offenders cautioned for burglary and all indictable offences, England and Wales, 1999 (from Home Office 2000: 108)*

| Ages | 10–11 | 12–14 | 15–17 | 18–20 | 21 or over | Total |
|---|---|---|---|---|---|---|
| *Males:* | | | | | | |
| Burglary | 87 | 62 | 27 | 8 | 5 | 19 |
| All indictable | 87 | 69 | 45 | 31 | 22 | 31 |
| *Females:* | | | | | | |
| Burglary | (100)[4] | 80 | 52 | 28 | 24 | 46 |
| All indictable | 96 | 87 | 64 | 43 | 36 | 48 |

Taking all males sentenced for burglary in England and Wales in 1999, 12% received a probation order, 9% a community service order, 7% a supervision order and 7% a combination order. However, prison was a more likely disposition: 18% were sent to a young offender institution and 31% to prison (Home Office 2000: 170). This overall incarceration rate of 49%[5] is well below that for those convicted of robbery but more than for those convicted of indictable violence offences or fraud and forgery.

The extensive use of imprisonment for burglars reflects a growing willingness to sentence offenders in general to incarceration, combined with an assumption that this is what the public wants. Therefore, before focusing in more detail on custodial and noncustodial sentences, the following section is devoted to a discussion of public attitudes towards sentencing burglars.

## Public attitudes towards sentencing

Public attitudes towards sentencing are an important ingredient of the sentencing process, especially in countries where media attention focuses on crime and where law and order policy is made a party political issue. Thus in Britain, the period since the late 1970s has variously seen the two main political parties vying to outbid one another as the party that is most 'tough on crime'.

International data, however, suggest considerable differences between countries in public perceptions of the appropriateness of different sentences. This is well illustrated in findings from the ICVS (del Frate 1998; Mayhew and van Dijk 1997). Here respondents were invited to say what they felt was the most appropriate sentence for 'a man aged 21 who is found guilty of burglary for a second time, having stolen a colour television'. Combining the 1992 and 1996 surveys, del Frate (1998: 111) demonstrated marked regional differences, with imprisonment the preferred sentence in Asia (77%) and Africa (70%), Latin America (50%) and countries in transition (39%), and community service orders being the most common choice in Europe and the New World. However, as is clear from Table 11.3, prison was favoured by a majority of respondents from the USA, and over 40% from the British Isles and Canada, although it received scant support from other European nations, where community service orders (CSOs) were by far the most endorsed option. Moreover, comparison with earlier ICVSs indicated that a gradual increase in support for imprisonment in Britain and Canada was not replicated in continental Europe.

*Table 11.3: Percentage of respondents opting for different sentences for a recidivist burglar (from Mayhew and van Dijk 1997: 56)*

|                   | Fine | Prison | CSO |
|-------------------|------|--------|-----|
| England and Wales | 8    | 49     | 39  |
| Scotland          | 13   | 48     | 27  |
| Northern Ireland  | 15   | 49     | 28  |
| Switzerland       | 10   | 9      | 61  |
| France            | 9    | 11     | 68  |
| Finland           | 15   | 18     | 49  |
| Sweden            | 13   | 22     | 50  |
| Austria           | 14   | 10     | 60  |
| Canada            | 8    | 43     | 30  |
| USA               | 8    | 56     | 23  |

Further information on public opinion in England and Wales is available from the BCS. Reporting on the 1996 BCS, Hough and Roberts (1998) noted that whilst four out of five respondents felt that sentences were too lenient and most condemned judges and magistrates as out of touch with the public, it was in fact the public that was out of touch with sentencing practices. For example, 55% of those interviewed underestimated the use of imprisonment for adult male burglars by at least 30%. Respondents were also presented with a real case of a daytime burglary of an empty house belonging to an elderly man, involving an offender with previous convictions and the theft of a video and television. The case in question actually attracted a two-year prison sentence. Asked what they felt would be the most appropriate sentence, 54% opted for imprisonment, with a CSO, fine and suspended sentence the next most common choices. Perhaps surprisingly, burglary victims were no more punitive than other respondents.

The 1998 BCS similarly revealed low levels of public awareness of both crime and sentencing policy, with police and courts both criticised for their leniency. In this case, though, the emphasis in the survey was on youth justice (Mattinson and Mirrlees-Black 2000). Respondents were invited to choose the most appropriate way of dealing with an offence committed by a male offender, aged either 10 or 15, who was either a first offender or recidivist. Respondents were each offered one of three offence scenarios: shoplifting, burglary and a 'serious attack on a teacher'. Not surprisingly, burglary attracted more severe suggestions than shoplifting, but less than for violence.

Closer consideration of Table 11.4 reveals a number of themes. First, respondents were most severe in their judgements where the burglar was older and a persistent offender (i.e. had committed at least three previous offences). Second, persistence had a more significant impact on severity than did age; that is, a 10-year-old persistent offender was deemed worthy of a tougher sentence than a 15-year-old first offender. Third, imprisonment in a young offender institution was favoured by a majority in the case of the 15-year-old persistent offender. Fourth, in contrast, imprisonment was almost universally rejected for a first offender. Finally, respondents were, overall, more punitive than the police/YOTs[6] (*vis-à-vis* cautioning) and courts (*vis-à-vis* sentencing) in these cases, and more punitive towards the 15-year-old 'persistent' offender than they were towards the recidivist burglar described above.

Table 11.4: Percentages opting for different ways of dealing with a juvenile burglar (from Mattinson and Mirrlees-Black 2000: 3)

|  | 10-year-old | | 15-year-old | |
|  | First time | Persistent | First time | Persistent |
| --- | --- | --- | --- | --- |
| Caution | 25 | 6 | 22 | 3 |
| Reparation order | 22 | 2 | 16 | 1 |
| Community sentence | 33 | 47 | 42 | 29 |
| Imprisonment | 3 | 32 | 9 | 59 |

Victims were also asked to say how they felt the perpetrator of *their* crime should be dealt with. About a third of victims of burglary with entry felt prison was the most appropriate sentence, similar to victims of muggings, and more punitive than for many types of violence. Overall, though, victims expressed considerable support for restorative or reparative justice (Mattinson and Mirrlees-Black 2000). Moreover, sentencing severity was considered an effective means of tackling crime by only a minority of people, with increased discipline within the family and reductions in unemployment considered more effective (Hough and Roberts 1998).

Findings from the 1996 and 1998 BCSs thus suggested that the public in England and Wales supported tough sentencing policy, but under-estimated how tough sentences currently were. At the same time, however, crime prevention approaches were seen as more effective, and more constructive sentencing options, such as reparation, received widespread endorsement. Before considering the use of noncustodial sentences for burglars, however, the following section focuses on the use of imprisonment.

**Imprisonment**

Given that detection rates for burglary are so low, the impact of sentencing on burglary rates is likely to be minimal. Nevertheless, sentencing strategies reflect (government) perceptions of the seriousness of burglary (or, perhaps, government perceptions of what the public wants) and specific programmes may impact upon individual burglars so as to affect their chances of re-offending. What then of the use of imprisonment?

Cross-national comparisons of rates of imprisonment are fraught with difficulties (Pease 1994; Walker *et al* 1990). However, there is an increasing amount of data available on the numbers in prison in different countries, albeit little of this allows us to distinguish burglary from other offences (Flynn 2001; Walmsley 2000). What it does show, however, is that the use of imprisonment is extensive in Russia and the USA (730 and 680 prisoners per 100,000 population respectively in 1999). England and Wales, with a rate of 125, imprisoned far less offenders by world standards, but rated second only to Portugal in Western Europe.

More detailed information on the use of imprisonment for those committing burglaries is available for some Western societies. For example, Lynch's (1987) comparison of England and Wales, the USA and Canada in the early 1980s argued that the proportions receiving a prison sentence were not that different once contrasting national crime rates were taken into account. Taking the number of burglars imprisoned as a proportion of those arrested Lynch concluded that the differences between Canada (23%), England (30%) and the USA (35%) were not excessive. However, elsewhere Lynch *et al* (1994), comparing the USA and England and Wales, provided other evidence that undermined these conclusions. For example, in the USA only 16% of imprisoned burglars were serving sentences of three years or less, compared with 81% in England and Wales.

More recently, Langan and Farrington (1998: 22–23) demonstrated that while imprisonment was a common sentence for burglars in both the USA and England and Wales, it was used more sparingly in the latter. In 1994/1995 60% of convicted burglars received prison sentences in the USA compared with 38% in England and Wales. In both countries, use of imprisonment had risen since 1981 (from 54% in the USA and 29% in England and Wales). The average sentence imposed (43 months compared to 15 months) and served (18 months compared to 6 months) was also greater in the USA (*ibid* 30–33). However, given the low detection rates, only a minute proportion of burglars ended up in prison. The researchers (*ibid* 28–29) estimated that for every 1,000 burglars, only eight ended up in prison in the USA and only two in England and Wales!

Langan and Farrington (1998: 38–40) also assessed the relationship between rates of burglary (using police statistics and victim survey data) and the risk and severity of punishment. In both countries, there was a close negative correlation between the burglary rate and the risk of conviction; that is, a fall in convictions was associated with a rise in burglary. In the USA, but not England and Wales, there was also a negative relationship between burglary rates and *use* of imprisonment (but not sentence length). These relationships were stronger and more consistent in the case of burglary than many other offences, this being attributed by the authors to the fact that many burglaries were planned.

However, although this implied that in the USA prison was a deterrent, overall the figures demonstrated that certainty *of detection* had a greater deterrent effect than did level *of punishment*.

Cromwell, Olson and Avary (1991), in their interviews with burglars, also noted the balance between certainty of detection and severity of punishment. Burglars saw imprisonment, particularly a long sentence, as more of a deterrent than probation (see also Rengert and Wasilchick 2000). However, detection was seen as a more important deterrent than punishment alone:

> Severity of punishment has little, if any, impact on the risk–gain calculus of the young offender – until the probability of punishment becomes greater. (*ibid* 86)

Interestingly, subjects felt that once they had been apprehended a few times and their *modus operandi* had become familiar to the police, their chance of being detected again increased. Consequently, some who were deterred by the prospect of a long prison sentence committed less serious crimes, like shoplifting, which they felt would not provoke a prison sentence should they be caught.

Nevertheless, primary crime prevention was considered more effective than tertiary prevention:

> Except under certain circumstances, crime prevention strategies at the community level, such as increased levels of prosecution, or at the state level, such as increasing statutory penalties for burglary, were not perceived by the informants as being as effective as micro-level strategies instituted by the residents of a potential target site, such as buying a dog or installing an alarm (Cromwell, Olson and Avary 1991: 89).

One innovation that has caused the likelihood of incarceration in the USA to increase is the so-called 'three strikes' laws. 'Three strikes' policies were introduced to California in 1994. Proposition 184 led to a doubling of sentences for a 'second strike' and a mandatory '25 years to life' in cases involving a third felony conviction. Similar legislation was introduced in other states and – in cases of violent felonies only – by the Federal government. The key justification for such legislation appears to have been the principle of incapacitation; that is, offenders who are locked away are unable to reoffend, thus reducing crime levels. However, while crime may be reduced, there is disagreement over the extent of any fall that can be attributed to the 'three strikes' policy (Henham 1997). Be that as it may, the result of such policies is that the prison population has increased relative to those on probation or parole (Bonczar and Glaze 1999).

Prison is clearly a more likely sentence for burglars in the USA than in England and Wales, but – as the above illustrates – the courts in England and Wales have also shown a greater willingness to imprison burglars in recent years. Just as government views on the usefulness and appropriateness of prison as a sentence have been adjusted on a number of occasions of late, so views on its applicability for burglars have changed. In the late 1980s, as noncustodial sentences were encouraged, two trends became evident. First, a distinction was made between household and corporate burglary, with the latter seen as less serious and thus less meritorious of a prison sentence. Then, with the 1991 Criminal Justice Act, community punishment was seen as a suitable option for most burglars. However a subsequent government u-turn saw prisons decreed effective by the then Home Secretary, Michael Howard. With the threat of an English equivalent to the US three strikes rule, it appeared that prison had been re-established as the appropriate sentence for burglary. The new Labour (or New Labour) government of 1997, keen to portray itself as tough on crime, continued the Conservatives' expansion policy and the numbers in prison rose to an all-time high of 65,300 in 1998, having risen by 47% since 1993 (Cullen and Minchin 2000).

The introduction of Home Detention Curfews (using electronic monitoring) for offenders near the end of their sentence reduced the prison population in England and Wales to 64,770 in 1999 (Cullen and Minchin 2000), although it was infrequently used for high risk offenders, including burglars (Mortimer 2001). At this time, 18% (8,622) of male sentenced prisoners had been convicted of burglary, compared with only 6% (158) of females, although in each case both the proportion and number of burglars in prison had increased since 1998. The overall male incarceration rate of 49% demonstrates a dramatic increase in the use of prison for burglars during the late 1990s, reflecting successive governments' targeting of household burglary.

In marked contrast, however, prison was demonstrably ineffective in preventing burglars reoffending on release. No fewer than 76% of burglars released from prison in 1996 were reconvicted within two years, a higher figure than for any other offence category (see Figure 11.1).

It is, indeed, widely accepted that while imprisonment might reduce burglary by removing potential offenders from circulation, it has little impact on reoffending (Sherman et al 1997). What then of noncustodial alternatives?

*Figure 11.1: Percentage of offenders released from prison in 1996 who were reconvicted within two years (Cullen and Minchin 2000: 4)*

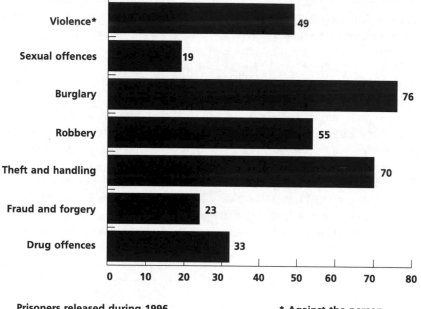

Prisoners released during 1996                    * Against the person

## Noncustodial alternatives

Probation orders and community service orders (CSOs) have generally been seen as constructive, but a soft option in the eyes of both the public and offenders. Thus the burglars interviewed by Cromwell, Olson and Avary (1991) were generally dismissive of probation, feeling that probation officers were under too much pressure to impose any meaningful supervision:

> The perception of probation as free crime was widespread. As a sanction, probation was perceived as a suspended sentence with almost no negative consequences. The informants we interviewed regularly committed crimes and used drugs while on probation – and parole. Few of them felt any pressure to cease or even reduce their criminal activities during their probationary period. The general perception was that probation and parole officers were overworked, understaffed and underfunded (*ibid* 84).

Probation was originally conceived in the USA and England and Wales as a means of diverting minor offenders out of the court process. It subsequently became the lynchpin of the treatment philosophy (McWilliams 1986). Then, as the treatment approach became discredited, its *raison d'être* became further undermined. The response has been to 'toughen up' probation and use community punishment as a mechanism for reducing reoffending. Thus intensive probation became established in the USA in the 1980s to provide more intensive, regular supervision, with a variety of additional requirements attached to the order (Byrne 1990; Erwin and Bennett 1990; Mair 1996b; Petersilia 1990; Petersilia and Turner 1991).

Although probation caseloads in England and Wales never approached those across the Atlantic, similar pressures to 'toughen up' were exerted by government on somewhat reluctant probation services. The 1982 Criminal Justice Act provided for additional conditions to be attached to a probation order where appropriate and the 1991 Criminal Justice Act extended these and created the combination order as a combination of probation and community service (Smith 1996). Intensive probation was then established on an experimental basis in eight probation areas in 1990 (Mair 1996b; Mair *et al* 1994, 1995). Intensive probation was never extended nationally, but it did provide the basis for the emergence of accredited programmes as a key feature of probation work with offenders. Based on the cognitive-behavioural model developed by Ross, Fabiano and Ross (1989) in Canada, the 'what works' orthodoxy of the new, national probation service in England and Wales assumes the availability of a coherent menu of programmes geared to address the offending patterns displayed by offenders and the specific offences they have committed (Chapman and Hough 1998; McGuire 1995; Wallis 1999).

In England and Wales, the community service order was introduced as an appropriate sentence for 'imprisonable offences', but not exclusively as an alternative to prison. Extensive monitoring of the imposition of orders in the 1970s suggested that about half those given a CSO would otherwise have received a prison term, with the remainder drawn from other noncustodial sentences (Pease and McWilliams 1980). However, the 1991 Criminal Justice Act extended the use of CSOs for those lower on the tariff, and monitoring of sentencing patterns during the 1990s indicated that – compared with probation orders – CSOs were being given to those with less extensive criminal records and less problematic social backgrounds (Kershaw 1999; May 1999).

Nevertheless, in England and Wales the period since the mid-1980s also saw a marked toughening up of the standards applying to community service in an attempt to make it appear a more attractive alternative to imprisonment (Hine and Thomas 1996). When first introduced, guidance about its operation and organisation was minimal. This changed in 1989 with the introduction of national standards; one consequence of this was an increase in the number of those on a CSO who were breached; another was a shift in the typical order, with group placements becoming more common and individual placements being 'earned' rather than allocated automatically. The introduction of the combination order in the 1991 Criminal Justice Act provided further opportunities for tougher community sentencing.

The 1991 Act also opened up the opportunity for electronic monitoring, and this was extended following the 1994 Criminal Justice and Public Order Act and the 1997 Crime (Sentences) Act (Mair and Nee 1990; Mortimer and Mair 1997; Mortimer and May 1998; Mortimer *et al* 1999; Nellis 1991; Walter, Sugg and Moore 2001). While both probation and community service *originated* as constructive alternatives to custody, electronic monitoring has a traditionally more explicitly punitive *raison d'être*. Initiated by Judge Jack Love in Florida in the early 1980s, it is still very much a minority sentence in the USA, and tends to be concentrated in Florida and Michigan.

In England and Wales, tougher, more demanding community punishments – new style CSOs and probation with conditions attached – have replaced other community alternatives – traditional community service and probation, and suspended sentences – as the use of imprisonment has risen. How has this affected the use of community punishment for burglars?

Intensive probation was clearly seen as an appropriate disposal for burglars: during the experimental period no less than 42% of those considered suitable for IP had committed burglary (Mair *et al* 1995). Individualised programmes involving a 'personal action plan' were also considered a particularly suitable approach to confronting offending behaviour in cases of burglary, and also may be used to restrict burglars' movements during the periods when they choose to commit their offences (for the USA, see Rengert and Wasilchick 2000). At the same time, although rather less of those tagged have been currently charged with burglary (around 17%), a majority have a prior record of burglary offences (Sugg, Moore and Howard 2001), burglary comprises one of the most common offence types amongst those tagged, and electronic monitoring may be viewed as an opportunity to prevent offence patterns such as night-time burglaries (Mortimer and May 1998; Mortimer *et al* 1999; Walter, Sugg and Moore 2001).

The new 'accredited programmes' within probation are the subject of ongoing evaluation. However, recent comparisons of recidivism rates for different sentences in England and Wales suggest few grounds for optimism, with minimal differences between custodial and noncustodial sentences, and between alternative community sentences, once criminal records and offence types are taken into account (recidivism rates being particularly high for burglars) (Kershaw 1999; Lloyd, Mair and Hough 1994; May 1999).

In the USA, MacKenzie *et al* (1999) have recently provided a more optimistic assessment of probation, especially for property offences like burglary. They noted a reduction during probation in the kinds of behaviour likely to promote reoffending, and a fall in self-reported burglary from 6.5% to 0.9%, with the number of burglaries per offender declining from 67.3 per annum before probation to 3.0 per annum during probation. Interestingly, they detected no differences between traditional and newer forms of probation. On the other hand, Sherman *et al* (1997) found that programmes directed at offenders' problems and needs had a better rate of success.

While the more recent 'accredited programmes' offered by the probation service provide an extension of both the punitive and the offence-directed aspects of intensive probation, a more constructive alternative may be the restorative justice developments initiated by New Labour. Mediation and/or reparation has been used for a considerable time, but has received more interest since the 1970s (Mawby and Walklate 1994; Umbreit 1999).

Two approaches may be offered as examples. First, burglars may be enrolled in victim–offender mediation processes. In the USA, Galaway (1986) described an example of this operating in Minnesota as a Victim Offender Reconciliation Project (VORP). Somewhat differently, the now defunct Victim/Burglar Group operated in Plymouth by the probation service (Mawby and Nation 1993; Nation and Arnott 1991) provided a structured programme for convicted burglars subject to a probation order, part of which involved them in group discussions with burglary victims. This provided the opportunity for victims to express their anger and fears, albeit towards someone other than 'their' burglar, and feedback demonstrated that most felt they benefited from the experience. Additionally, being confronted by victims proved beneficial to offenders, who were forced to confront and re-evaluate their actions. Following Sykes and Matza (1957), one of the advantages of such programmes was that they enabled probation officers to challenge 'techniques of neutralisation'. That is, burglars were less able to hide behind excuses that 'victims can afford it' or 'it didn't really affect the victim', and instead were left with the clear message that their actions had impacted on their victims.

It is possible that youth justice initiatives currently being evaluated in England and Wales will maintain such constructive approaches to burglary. However, for older burglars, government policies, steered by public opinion – or at least government perceptions of public opinion – have identified imprisonment and new forms of community punishment as the most appropriate ways of tackling burglary.

## Targeting drug misusers

Given the close association between burglary and drug misuse (see chapter 5), and recent findings that offenders with a drug problem are highly likely to reoffend (May 1999), a number of recent initiatives have focused on providing treatment programmes for property offenders who commit offences to subsidise a drug habit. In England and Wales, Drug Treatment and Testing Orders (DTTOs), introduced under the Crime and Disorder Act 1998, have been piloted in three areas of the country and subsequently extended countrywide. DTTOs are a requirement of the court, whereby the offender, under probation supervision and with support from specialist drug agencies, undergoes regular drug testing. In his preliminary evaluation, Turnbull (2000) found that DTTOs were most commonly deployed in cases of shoplifting. Urine test results and interviews with offenders and other key players, however, suggested that the orders were successful in leading to a reduction in drug misuse, expenditure on illegal substances, and consequently offending. For example, average weekly expenditure on drugs fell from £400 to £30, and self-reported offending fell to under 10% of previous levels. US evaluations also give grounds for cautious optimism (Sherman *et al* 1997).

A slightly different approach was adopted somewhat earlier in Devon through the Fast Track programme. This was a multi-agency initiative aimed at property offenders who commit offences to feed a drug habit. The idea here was that offenders, the majority of whom had been arrested for burglary, could be given priority in being placed on a drug treatment programme, participation in which was a condition of a probation order. If the treatment was effective and the offender was either weaned off drugs or stabilised on prescribed drugs, then the motivation for burglary would be weakened (Barton and Mawby 1997). Preliminary analysis of Fast Track concluded that it had successfully met its objectives and highlighted multi-agency cooperation as a successful feature of the initiative (Barton 1999; Barton and Mawby 1997). Moreover, it had demonstrated its success without resort to the more punitive approach illustrated by DTTOs and the community punishment philosophy.

## Summary

The deterrent qualities of punishment, and the effectiveness of alternative sentences, is however limited by traditionally low detection rates. The fact that so few burglaries are cleared up is scarcely surprising, and owes more to the nature of the offence than to police failings. Nevertheless, evaluations of policework suggest that it may be possible to improve detection rates for crimes like burglary.

While a high proportion of very young burglars are cautioned, most burglars who are arrested are prosecuted and subject to either a prison sentence or – in England and Wales and the USA – recently toughened community punishments. In some respects, new community programmes may provide a more focused approach to reducing reoffending by burglars, since they more explicitly address the offending behaviour. However, the movement towards community punishment and 'what works' is essentially punitive, and consequently the constructive element of different initiatives is highly circumscribed. Approaches that are based on restorative justice are in marked contrast.

Overall sentencing alternatives are inevitably restricted in their effectiveness. Consequently, crime prevention and burglary reduction programmes provide the best chance of reducing burglary *rates*, and an improved service for victims from police and specialist agencies provide means of reducing the *impact* of burglary.

A decline in burglary rates in England and Wales in recent years is one illustration that burglary reduction programmes have been effective. Addressing how these might be adapted to other crimes is, perhaps, a more constructive way forward, than an approach that sees more punitive sentencing as the solution.

## Notes

1  In fact, in 1999 clear-ups that resulted from prison visits – at that time accounting for a third of all burglary detections – were excluded from detection statistics (Home Office 2000: 30).
2  Although Sutton (1998a) (see chapter 5) found little evidence that much fencing took place at car boot sales.
3  An international review of evaluation research came to a similar conclusion: see Sherman *et al* (1997).
4  Numbers too small to cite with confidence.
5  In the same year some 25% of female burglars convicted in the courts were imprisoned.
6  Since 2000 pre-court decision making on young offenders has passed from the police to multi-agency Young Offender Teams (YOTs).

# Afterword

Burglary is a crime that is both relatively common and impacts upon victims in a number of ways. Moreover, evidence from the ICVS and our own research confirms this picture across a wide range of countries. In England and Wales and North America, at least, repeat victimisation is also common. It is, therefore, scarcely surprising to find that public concern over burglary is widespread. The level of support and sympathy evoked for Tony Martin, the Lincolnshire recluse who shot and killed an intruder, is indicative of this.

Ironically, at the time of the Martin case, the British government was midway through a series of initiatives aimed at reducing levels of burglary. And most of the evidence to date suggests that these have been successful. Residential burglary rates across the country have declined, and rates in targeted areas have fallen even more. While the effect of incarceration and community punishments is likely to be limited, if only by the small proportion of burglars who are caught, comprehensive burglary reduction programmes that combine target hardening with community based approaches appear to have been successful. At the same time, improvements in police procedures and the expansion of victim assistance programmes direct help at those who have been burgled.

In general, this text aims to provide an international review of the topic. In some respects, though, the focus is inevitably on the situation in England and Wales. Here, the priority afforded by successive governments to tackling burglary may offer lessons to some other countries. For example, Victim Support in Britain is distinctive in prioritising burglary victims, yet – as we have seen – burglary affects people in similar ways in countries without victim assistance programmes, or where programmes do not target burglary. There is thus a strong argument for providing more help for burglary victims in other countries. Another example relates to the extensive nationally led burglary reduction initiatives in England and Wales that could provide models of effective intervention for adoption elsewhere.

The lessons of this text, however, stretch further than the subject of burglary. Burglars are not uniquely distinct from other offenders; other crimes impact on victims in similar, though not identical, ways; and issues relating to fear, differential risk, and repeat victimisation, apply to crimes in general. The approaches to reducing the risk and impact of crime that have been successfully applied to burglary may, therefore, be usefully adapted and applied to other offences. Equally, while it has been my intention to use burglary as an example on which to pin a number of themes *vis-á-vis* crime and criminal justice policy, I hope that the reader will draw ideas from the different chapters that better inform an understanding of the nature of crime and policy responses.

# References

Allatt, P. (1984) 'Residential security: containment and displacement of burglary', *Howard Journal*, **23**, 99–116.

Anderson, D., Chenery, S. and Pease, K. (1995) *Biting back: tackling repeat burglary and car crime*. London: Home Office (Crime Detection and Prevention Series, no. 58).

Ashton, J., Brown, I., Senior, B. and Pease, K. (1998) 'Repeat victimisation: offender accounts', *International Journal of Risk, Security and Crime Prevention*, **3**, 269–279.

Audit Commission (1996) *Streetwise: effective police patrol*. London: HMSO.

Baldwin, J. and Bottoms, A.E. (1976) *The urban criminal*. London: Tavistock.

Barclay, G.C. and Tavares, C. (2000) *International comparisons of criminal justice statistics 1998*. London: Home Office (Home Office Statistical Bulletin 04/00).

Barker, M. (2000) 'The criminal range of small-town burglars', pp. 57–73 in Canter, D. and Alison, L. (eds.) *Profiling property crimes*. Aldershot: Ashgate/Dartmouth.

Barton, A. (1999) 'Breaking the crime/drugs cycle: the birth of a new approach?', *Howard Journal*, **38.2**, 144–157.

Barton, A. and Mawby, R.I. (1997) *Breaking the drug/crime link: a preliminary evaluation of Fast-Track*. Plymouth: University of Plymouth (Criminology and Criminal Justice: Research paper 2).

Bayley, D.H. (1994). *Police for the future*. New York: Oxford University Press.

Bayley, D.H. (1989). 'Community policing in Australia', pp. 63–82 in Chappell, D. and Wilson, P. (eds) Australian policing: contemporary issues. London: Butterworth.

Beaton, A., Cook, M., Kavanagh, M. and Herrington, C. (2000) 'The psychological impact of burglary', *Psychology, Crime and Law*, **6**, 33–43.

Beck, A. and Willis, A. (1991) *Burglary in Currys and Comet: a comparative analysis*. Centre for the Study of Public Order, University of Leicester, Leicester.

Bennett, T. (1987) 'Neighbourhood watch: principles and practices', pp. 31–51 in Mawby, R.I. (ed.) *Policing Britain*. Plymouth: Plymouth Polytechnic.

Bennett, T. (1990) *Evaluating neighbourhood watch*. Aldershot: Gower.

Bennett, T. and Durie, L. (1999) *Preventing residential burglary in Cambridge: from crime audits to targeted strategies*. London: Home Office (Police Research Series, Paper no. 108).

Bennett, T. and Wright, T. (1984) *Burglars on Burglary*. Aldershot: Gower.

Block, R. (1987) 'A comparison of victimization, crime assessment and fear of crime in England/Wales, the Netherlands, Scotland and the United States', paper to American Society of Criminology annual conference, Montreal.

Blumstein, A., Cohen, J., Das, S. and Moitra, S. (1988) 'Specialisation and seriousness during adult criminal careers', *Journal of Quantitative Criminology*, **4**, 303–345.

Bolin, D.C. (1980) 'The Pima County victim witness program: analysing its success', *Evaluating Change, special issue*, 120–126.

Bonczar, T.P. and Glaze, L.E. (1999). 'Probation and parole in the United States, 1998', *US Department of Justice, Bureau of Justice Statistics Bulletin*.

Bottomley, A.K. and Coleman, C.A. (1981) *Understanding crime rates*. Farnborough: Saxon House.

Bottoms, A.E. and Costello, A. (2001) 'Offenders as victims of burglary and other property crimes', paper to 10th International Seminar on Environmental Criminology and Crime Analysis, Liverpool, June.

Bottoms, A.E., Mawby, R.I. and Walker, M. (1987) 'Localised crime survey in contrasting areas of a city', *British Journal of Criminology*, **27.2**, 125–154.

Bowers, K.J. (2001) 'Small business crime: the evaluation of a crime prevention initiative', *Crime prevention and community safety: an international journal*, **3.1**, 23–42.

Bowers, K.J., Hirschfield, A. and Johnson, S.D. (1998) 'A case study of nonresidential repeat burglary on Merseyside', *British Journal of Criminology*, **38**, 429–452.

Bridgeman and Sampson (1994). *Wise after the event: tackling repeat victimisation*. London: National Board for Crime Prevention.

Bright, J. (1991) 'Crime prevention: the British experience', pp. 62–86 in Stenson, K. and Cowell, D. (eds.) *The politics of crime control*. London: Sage.

Bright, J. (1985) *After entry phones: improving management and security in multi-storey blocks*. London: NACRO.

Brown, B. (1995) *CCTV in town centres: three case studies*. London: Home Office (Crime Detection and Prevention Series, paper no. 68).

Budd, T. (1999) *Burglary of domestic dwellings: findings from the British Crime Survey*. London: Home Office (Home Office Statistical Bulletin, issue 4/99).

Bunt, P. (1999) *The changing face of policing: local issues in national perspective*. PhD, University of Plymouth.

Bunt, P. and Mawby, R. I. (1994) 'Quality of Policing', *Public Policy Review*, **2.3**, 58–60.

Burquest, Farrell, G. and Pease, K. (1992) 'Lessons from schools', *Policing*, **8**, 148–155.

Burrows, J. (1988) *Retail crime: prevention through crime analysis*. London: Home Office (Crime Prevention Unit, paper no. 11).

Burrows, J. (1988) *Making crime prevention pay: initiatives from business*. London: Home Office (Crime Prevention Unit, paper no. 27).

Burrows, J. (1986) *Investigating burglary: the measurement of police performance*. London: HMSO (Home Office Research Study no. 88).

Burrows, J., Ekblom, P. and Heal, K. (1979). *Crime prevention and the police*. London: HMSO (Home Office Research Study no. 55).

Burrows, J. and Tarling, R. (1982) *Clearing up crime*. London: HMSO (Home Office Research Study no. 73).

Butler, G. (1994) 'Commercial burglary: what offenders say', pp. 29–41 in M. Gill (ed.) *Crime at work*. Leicester: Perpetuity Press.

Button, M. and George, B. (1994) 'Why some organisations prefer in-house to contract security staff', pp 209–223 in Gill (ed.) *op cit*.

Byrne, J.M. (1990) 'The future of intensive probation supervision and the new intermediate sanctions', *Crime and Delinquency*, **36.1**, 6–41.

Canter, D. and Alison, L. (2000) 'Profiling property crimes', pp. 1–30 in Canter, D. and Alison, L. (eds.) *Profiling property crimes*. Aldershot: Ashgate/Dartmouth.

Chapman, T. and Hough, M. (1998) *Evidence based practice: a guide to effective practice*. London: Her Majesty's Inspectorate of Probation.

Chesney, S. and Schneider, C.S. (1981) 'Crime victim crisis centres: the Minnesota experience', pp. 399–404 in B. Galaway, and J. Hudson (eds.) *Perspectives on Crime Victims*. St Louis: C.V. Mosby.

Clarke, R.V., Perkins, E. and Smith, D.J. (2001) 'Explaining repeat residential burglaries: an analysis of stolen property', pp. 119–132 in Farrell, G. and Pease, K. (eds.) *Repeat victimization*. Monsey, NJ: Criminal Justice Press (Crime Prevention Studies, 12).

Clarke, R. (1980) '"Situational" crime prevention: theory and practice', *British Journal of Criminology*, **20**, 136–145.

Cochran, D., Corbett, R.P. and Byrne, J.M. (1986) 'Intensive probation supervision in Massachusetts: a case study in change', *Federal Probation*, **L.2**, 32–41.

Cohen, L. and Cantor, D. (1981) 'Residential burglary in the United States: life-style and demographic factors associated with the probability of victimization', *Journal of Research in Crime and Delinquency*, **18**, 113–127.

Cohen, L., Kluegel, J.R. and Land, K. (1981) 'Social inequality and predatory criminal victimization: an exposition and test of a formal theory', *American Sociological Review*, **46**, 505–524.

Coleman, A. (1985). *Utopia on trial*. London: Hilary Shipman.

Coupe, T. and Griffiths, M. (1997) *Solving residential burglary*. London: Home Office (Crime Detection and Prevention Series, paper no. 77).

Crawford, A., Jones, T., Woodhouse, T., and Young, J. (1990) *Second Islington Crime Survey*. London: Middlesex Polytechnic.

Cromwell, P. (1991) 'The burglar's perspective', pp. 35–50 in Roberts, A.R. (ed.) *Critical issues in criminal justice*. London: Sage.

Cromwell, P.F., Olson, J.N. and Avary, D'A.W. (1991) *Breaking and entering*. Newbury Park, CA: Sage.

Cullen, C. and Minchin, M. (2000) 'The prison population in 1999: a statistical review', *Home Office Research and Statistics Directorate, Research Findings no. 118*.

Dale, P. and Mawby, R.I. (1994). 'Backing the bobby', *Police Review*, 2, September, 26–28.

Davidoff, L. (1993) 'Performance indicators for the police service', *Focus on Police Research and Development*, **3**, 12–17.

Davis, R.C. (1987) 'Studying the effects of services for victims in crisis', *Crime and Delinquency*, **33**, 520–531.

Davis, R.C. and Henley, M. (1990) 'Victim service programs', pp. 157–71 in A.J. Lurigio, A.J., Skogan, W.G. and Davis, R.C. (eds.) *Victims of Crime: Problems, Policies, and Progress*. Newbury Park, CA: Sage.

Davis, R.C., Lurigio, A.J. and Skogan, W.G. (1999) 'Services for victims: a market research study', *International Review of Victimology*, **6**, 101–115.

Dijk, J.J.M. van (1989) 'The challenge of quality control: Victim Support in the Netherlands', unpublished paper.

Dijk, J.J.M. van (1985) 'Regaining a sense of community and order', in Council of Europe (ed.) *Research on crime victims*. Strasbourg: Council of Europe.

Dijk, J.J.M. van and Terlouw, G.J. (1996) 'An international perspective of the business community as victims of fraud and crime', *Security Journal*, 7, 157–167.

Ditton, J. *et al* (1999) 'Reactions to victimisation: why has anger been ignored?' *Crime Prevention and Community Safety: an international journal* 1.3, 37–54.

Dobinson, I. (1986) 'Drug related burglary in New South Wales', pp. 222–232 in Mukherjee, S.K. and Jorgensen, L. (eds.) *Burglary: a social reality.* Australian Institute of Criminology, conference proceedings.

Doening-Striening, G. (1989) 'The advantages of Weisser Ring's approach to Victim Support compared with state policy', pp. 48–51 in First European Conference of Victim Support Workers *Guidelines for Victim Support in Europe.* Utrecht, the Netherlands: VLOS.

Donald, I. and Wilson, A. (2000) 'Ram raiding: criminals working in groups', pp. 191–246 in Canter, D. and Alison, L. (eds.) *The social psychology of crime: groups, teams and networks.* Aldershot: Ashgate.

Dowds, L. and Mayhew, P. (1994) 'Participation in neighbourhood watch: findings from the British Crime Survey', *Home Office Research and Statistics Department, Research Findings 11.*

Dugan, L. (1999) 'The effect of criminal victimization on a household's moving decision', *Criminology*, **37.4**, 903–928.

Ekblom, P., Law, H. and Sutton, M. (1996a) *Domestic burglary schemes in the Safer Cities programme*, Home Office Research and Statistics Department, Research Findings No. 42.

Ekblom, P., Law, H. and Sutton, M. (1996b) *Safer Cities and domestic burglary*, London: Home Office (Home Office Research Study No. 164).

Ellingworth, D., Farrell, G. and Pease, K. (1995) 'A victim is a victim is a victim? Chronic victimisation in four sweeps of the British Crime Survey', *British Journal of Criminology*, **35.3**, 360–365.

Ellingworth, D. and Pease, K. (1998) 'Movers and breakers: household property crime against those moving home', *International Journal of Risk, Security and Crime Prevention*, **3.1**, 35–42.

Erwin, B.S. (1986) 'Turning up the heat on probationers in Georgia', *Federal Probation*, **L.2**, 17–24.

Erwin, B.S. (1990) 'Old and new tools for the modern probation officer', *Crime and Delinquency*, **36.1**, 61–74.

Evans, D.J. (1992) 'Left realism and the spatial study of crime', pp. 36–59 in Evans, D.J., Fyfe, N.R. and Herbert, D.T. (eds.) *Crime, policing and place: essays on environmental criminology.* London: Routledge.

Evans, D.J. (1989). 'Geographical analysis of residential burglary', pp 86-107 in Evans, D.J. and Herbert, D.T. (eds.) *The geography of crime.* London: Routledge.

Evans, D.J. and Fletcher, M. (1998) 'Residential burglary within an affluent housing area', *International Journal of Risk, Security and Crime Prevention*, **3.3**, 181–191.

Evans, D.J. and Oulds, G. (1984) 'Geographical aspects of the incidence of residential burglary in Newcastle-under-Lyme, UK', *TESG*, **75.5**, 344–355.

Farrell, G. (1992). 'Multiple victimisation: its extent and significance', *International Review of Victimology*, **2**, 85–102.

Farrell, G. and Bouloukos, A.C. (2001) 'International overview: a cross-national comparison of rates of repeat victimization', pp. 5–25 in Farrell and Pease, *op cit.*

Farrell, G. and Pease, K. (1993). *Once bitten, twice bitten: repeat victimisation and its implications for crime prevention.* London: HMSO (Home Office Crime Prevention Unit Paper no. 46).

Farrell, G., Phillips, C. and Pease, K. (1995) 'Like taking candy: why does repeat victimisation occur?', *British Journal of Criminology,* **35**, 384–399.

Farrington, D.P. and Lambert, S. (1994) 'Differences between burglars and violent offenders', *Psychology, Crime and Law,* **1**, 107–116.

Farrington, D.P. and Lambert, S. (2000) 'Statistical approaches to offender profiling', pp. 233–273 in Canter, D. and Alison, L. (eds.) *Profiling property crimes.* Aldershot: Ashgate/Dartmouth.

Felson, M. and Cohen, L.E. (1980) 'Human ecology and crime: a routine activity approach', *Human Ecology,* **8.4**, 389–405.

Findlay, A., Rogerson, R., Paddison, R. and Morris, A. (1989) 'Whose quality of life?', *The Planner,* **75.15**, 21–22.

Fisher, B. (1991) 'A neighbourhood business area is hurting: crime, fear of crime and disorders take their toll', *Crime and Delinquency,* **37.3**, 363–373.

Flynn, K. (2001) 'Surfing the Crime Net: the use of imprisonment worldwide' *Crime Prevention and Community Safety: an international journal,* **3.2**, 65–69.

Fogel, D. (1994) *Policing in Central and Eastern Europe.* Helsinki: HEUNI.

Folland, D. and Mawby, R.I. (forthcoming) 'Explaining the extent of burglary from static caravans'.

Forrester, D., Chatterton, M. and Pease, K. (1988). *The Kirkholt Burglary Prevention Project, Rochdale.* London: HMSO (Crime Prevention Unit Paper no. 13).

Forrester, D., Frenz, S., O'Connell, M. and Pease, K. (1990) *The Kirkholt Burglary Prevention Project, phase* 2. London: Home Office (Crime Prevention Unit Paper no. 23).

Foster, J. and Hope, T. (1993) *Housing, community and crime: the impact of the priority estates project.* London: Home Office (Home Office Research Study no. 131).

Frate, A.A. del (1998) *Victims of crime in the developing world.* Rome: UNICRI.

Frate, A.A. del, Zvekic, U. and Dijk, J.J.M. van (1993) *Understanding crime: experiences of crime and crime control.* Rome: UNICRI.

Friedman, K., Bischoff, H. Davis, R.C. and Person, A. (1982) *Victims and helpers: reactions to crime.* Washington, DC: US Government Printing Office.

Galaway, B. (1986) 'Implementing a penal-corrective process with juvenile burglary offenders and their victims', paper to Second World Congress of Victimology, Orlando.

Garofalo, J. (1979) 'Victimisation and fear of crime', *Journal of Research in Crime and Delinquency* **16**, 80–97.

Gay, M.J., Holton, C. and Thomas, M.S. (1975) 'Helping the victims', *International Journal of Offender Therapy and Comparative Criminology,* **19**, 263–9.

Genn, H. (1988) 'Multiple victimisation', pp. 90–100 in Maguire, M. and Pointing, J. (eds.) *Victims of crime: a new deal?* Milton Keynes: Open University Press.

Gill, M., Hart, J., Livingstone, K. and Stevens, J. (1996) *The crime allocation system: police investigations into burglary and auto crime.* London: Home Office (Police Research Series paper no. 16).

Gill, M.L. and Mawby, R.I. (1990) *Volunteers in the criminal justice system.* Milton Keynes: Open University Press.

Gilling, D. (1994) 'Multi-agency crime prevention in Britain: the problem of combining situational and social strategies', pp. 231–248 in Clarke, R. (ed.) *Crime prevention studies, Volume 3.* Monsey, NY: Criminal Justice Press.

Gottfredson, M. (1984) *Victims of crime: the dimensions of risk.* London: HMSO (Home Office Research study no. 81).

Graham, J. and Bennett, T. (1995) *Crime prevention strategies in Europe and North America.* Helsinki, Sweden: European Institute for Crime Prevention and Control.

Greenville Police Department (1979) *Project U.F.O.* Rockville, MD: NCJRS, National Institute of Justice.

Greenwood, P. and Chaiken, J. (1977) *The criminal investigation process.* Lexington, MA: D.C. Heath.

Groenhuijsen, M. (1990) 'Victim Support for road traffic accident victims', paper to National Association of Victim Support Schemes, annual conference, Warwick.

Hauber, A.R. and Zandbergen, A. (1991) 'Victim assistance in police stations on the move: an experiment of victim assistance in police stations, *International Review of Victimology,* **2**, 1–13.

Henham, R. (1997) 'Anglo-American approaches to cumulative sentencing...', *Howard Journal,* **36.3**, 263–283.

Herbert, D. and Darwood (1992) 'Crime awareness and urban neighbourhoods', pp. 145–163 in Evans *et al* (eds.) *op cit.*

Herbert, D. (1982) *The geography of urban crime.* London: Longman.

Hindelang, M., Gottfredson, M.R. and Garafalo, J. (1978) *Victims of personal crime: an empirical foundation for a theory of personal victimization.* Cambridge, MA: Ballinger.

Hine, J. and Thomas, N. (1996) 'Evaluating work with offenders: community service orders', pp. 133–151 in McIvor (ed.) *op cit.*

Home Office (2000) *Criminal statistics: England and Wales, 1999.* London: HMSO (Cm 5001).

Home Office (1995) *Review of police core and ancillary tasks.* London: HMSO.

Home Office Standing Conference on Crime Prevention (1989) *Report of the Working Group on Fear of Crime.* London: Home Office.

Hope, T. (1988) 'Support for neighbourhood watch: a British Crime Survey analysis', pp. 146–161 in Hope, T. and Shaw, M. (eds.) *Communities and crime reduction.* London: HMSO.

Hope, T. (1982) *Burglary in schools: the prospects for prevention.* London: Home Office (Research and Planning Unit, paper no. 11).

Hough, M. (1995). *Anxiety about crime: findings from the 1994 British Crime Survey.* London: Home Office (Home Office Research Study no. 147).

Hough, M. and Mayhew, P. (1983). *The British Crime Survey.* London: HMSO (Home Office Research Study no. 76).

Hough, M. and Roberts, J. (1998) 'Attitudes to punishment: findings from the 1996 British Crime Survey', *Home Office Research and Statistics Directorate, Research Findings no. 64.*

Husain, S. (1988) *Neighbourhood watch in England and Wales.* London: Home Office (Home Office Crime Prevention Unit, no. 12).

Inciardi, J.A. (ed.) (1981) *The drugs crime connection.* Beverly Hills, CA: Sage.

Jackson, H.M. and Winchester, S.W.C. (1982) *Residential burglary.* London: Home Office (Home Office Research Study no. 74).

Jacques, C (1994) 'Ram-raiding: the history, incidence and scope for prevention', pp. 42–55 in Gill (ed.) *op cit.*

Jasinski, J. and Siemaszko, A. (eds.) (1995) *Crime control in Poland*. Warsaw: Oficyna Naukowa.

Johnson, B.D. *et al* (1985) *Taking care of business: the economics of crime by heroin abusers*. Lexington, MA: Lexington.

Johnson, J.H. *et al* (1973) 'The recidivist victim: a descriptive study', *Criminal Justice Monograph, volume 5.1*. Huntsville, TX: Sam Houston State University.

Johnston, L. (1999) 'Private policing: uniformity and diversity', pp. 226–238 in Mawby, R.I. (ed.) *Policing across the world: issues for the twenty-first century*. London: UCL Press.

Johnston, L. (1992) *The rebirth of private policing*. London: Routledge.

Johnston, V. *et al* (1994) 'Crime, business and policing on industrial estates, pp. 102–124 in Gill (ed.) *op cit*.

Jones, T., Maclean, B. and Young, J. (1986) *The Islington crime survey*. London: Gower.

Jones, T. and Newburn, T. (1995). 'How big is the private security sector?'. *Policing and Society*, 5, 221–232.

Joutsen, M. (1987) *The role of the victim of crime in European criminal justice systems*. Helsinki, Finland: HEUNI.

Joyner, M. (1999) 'Surfing the crime net: domestic violence', *Crime Prevention and Community Safety: an international journal*, **1.2**, 51–58.

Kershaw, C. *et al* (2000) *The 2000 British Crime Survey*. London: HMSO (HO Statistical Bulletin 18/00).

Kershaw, C. (1999) 'Reconviction of offenders sentenced or released from prison in 1994', *Home Office Research and Statistics Directorate, Research Findings no. 90*.

Kilpatrick, D.G. *et al* (1987) 'Criminal victimization: lifetime prevalence, reporting to the police, and psychological impact', *Crime and Delinquency*, **33.4**, 379–389.

King, M. (1987) 'A counsel of prevention', *New Statesman*, 23 October, 15–16.

King, M. (1988) *How to make social crime prevention work: the French experience*. London: NACRO.

Kinsey, R., Lea, J. and Young, J. (1986) *Losing the fight against crime*. London: Blackwell.

Kleemans, E.R. (2001) 'Repeat burglary victimization: results of empirical research in the Netherlands', pp. 53–68 in Farrell and Pease, *op. cit*.

Klein, M.W. (1984) 'Offence specialisation and versatility among juveniles', *British Journal of Criminology*, **24**, 184–194.

Klockars, C.B. (1974) *The professional fence*. New York: Free Press.

Kock, E., Kemp, T. and Rix, B. (1996) *Disrupting the distribution of stolen electrical goods*. London: Home Office (Crime Detection and Prevention Series, paper 69).

Kruissnik, M. (1995) *Inbraak in Bedrijven*. Den Haag, Netherlands: DCP.

Lab, S. (1992) *Crime prevention: approaches, practices and evaluations*. Cincinnati, OH: Anderson.

Langan, P.A. and Farrington, D.P. (1998) *Crime and justice in the United States and in England and Wales, 1981-96*. Washington, DC: US Department of Justice, Bureau of Justice Statistics. (See also at www.ojp.usdoj.gov/bjs/abstract/cjusew96.htm.)

Langworthy, R.H. (1989) 'Do stings control crime? An evaluation of a police fencing operation', *Justice Quarterly*, **6.1**, 27–45.

Laycock, G. (1985) *Reducing burglary: a study of chemists' shops*. London: Home Office (Crime Prevention Unit, paper no. 1).

Laycock, G. and Tilley, N. (1995) *Policing and neighbourhood watch: strategic issues*.

London: Home Office (Crime Detection and Prevention Series no. 60).

Lewis, H. (1989) *Insuring against burglary losses*. London: Home Office (Home Office Research and Planning Unit, Paper no. 52).

Liege, M-P de (1988) 'The fight against crime and fear: a new initiative in France', pp. 254–259 in Hope, T. and Shaw, M. (eds.) *Communities and crime reduction*. London: HMSO.

Liska, A.E., Sanchirico, A. and Reed, M.D. (1988) 'Fear of crime and constrained behaviour: specifying and estimating a reciprocal effects model', *Social Forces*, **66**, 827–837.

Lloyd, C., Mair, G. and Hough, M. (1994) 'Explaining reconviction rates: a critical analysis', *Home Office Research and Statistics Directorate, Research Findings no. 12*.

Lurigio, A.J. (1987) 'Are all victims alike? The adverse, generalized, and differential impact of crime', *Crime and Delinquency*, **33.4**, 452–467.

Lynch, J.P. (1987) 'Imprisonment in four countries', *US Department of Justice, Bureau of Justice Statistics Special Report*.

Lynch, J.P. and Cantor, D. (1992) 'Ecological and behavioral influences on property victimization at home: implications for opportunity theory', *Journal of Research in Crime and Delinquency*, **29.3**, 335–362.

Lynch, J. et al (1991) 'Profiles of inmates in the US and England and Wales, 1991', *US Department of Justice, Bureau of Justice Statistics Special Report*.

MacKenzie, D.L. et al (1999) 'The impact of probation on the criminal activities of offenders', *Journal of Research in Crime and Delinquency*, **36.4**, 423–453.

Maguire, M. (1982) *Burglary in a dwelling*. London: Heinemann.

Maguire, M. (1980) 'Impact of burglary upon victims', *British Journal of Criminology*, **20.3**, 261–275.

Maguire, M. and Corbett, C. (1987) *The Effects of Crime and the Work of Victim Support Schemes*. Aldershot: Gower.

Maguire, M. and Kynch, J. (2000) *Public perceptions and victims' experiences of Victim Support: findings from the 1998 British Crime Survey*. London: Home Office.

Mair, G. (1996a) 'Developments in probation in England and Wales', pp. 25–38 in McIvor, G. (ed.) *op cit.*

Mair, G. (1996b) 'Intensive probation, pp. 120–132 in McIvor, G. (ed.) *op cit.*

Mair, G. et al (1994) *Intensive probation in England and Wales*. London: Home Office (Home Office Research Study no. 134).

Mair, G., Lloyd, C., Nee, C. and Sibbitt, R. (1995) 'Intensive probation in England and Wales: an evaluation', *Home Office Research and Statistics Directorate, Research Findings no. 15*.

Mair, G. and Nee, C. (1990) *Electronic monitoring*. London: HMSO.

Matsaers, P. (1996) *Woninginbraak* (Residential burglary: summary in English). Den Haag: CIP-gegevens Koninklijke Bibliotheek.

Mattinson, J. and Mirrlees-Black, C. (2000) 'Attitudes to crime and criminal justice: findings from the 1998 British Crime Survey', *Home Office Research and Statistics Directorate, Research Findings no. 111*.

Mawby, R.I. (2001) 'The impact of repeat victimisation on burglary victims in East and West Europe', pp. 69–82 in Farrell and Pease, *op cit.*

Mawby, R.I. (2000) 'Core policing: the seductive myth', pp. 107–123 in Leishman, F., Loveday, B. and Savage, S. (eds.) *Core issues in policing, second edition*. Harlow: Longman.

Mawby, R.I. (1999a) 'Providing a secure home for older residents: evaluation of an initiative in Plymouth.' *Howard Journal*, **38.3**, 313–327.

Mawby, R.I. (1999b) 'The changing force of policing in Central and Eastern Europe', *International Journal of Police Science and Management*, **2.3**, 199–216.

Mawby, R.I. (1998) 'Victims' perceptions of police services in East and West Europe', pp. 180–200 in Ruggiero, V., South, N. and Taylor, I. (eds.) *The new European criminology: crime and social order in Europe.* London: Routledge..

Mawby, R. I. (1997) *Evaluation of a burglary prevention initiative in Plymouth.* Plymouth: University of Plymouth (Criminology and Criminal Justice: Research Paper 1).

Mawby, R.I. (1992) 'Comparative police systems: searching for a continental model', pp. 108–132 in Bottomley, K., Fowles, T. and Reiner, R. (eds.) *Criminal justice: theory and practice.* London: British Society of Criminology.

Mawby, R.I. (1990a) 'Neighbourhood watch in the South West: a survey of scheme co-ordinators', unpublished paper.

Mawby, R.I. (1990b) *Comparative policing issues: the British and American experience in international perspective.* London: Routledge

Mawby, R.I. (1979) *Policing the city.* Farnborough: Saxon House.

Mawby, R.l., Brunt, P. and Hambly, Z. (2000) 'Fear of crime among British holidaymakers', *British Journal of Criminology*, **40.3**, 468–479.

Mawby, R.l., Brunt, P. and Hambly, Z. (1999) 'Victimisation on holiday: a British survey', *International Review of Victimology*, **6.3**, 201–211.

Mawby, R.I. and Gill, M. (1987) *Crime victims: needs, services and the voluntary sector.* London: Tavistock.

Mawby, R.I. and Gorgenyi, I. (1997) 'Break-ins to weekend homes: research in a Hungarian city', pp. 120–132 in Raska, E. and Saar, J. (eds.) *Crime and criminology at the end of the century.* Tallinn, Estonia: Estonian National Defence and Public Service Academy.

Mawby, R.I. *et al* (1999) 'Victims' needs and the availability of services: a comparison of burglary victims in Poland, Hungary and England', *International Criminal Justice Review*, **9**, 18–38.

Mawby, R. I. and Kirchoff, G. (1996). 'Coping with crime: a comparison of victims' experiences in England and Germany', pp. 55–70 in Francis, P. and Davies, P. (eds.) *Understanding victimisation: themes and perspectives.* Newcastle: University of Northumberland.

Mawby, R.I., Koubova, E. and Brabcova, I. (2000) 'Victims' needs and support for victims in Prague', *International Journal of the Sociology of Law*, **28**, 129–145.

Mawby, R.I. and Nation, D. (1993) 'Dialogues between victims and offenders: initiatives in an English city', paper to Eleventh International Congress on Criminology, Budapest.

Mawby, R. I., Ostrihanska, Z. and Wojcik, D. (1997) 'Police response to crime: the perceptions of victims from two Polish cities', *Policing and Society*, **7**, 1–18.

Mawby, R.I. and Simmonds, L. (2000) 'Addressing victims' needs: evaluation of Victim Support', paper to British Criminology Conference, Leicester, July.

Mawby, R. I. and Walklate, S. (1994) *Critical victimology.* London: Sage.

Mawby, R.I. and Walklate, S. (1997) 'The impact of burglary: a tale of two cities', *International Review of Victimology*, **4.4**, 267–295.

Maxfield, M.G. (1987) 'Household composition, routine activity and victimization: a comparative analysis', *Journal of Quantitative Criminology* **3.4**, 301–320.

May, C. (1999) 'The role of social factors in predicting reconviction for offenders on community penalties', *Home Office Research and Statistics Directorate, Research Findings no. 97.*

Mayhew, P., Clarke, R.V.G., Sturman, A. and Hough, J.M. (1976). *Crime as opportunity.* London: HMSO (Home Office Research Study no. 34).

Mayhew, P. *et al* (1979) *Crime in public view.* London: HMSO (Home Office Research Study no. 49).

Mayhew, P. and Dijk, J.J.M. van (1997) *Criminal victimisation in eleven industrialised countries.* Amstelveen, the Netherlands : WODC.

Mayhew, P., Elliott, D. and Dowds, L. (1989). *The 1988 British Crime Survey.* London: HMSO (Home Office Research Study no. 111).

McIvor, G. (ed.) (1996) *Working with offenders.* London: Jessica Kingsley.

McGuire, J. (ed.) (1995) *What works: reducing reoffending.* Chichester: Wiley.

McWilliams, W. (1986) 'The English probation system and the diagnostic ideal', *Howard Journal,* **25.4,** 241–260.

Merry, S. (2000) 'Crime analysis: principles for analysing everyday serial crime', pp. 299–318 in Canter, D. and Alison, L. (eds.) *Profiling property crimes.* Aldershot: Ashgate/Dartmouth.

Merry, S. and Harsent, L. (2000) 'Intruders, pilferers, raiders and invaders: the interpersonal dimension of burglary, pp. 31–56 in Canter, D. and Alison, L. (eds.) *Profiling property crimes.* Aldershot: Ashgate/Dartmouth.

Merseyside Police (1992) *Countywide burglary survey, 1992.* Liverpool: Force Inspectorate and Policy Support Unit.

Michael, A. (1993) *Safe as Houses? Burglary of Homes: an Analysis.* London: Labour Party.

Mirrlees-Black, C. (2001) 'Confidence in the criminal justice system: findings from the 2000 British Crime Survey', *Home Office Research, Development and Statistics Directorate, Research Findings no. 137.*

Mirrlees-Black, C. (1998) 'Rural areas and crime: findings from the British crime survey', *Home Office Research, Development and Statistics Directorate, Research Findings no. 77.*

Mirrlees-Black, C. and Allen, J. (1998) 'Concern about crime: findings from the 1998 British Crime Survey', *Home Office Research, Development and Statistics Directorate, Research Findings no. 83.*

Mirrlees-Black, C., Budd, T., Partridge, S. and Mayhew, P. (1998) *The 1998 British Crime Survey: England and Wales.* London: HMSO (HO Statistical Bulletin 21/98).

Mirrlees-Black, C., Mayhew, P. and Percy, A. (1996) *The 1996 British Crime Survey: England and Wales.* London: Home Office (Home Office Statistical Bulletin).

Mirrlees-Black, C. and Maung, N.A. (1994) 'Fear of crime: findings from the 1992 British Crime Survey', *Home Office Research and Statistics Department, Research Findings no. 9.*

Mirrlees-Black, C. and Ross, A. (1995). *Crime against retail and manufacturing premises: findings from the 1994 commercial victimisation survey.* London: Home Office (Home Office Research Study no. 146).

Morgan, C. (2001) 'Repeat burglary in a Perth suburb: indicator of short-term or long-term risk?', pp. 83–118 in Farrell and Pease, *op cit.*

Morgan, J. (1991) *Report on safer communities.* London: HMSO.

MORI (1994). *Public attitudes towards crime.* London: MORI (for *Reader's Digest*

*Magazine*).

Mortimer, E. (2001) 'Electronic monitoring of released prisoners: an evaluation of the Home Office Detention Curfew scheme', *Home Office Research and Statistics Directorate, Research Findings no. 139.*

Mortimer, E. and Mair, G. (1997) 'Electronic monitoring of curfew orders: the second year of the trials', *Home Office Research and Statistics Directorate, Research Findings no. 66.*

Mortimer, E. and May, C. (1998) 'Curfew orders with electronic monitoring: the first twelve months', *Home Office Research and Statistics Directorate, Research Findings no. 51.*

Mortimer, E., Pereira, E. and Walter, I. (1999) 'Making the tag fit: further analysis from the first two years of the trials of curfew orders', *Home Office Research and Statistics Directorate, Research Findings no. 105.*

Muir, M. (1999) 'Tackling bogus callers', *Focus on Police Research and Development*, **11**, 53–54.

Nation, D. and Arnott, J. (1991) 'House burglaries and victims', *Probation Journal*, **38.2**, 63–67.

National Board for Crime Prevention (1994) *Wise after the event: tackling repeat victimisation*. London: Home Office.

Nee, C. and Taylor, M. (1988) 'Residential burglary in the Republic of Ireland: a situational perspective', *Howard Journal*, **27.2**, 105–116.

Nellis, M. (1991) 'The electronic monitoring of offenders in England and Wales', *British Journal of Criminology*, **31.2**, 165–185.

Newman, O. (1973) *Defensible space*. London: Architectural Press.

Nicholson, L. (1995) *What works in situational crime prevention: a literature review*. Edinburgh: Scottish Office Central Research Unit.

Noakes, L. (2000) 'Private cops on the block: a review of the role of private security in residential communities', *Policing and Society*, **10**, 143–161.

Norris, F.H. and Kaniasty, K. (1994) 'Psychological distress following criminal victimization in the general population: cross-sectional, longitudinal, and prospective analysis', *Journal of Consulting and Clinical Psychology*, **62.1**, 111–123.

Norris, F.H. Kaniasty, K. and Thompson, M.P. (1997) 'The psychological consequences of crime', pp. 146–166 in Davis, R.C., Lurigio, A.J., and Skogan, W.G. (eds.) *Victims of crime*. London: Sage.

Painter, K. and Farrington, D.P. (1999) 'Improved street lighting: crime reducing effects and cost-benefit analyses', *Security Journal*, **12.4**, 17–32.

Pascoe, T. and Topping, P. (1997) 'Secured by design: assessing the basis of the scheme', *International Journal of Risk, Security and Crime Prevention*, **2.3**, 161–173.

Pease, K. (1997) 'Crime prevention', pp. 963–995 in Maguire, M., Morgan, R. and Reiner, R. (eds.) *The Oxford handbook of criminology*. Oxford: Clarendon Press.

Pease, K. (1991) 'The Kirkholt project: preventing burglary on a British public housing estate', *Security Journal*, **2.2**, 73–77.

Pease, K. (1994) 'Cross-national imprisonment rates', *British Journal of Criminology*, **34** (Special issue), 24–35, 116–130.

Pease, K. and McWilliams, W. (1984) *Community service by order*. Edinburgh: Scottish Academic Press.

Penn, H.S. and Hegner, Q.J. (1973) *Criminal histories of burglary and drug offenders in selected California counties, 1971*. Rockville, MD: National Institute of Justice.

Perrone, S. (2000) 'Crimes against small business in Australia: a preliminary analysis', *Australian Institute of Criminology, Trends and Issues no. 184* (www.aic.gov.au).

Petersilia, J. (1990) 'Conditions that permit intensive supervision programs to survive', *Crime and Delinquency*, **36.1**, 126–145.

Petersilia, J. (1988) 'Probation reform', pp 166–179 in Scott, J.E. and Hirschi, T. (eds.) *Controversial issues in criminal justice*. Beverly Hills, CA: Sage.

Petersilia, J. and Turner, S. (1991) 'An evaluation of intensive probation in California', *Journal of Criminal Law and Criminology*, **82.3**, 610–658.

Penn, H.S. (1973) *California: five year follow-up of 1966 juvenile burglary-involved drug arrestees*. California Department of Justice.

Polvi, N. *et al* (1990) 'Repeat break and enter victimisation: time course and crime prevention opportunity', *Journal of Police Science and Administration*, **17**, 8–11.

Polvi, N. *et al* (1991) 'The time course of repeat burglary victimisation', *British Journal of Criminology*, **31**, 411–414.

Phillips, T. and Walker, J. (1997) 'State differences in burglary victimisation in Australia: a research note', *Australian and New Zealand Journal of Sociology*, **33.1**, 91–100.

Poyner, B. and Webb, B. (1991) *Crime free housing*. Oxford: Butterworth-Architecture.

Ratcliffe, J.H. and McCullagh, M.J. (1999) 'Burglary, victimisation and social deprivation', *Crime Prevention and Community Safety: an international journal*, **1.2**, 37–46.

Raub, R.A. (1983) *A study of anti-fencing operations in Illinois – an analysis of their effectiveness*. Rockville, MD: NCJRS, National Institute of Justice.

Redshaw, J. and Mawby, R.I. (1996). 'Commercial burglary: victims' views of the crime and the police response', *International Journal of Risk, Security and Crime Prevention*, **1**, 185–193.

Reiss, A. (1967) *Measurement of the Nature and Amount of Crime*. President's Commission, Field Surveys III, Washington DC.

Rengert, G.F. (1981) 'Burglary in Philadelphia: a critique of an opportunity structure model', pp. 189–201 in Brantingham, P.J. and Brantingham, P.L. (eds.) *Environmental criminology*. Beverly Hills, CA: Sage.

Rengert, G.F. and Wasilchick, J. (2000) *Suburban burglary: a tale of two suburbs*. Springfield, IL: Charles C. Thomas.

Renooy, P.H. (1991) *Heling*. Den Haag, the Netherlands: Ministry of Justice (In Dutch).

Resick, P.A. (1987) 'Psychological effects of victimization: implications for the criminal justice system', *Crime and Delinquency*, **33.4**, 468–478.

Reppetto, T. (1974) *Residential crime*. Cambridge, MA: Ballinger.

Roberts, A.R. (1990) *Helping victims of crime*. London: Sage.

Robinson, M.B. (1998) 'Burglary revictimisation: the time period of heightened risk', *British Journal of Criminology*, **38**, 78–87.

Rock, P. (1990) *Helping Victims of Crime*. Oxford: Clarendon Press.

Roell, G. (1986) *Een inventarisatie van heling in Nederland*. Den Haag, the Netherlands: Ministry of Justice (In Dutch).

Ross, R., Fabiano, E. and Ross, B. (1989) *Reasoning and rehabilitation: a handbook for teaching cognitive skills*. Ottawa: the Cognitive Centre.

Rogerson, R., Findlay, A. and Morris, A. (1988) 'The best cities to live in', *Town and*

*Country Planning,* **57.10**, 270–273.

Rosenbaum, D.P. (1988). 'A critical eye on Neighborhood Watch: does it reduce crime and fear', pp. 126–145 in Hope, T. and Shaw, M. (eds.) *Communities and crime reduction.* London: HMSO.

Rosenbaum, D.P. (1987a) 'The theory and research behind Neighbourhood Watch: is it a kind of fear and crime reduction strategy?', *Crime and Delinquency,* **33.1**, 103–134.

Rosenbaum, D.P. (1987b) 'Coping with victimization: the effects of police intervention on victims' psychological readjustment', *Crime and Delinquency,* **33**, 502–519.

Rountree, P.W. and Land, K.C. (1996) 'Burglary victimization, perceptions of crime risk, and routine activities: a multilevel analysis across Seattle neighborhoods and census tracts', *Journal of Research in Crime and Delinquency,* **33.2**, 147–180.

Rubenstein, H., Murray, C., Motoyama, T. and Rouse, W.V. (1980) *The link between crime and the built environment.* Washington DC: National Institute of Justice.

Russell, J. (1990) *Home Office Funding of Victim Support Schemes – Money Well Spent?* London: HMSO (Home Office Research and Planning Unit paper no. 58).

Scarr, H. (1973) *Patterns of burglary.* Washington, DC: Government Printing Office.

Sherman, L. *et al* (eds.) (1997) *Preventing crime: what works, what doesn't, what's promising.* Washington, DC: Department of Justice. (See also www.ncjrs.org/works/index.htm.)

Shover, N. (1973) 'The social organization of burglary', *Social Problems,* **20**, 499–514.

Shover, N. (1991) 'Burglary', pp. 73–113 in Tonry, M. (ed.) *Crime and justice: a review of research.* Chicago: University of Chicago Press.

Shubert, A. (1981) 'Private initiative in law enforcement: associations for the prosecution of felons, 1744–1856', pp. 25–41 in Bailey, V. (ed.) *Policing and punishment in nineteenth century Britain.* London: Croom Helm.

Sims, L. and Myhill, A. (2001) 'Policing and public: findings from the 2000 British Crime Survey', *Home Office Research, Development and Statistics Directorate, Research Findings no. 136.*

Skogan, W. (1996) 'The police and public opinion in Britain', *American Behavioral Scientist,* **39**, 421–432.

Skogan, W. (1995) *Contacts between police and public: findings from the 1992 British Crime Survey.* London: Home Office (Home Office Research Study no. 134).

Skogan, W. (1990a) *Disorder and decline: crime and the spiral of decay in American neighborhoods.* New York: Free Press.

Skogan, W. (1990b) *The police and public in England and Wales: a British Crime Survey report.* London: Home Office (Home Office Research Study no. 117).

Skogan, W.G. and Wycoff, M.A. (1987) 'Some unexpected effects of a police service for victims', *Crime and Delinquency,* **33**, 490–501.

Smith, D. (1996) 'Social work and penal policy', pp. 6–24 in McIvor, G. (ed.) *op cit.*

South, N. (1988). *Policing for profit.* London: Sage.

Southgate, P., Bucke, T. and Byron, C. (1995). *The parish special constables scheme.* London: HMSO (Home Office Research Studies no. 143).

Sparks, R. (1981) 'Multiple victimisation: evidence, theory and future research', *Journal of Criminal Law and Criminology,* **72**, 762–778.

Sparks, R., Genn, H. and Dodd, D. (1977) *Surveying victims.* Chichester: Wiley.

Squires, P. (1998) 'Cops and customers: consumerism and the demand for police services. Is the customer always right?', *Policing and Society,* **8**, 169–188.

Steffensmeier, D.J. (1986) *The fence: in the shadow of two worlds.* Totowa, NJ: Roman and Littlefield.

Stockdale, J.E. and Gresham, P.J. (1995) *Combatting burglary: an evaluation of three strategies.* London: Home Office (Crime Detection and Prevention Series, paper no. 59).

Sugg, D., Moore, L. and Howard, P. (2001) 'Electronic monitoring and offending behaviour – reconviction results for the second year of trials of curfew orders', *Home Office Research and Statistics Directorate, Research Findings no. 141.*

Sutton, M. (1998a) 'Handling stolen goods and theft: a market reduction approach', *Home Office Research and Statistics Directorate, Research Findings no. 69.*

Sutton, M. (1998b) *Handling stolen goods: a market reduction approach.* London: HMSO (Home Office Research Study no. 178).

Swedish Crime Prevention Council (1978) *Fencing of stolen goods.* Stockholm, Sweden: Brottsforebyggande Radet (In Swedish).

Sykes, G. and Matza, D. (1957) 'Techniques of neutralisation', *American Sociological Review,* **22**, 664–673.

Tarling, R. and Davison, T. (2000) *Victims of domestic burglary: a review of the literature.* London: Victim Support.

Taylor, B. and Bennett, T. (1999) *Comparing drug use rates of detained arrestees in the United States and England.* Washington, DC: US Department of Justice.

Taylor, M. and Hirst, J. (1995) *Initial scene visits to house burglaries. London:* Home Office (Police Research Series Paper no. 14).

Tilley, N. (1993a) *After Kirkholt – theory, method and results of replication evaluations.* London: Home Office (Crime Prevention Unit Paper no. 47).

Tilley, N (1993b) *The prevention of crime against small business: the Safer Cities experience.* Home Office (Crime Prevention Unit Paper no. 45), London.

Tilley, N. (1992). *Safer cities and community strategies.* London: Home Office (Crime Prevention Unit Paper no. 38).

Tilley, N. and Hopkins, M. (1998) *Business as usual: an evaluation of the small business and crime initiative.* London: Home Office (Police Research Series, Paper no. 95).

Tilley, N. and Webb, J. (1994) *Burglary reduction: findings from Safer Cities schemes.* London: Home Office (Crime Prevention Unit Paper no. 51).

Timoranszky, P. (1992) *Rendeszeti, Tanulmanyok.* Budapest: BM Rendeszeti, Kutatointezet.

Titus, R.M. (1999) 'Personal opinion: declining residential burglary rates in the USA', *Security Journal,* **12.4**, 59–63.

Trainum, J., Brown, and Smith, R. (1991) 'ROPing in fences', *FBI Law Enforcement Bulletin,* **60.6**, 6–10.

Trickett, A. *et al* (1995) 'Crime victimisation in the eighties: changes in area and regional inequality', *British Journal of Criminology,* **35**, 343–359.

Trickett, A. *et al* (1992) 'What is different about high crime areas?' *British Journal of Criminology,* **32**, 81–90.

Trickett, A., Osborn, D.R. and Ellingworth, O. (1995) 'Property crime victimisation: the roles of individual and area influences', *International Review of Victimology,* **3**, 273–295.

Turnbull, P.J. (1999) 'Drug treatment and testing orders – interim evaluation', *Home Office Research and Statistics Directorate, Research Findings no. 106.*

Turner, E. and Alexandrou, B. (1997) 'Neighbourhood watch co-ordinators', *Home Office Research and Statistics Department, Research Findings no. 63*.

Umbreit, M.S. (1999) *Victim meets offender: the impact of restorative justice and mediation*. New York: Criminal Justice Press.

US Department of Justice (1979) *What happened – an examination of recently terminated anti-fencing operations*. Rockville, MD: NCJRS, National Institute of Justice.

Valkova, J. (1998) 'The international crime victim survey in the Czech Republic 1996', pp. 179–195 in Hatalak, O., Frate, A.A. del and Zvekic, U. (eds.) *The international crime victim survey in countries in transition: national reports*. Rome: UNICRI.

Victim Support (1999) *Annual Report 1999*. London: Victim Support.

Victim Support (1995) *Codes of practice*. London: Victim Support.

Walker, J. (1996) 'Crime prevention by businesses in Australia', *International Journal of Risk, Security and Crime Prevention*, **1.4**, 279–291.

Walker, J., Collier, P. and Tarling, R. (1990) 'Why are prison rates in England and Wales higher than in Australia?', *British Journal of Criminology*, **30.1**, 24–35.

Walker, S. (1992) *The police in America: an introduction*. New York: McGraw-Hill.

Waller, I. and Okihiro, N. (1978) *Burglary: the victim and the public*. Toronto: University of Toronto Press.

Wallis, E. (1999) 'The probation service of the future', *NAPO News*, December, 4.

Walmsley, R. (2000) 'World prisons population list', *Home Office Research and Statistics Directorate, Research Findings (second edition), no. 116*.

Walsh, D. (1986) *Heavy business*. London: Routledge and Kegan Paul.

Walsh, D. (1980) *Breakins: burglary from private homes*. London: Constable.

Walsh, M.E. (1976) *Strategies for combatting the criminal receiver of stolen goods – an anti-fencing manual for law enforcement agencies*. Rockville, MD: NCJRS, National Institute of Justice.

Walter, I., Sugg, D. and Moore, L. (2001) 'A year on the tag: interviews with criminal justice practitioners and electronic monitoring staff about curfew orders, *Home Office Research and Statistics Directorate, Research Findings no. 140*.

Webb, J. (1997) 'Direct Line Homesafe: an evaluation of the first year'. Unpublished paper.

Weiner, K.A., Stephens, C.K. and Besachuk, D.L. (1983) 'Making inroads into property crime – an analysis of the Detroit anti-fencing program', *Journal of Police Science and Administration*, **11.3**, 311–327.

Wemmers, J.M. and Zeilstra, M.I. (1991) 'Victims services in the Netherlands', *Dutch Penal Law and Policy*, **3**. The Hague: Ministry of Justice.

Whyley, C., McCormick, J. and Kempson, E. (1998) *Paying for peace of mind: access to home contents insurance for low-income households*. London: Policy Studies Institute.

Wiersma, E. (1996) 'Commercial burglars in the Netherlands: reasoning decision-makers?', *International Journal of Risk, Security and Crime Prevention*, **1.3**, 217–225.

Wilkinson, C. and Maguire, M. (1993) *Contacting victims*. London: Home Office.

Winkel, F.W. (1991) 'Police responses aimed at alleviating victims' psychological distress and at raising prevention-awareness: some grounded intervention programmes', paper to annual conference of Law and Society Association, Amsterdam.

Winkel. F.W. (1989) 'Responses to criminal victimization: evaluating the impact of a police assistance programme and some social psychological characteristics, *Police*

*Studies*, **12.2**, 59–72.

Witterbrood, K. and Nieuwbeerta, P. (2000) 'Criminal victimization during one's life course:the effects of previous victimization and patterns of routine activities', *Journal of Research in Crime and Delinquency*, **37.1**, 91–122.

Wojcik, D., Walklate, S., Ostrihanska, Z., Mawby, R. I. and Gorgenyi, I. (1997) Security and crime prevention at home: a comparison of victims' response to burglary in England, Poland and Hungary', *International Journal of Risk, Security and Crime Prevention*, **2.1**, 38–48.

Wright, R. and Decker, S.H. (1994) *Burglars on the job*. Boston: Northeastern University Press.

Wright, R., Decker, S.H., Redfern, A.K. and Smith, D.L. (1992) 'A snowball's chance in hell: doing fieldwork with active residential burglars', *Journal of Research in Crime and Delinquency*, **29.2**, 148–161.

Yeo, H. and Budd, T. (2000) 'Policing and the public: findings from the 1998 British Crime Survey', *Home Office Research, Development and Statistics Directorate, Research Findings no. 113*.

Young, M.A. (1990) 'Victim assistance in the United States: the end of the beginning', *International Review of Victimology*, 1, 181–199.

Ziegenhagen, E. (1976) 'The recidivist victim of violent crime', *Victimology: an international journal*, **1**, 538–550.

Zvekic, U. (1998) *Criminal victimisation in countries in transition*. Rome: UNICRI.

Zveric, U. (1996) 'Policing and attitudes towards police in countries in transition', pp. 45–59 in Pagon, M. (ed.) *Policing in Central and Eastern Europe: comparing firsthand knowledge with experience from the West*. Ljubljana, Slovenia: College of Police and Security Studies

# Index

*Introductory Note*
*Added to page number, f denotes a figure, t denotes a table.*